THEORIZING HISTORIES OF RHETORIC

Theorizing Histories of Rhetoric

Edited by Michelle Ballif

Southern Illinois University Press
Carbondale and Edwardsville

16 15 14 13   4 3 2 1

Library of Congress Cataloging-in-Publication Data

Theorizing histories of rhetoric / edited by Michelle Ballif.
    p. cm.
Includes bibliographical references and index.
ISBN 978-0-8093-3210-6 (pbk. : alk. paper)
ISBN 0-8093-3210-8 (pbk. : alk. paper)
ISBN 978-0-8093-3211-3 (ebook)
ISBN 0-8093-3211-6 (ebook)
1. Rhetoric—History. 2. Rhetoric. I. Ballif, Michelle, 1964–
PN183.T48 2012
808.009—dc23   2012029747

for
(this)

Victor

(over nothingness)

CONTENTS

CONTENTS

ACKNOWLEDGMENTS

I would like to acknowledge all those who have shared in this risk: Karl Kageff, editor in chief of Southern Illinois University Press, for encouraging support, along with the two anonymous reviewers of this project, who helped me better frame and conceive the collection and who provided productive feedback to the contributors; Victor J. Vitanza, for the conditions of possibility for this project and for the "beautiful ride" through the fecund period of theorization, including a "front seat" at the 1989 conference in Arlington; all the authors included in this volume, for their insightful contributions, for inspiring e-mail conversations, and for pressing me to think, further, about what writing histories of rhetoric could mean; Sharon Crowley, for her—as ever—curmudgeonly grace and graciousness; and Larry Nackerud, for all.

INTRODUCTION

Michelle Ballif

A lthough the reclamation of the ancient rhetorical tradition was of interest to scholars of rhetoric, composition, and communication during much of the latter half of the twentieth century, this interest transformed into a central preoccupation during the decades of the 1980s and 1990s, producing a plethora of publications on the history of rhetoric. More specifically, the scholarship of this time generated an intense and engaged conversation amongst scholars in which they dialogued and theorized about the *historiography* of such reclamation work. That is, they asked: What does it mean to write histories of rhetoric? What methods are to be used? For what purposes are such histories to be composed? And what are the ideological motivations for writing such histories? More publications ensued, all working to theorize—or *metatheorize*— not only what it might mean to *write* histories of rhetoric, but what it might mean to *rewrite* histories of rhetoric by regendering them or by revising them.

During the decades of the 1980s and 1990s, such conversations were prominent and ubiquitous—in the journals and at our conventions. In the field of communication, for example, in a number of publications, John Poulakos and Ed Schiappa argued back and forth over what a history of rhetoric could be, when the very term "sophistic rhetoric" was contested; likewise, Barbara Biesecker and Karlyn Kohrs Campbell battled over what a history of rhetoric might be when woman, as a (rhetorical) subject, was interrogated. And in rhetoric and composition, in the spring of 1988, a number of scholars—eight to be exact—joined a panel discussion entitled "The Politics of Historiography," which was attended by hundreds of participants of the Conference on College Composition and Communication. The presentation—with further reflection—was published in *Rhetoric Review*, as the infamous "Octalog," a discussion that is ranked as *Rhetoric Review*'s most highly requested reprint. Indeed, so vociferous (and often heatedly so) was this particular scholarly conversation that during this period, as Arthur E. Walzer and David Beard note, publications "engaging historiographical debates outnumbered articles in traditional history in rhetoric-centered journals" (17).

In the fall of 1989, hailing an audience from both communication studies and rhetoric and composition, Victor J. Vitanza hosted a richly productive conference that centered on theoretical and methodological issues attendant to the practice of writing histories of rhetoric, resulting in the publication in 1994 of *Writing Histories of Rhetoric*, a collection of essays composed by a select number of conference attendees. This present collection is an attempt to rewrite, retheorize that volume, specifically by querying: Where did all the theory go? That is, what happened to the impassioned fervor generated in the 1980s and 1990s regarding the *theorization* of theories of writing histories of rhetoric? The fervor/fever is documentable: one need only review the number of publications on the topic and review Sharon Crowley's "history" of the period ("Let Me Get This Straight") in the aforementioned Vitanza collection to understand that to write histories of rhetoric demanded a theoretical investigation into the metatheory of historiography.

After this fertile period of *theorization*, the writing of histories—of rhetoric, of composition, of communication—exploded: archives were stormed, archaeological sites probed, originary figures investigated in ethnographic detail. And volumes and volumes and volumes of histories were subsequently and continue to be produced. Open the pages of the recently published *The Present State of Scholarship in the History of Rhetoric*, edited by Lynée Lewis Gaillet with Winifred Bryan Horner, and be prepared to be awed by the number and quality of histories of rhetorics that have been generated since the original 1990 edition of that work.

Yet the impassioned discussion and the metatheorization that engendered these past two decades of historiographical productivity have largely fallen silent, as historians have gone about their business of *doing* history, *writing* history without articulating a fervored sense of exigency about *theorizing* the doing of history, the writing of history. To be sure, these published histories of rhetoric, these disciplinary histories of composition and communication, these histories of rhetorical and pedagogical practices, have greatly enriched our discipline, and I share the hope with others in our field that this rich historiographical production continues. Yet perhaps I am suggesting it is (un)time to focus, once again, specifically on the *theory* of historiography: to ask difficult questions about the purposes and methodologies of writing histories of rhetorics, broadly defined. This collection, then, aims to provoke us to question what it means, what it should mean, what it could mean to write histories of rhetoric, composition, communication.

For approximately two decades, Victor J. Vitanza has maintained that "we," historians of rhetoric, have an obligation to search for "the third man" or "the third woman"—for that which has been "systematically excluded" from "*The* History of Rhetoric" ("Taking A-Count" 181). This third is that which must be excluded for communication or community or identity of any kind to be achieved, including the identity of "*The*" "History" of "Rhetoric." As Vitanza's work has ceaselessly demonstrated, the excluded third "is symptomatic of the logic of the dialectic: *the* epistemic motor of Western thought, which establishes some *positive* ('The Good,' 'The True,' 'The Beautiful') through a *negation* of the Other and an *exclusion* of all that can't be *synthesized*" (Ballif, "Victor J. Vitanza" 338). Hence, according to this logic, to write *any history* (of rhetoric) demands "systematic exclusions" of figures, of events, of artifacts, of whatever cannot be accounted for or synthesized by the historical narrative. The ethical task, then, is to search for, to attend to, these exclusions, these "unaccountable refugees of cognitive regimens" (Ronell, "Is It Happening?" 324). As David Carroll writes, "The obligation of and to" this excluded third of historicized "memory . . . would thus not be phrased as 'Never forget.' Rather it would be, 'Never forget that in all memory there is 'the Forgotten'—to which we are obliged as much as, if not more than, to the remembered past'" (24).

The field of rhetoric studies has taken up this challenge to remember the excluded third with great energy, manifesting itself in a rich body of so-called "recovery work," of rewriting the history of rhetoric to include excluded (or demonized) figures such as women, Sophists, and non-Western rhetors (again, I direct you to Gaillet's *The Present State of Scholarship* for a comprehensive bibliographic survey of such historiographic work).

Yet Vitanza has further admonished and warned us that our task, as historians, will only become "more difficult" when we *do* historicize "the third man" ("Taking A-Count" 181), because—again—*any history*, any remembrance or memorial, is composed precisely by forgetting, and in *any history,* any memory, "there is 'the Forgotten'" (Carroll 24). As Lauren Berlant and Michael Warner cleverly note, "Memory is the Amnesia You Like" (549; see also Morris and Rawson, this volume). That is, accounting for "the third man," writing "the third man" into history, inevitably produces *more third men.*

Acknowledging this conundrum, "we" historians are confronted with an exigency, inviting us to retheorize (the) writing of histories of rhetoric. The work of the authors here collected asks us to retheorize by provoking us to search, again, for the excluded third—but specifically for the excluded third *methodology*—of writing histories of rhetoric. That is, these essays query the ways our established historiographic methodologies always already preclude and occlude the excluded third and invite us to envision alternative methodologies to attend to "the Forgotten," and thereby to write the future of what will have been the field of rhetoric studies.

Richard Leo Enos, for example, in his entry "Theory, Validity, and the Historiography of Classical Rhetoric," argues that historiographical methods have privileged the "literary" or the textual and in the process overlooked material artifacts as evidence, resulting in histories that are not only Athens-centric but necessarily limited in their ability to account for the cultural context and "mentality" that generated and gave rise to specific rhetorical practices.

Steven Mailloux, in "Enactment History, Jesuit Practices, and Rhetorical Hermeneutics," asks us to employ a methodology of rhetorical hermeneutics as "enactment" to aid us in interpreting "past practices" that present themselves as foreign—or other—in a way that avoids appropriating that otherness for our own interpretive purposes. LuMing Mao, in "Writing the Other into Histories of Rhetorics," also attends to the historiographic problem of speaking for the other without appropriation. He theorizes an art of recontextualization that allows a historian to read/write "other" rhetorical histories "on its own terms," as demonstrated through his reading of the *Daodejing* and the rhetoric of the *Dao*.

In "Releasing Hold," Jessica Enoch investigates "what is left out of the dominant narrative told about feminist historiography." That is, although the two, central methodologies employed by feminist historiographers— recovery and rereading—have yielded "robust" histories, Enoch queries the exclusions and surplus resulting in these two approaches, including excluded methodologies—which she calls "outliers"—and interrogates how these excluded methodologies might "speak back to the larger project of feminist historiography."

Charles E. Morris III and K. J. Rawson, in "Queer Archives/Archival Queers," ask how rhetorical historiography might be complicit in an "ongoing disciplinary heteronormative omission" and invite us to examine "the archive" with a queer eye. The stakes for such a methodological approach are no less than the construction of nondiscriminatory, socially "constitutive narratives."

Debra Hawhee and Christa J. Olson explore the possibilities and challenges of "writing history across time and space" in their entry, "Pan-historiography."

Expressing a desire to put histories, artifacts, and archives in "motion," they argue for extended histories that stretch, temporally, beyond the "disciplinary trend" of "restricted or focused histories," which—although without disparaging the value of such synchronic studies—might elide an understanding of or "attention to residual accumulation of *topoi*, beliefs, and strategic practices" that only a spanning, diachronic approach can reveal.

In "Stitching Together Events," Byron Hawk resists historiographical practices that appropriate events into tidy narratives, limiting "possible readings," in order to establish a truth and a "specific historical *telos*." In contrast, Hawk envisions a networked historiography that would "version" "emergent possibilities" through the lens of jazz improvisation and complexity theory to produce histories that "perform events in present rhetorical situations, and that feed back into the present to produce multiple lines of flight to the future." Likewise, Jane S. Sutton risks the future—and our Aristotelian past, in her essay, "Rhetoric's Nose," in which she allows herself to be "caught unawares," and she invites rhetoric—and the historiography of such—to open itself to its (excluded) problematic relation to the "semantic domain of the unexpected, the exception, and the accidental."

In my entry, "Historiography as Hauntology," I take up a Derridean challenge by proposing a historiographical method of conversing with the dead—with those figures that inhabit the threshold of our understanding and that unsettle our understanding of the "past," and thereby invite us to refigure the "future," as not-yet, ethically. Also writing "the future," G. L. Ercolini and Pat J. Gehrke posit, in "Writing Future Rhetoric," that most histories written with a predictive claim "obviate and forestall the potentialities of the future." They offer, in contrast, the historiographical method as writing the future "as a transgressive act of self-experimentation," as a "ficture"—that "provide[s] futures that are at once fictive and yet offer the possibility of a fissure with our present, with our relationships to time, and to ourselves." And Victor J. Vitanza provides us with a seminar, complete with readings, assignments, and "test drives," in "A Philology for a Future Anterior." Desiring to refigure classical philology (heretofore figured as the "scientific, modernist set" of "principles and lawful tools *to know* the past") in the future anterior tense, Vitanza invites us to rethink, reread, and rewrite histories of rhetoric through a transvaluation of the (un)timely, which amounts to *willing* "to have begun histories for the advancement of *living*."

As Jessica Enoch writes, "I'm interested in . . . think[ing] beyond (or at least put[ting] pressure on) both the dominant modes of practice as well as the overarching goal of feminist scholarship." The contributors, in multiple ways, likewise—to appropriate Enoch—have put pressure on dominant modes of historiographic practice as well as the overarching goal of writing histories by attempting to "think beyond." Such a thinking invites historians to "break with the determination of reality exclusively in terms of cognition and the rules of knowledge used to determine it" (Carroll 23). That is, according to Jean-François Lyotard: "The historian . . . must risk lending his or her ear to what is not presentable under the rules of knowledge. Every reality entails this exigency insofar as it entails possible unknown meanings" (qtd. in Carroll 23).

Retheorizing writing histories of rhetoric, I am suggesting, asks that "we" historians challenge our methodological approaches, to wonder if, in our effort to recover "the third man" (or woman), we are not merely "neutralizing or domesticating the senseless" (Ronell, "Is It Happening?" 325), according to the "rules of knowledge" that govern our current methodologies. Rather, I am further suggesting, we might tarry in the wonder of the unpresentable with wonder. However that which presents itself as unpresentable often appears as, is taken as, is understood as, *monstrous* (see Derrida, "Passages"). And as the great epistemic project of the West has been to "de-monster" our thinking (see Vitanza, *Negation* 160), the greater challenge is to *think monstrously*. Etymologically, one might be surprised to learn that "to think" and "monster" share a common root. According to *The American Heritage Dictionary of Indo-European Roots,* the root "men-" indicates "to think; with derivatives referring to various qualities and states of mind and thought" (54). Following related derivations, including Old English and Greek words for memory and Latin words for remembrance (54), we come to the O-grade form ("mon-"), which brings us to the Latin words *monument, admonish, demonstrate,* and—yes—*monster* (Watkins 54; see also Vitanza, *Negation* 148). To think *monsters*, to remember *monsters,* however, is not to construct *taxonomies* of monsters, such as that composed by Ambroise Paré. To think monsters, to remember monsters, to historicize monstrously, on the contrary, is to wonder at "singularity."

According to Caroline Walker Bynum, "we write the best history when the specificity, the novelty, the awe-fulness . . . bowls us over with its complexity" (74). "Amazement," she also writes, "is suppressed by the citing of too many cases, the formulation of general laws. . . . Wonder is at the singular" (73). To retheorize writing histories of rhetoric, once again, is to think beyond that which presents itself or is made to present itself "according to classical values of presentation" (Ronell, "Is It Happening?" 325), which is to think beyond, of course, those very values of re/presentation and rules of cognition that govern our historiographical practices.

What such a wonderful, monstrous historiography would do is, in Lyotard's words, "bear witness [to the unrepresentable]. . . . It does not say the unsayable, but says that it cannot say it" (qtd. in Carroll 24). It says, "I don't even know how to tell this story. All I know how to do is to tell that I no longer know how to tell this story" (25). This "insufficiency" to the task of writing histories (of rhetoric) becomes the condition of possibility of the impossibility of writing histories (of rhetoric). This "modest possibility" (Carroll) engendered by epistemological humility is the "gesture of traversing peril and running a risk—a risk that does not know and cannot tell where it's going" (Ronell, "Slow Learner" 265). And this is the risk that *theorizing* writing histories of rhetoric embraces—for our past, our present, and our future (anterior).

1

THEORY, VALIDITY, AND THE HISTORIOGRAPHY OF CLASSICAL RHETORIC: A DISCUSSION OF ARCHAEOLOGICAL RHETORIC

Richard Leo Enos

All these are questions which we cannot answer; the facts were known to the writer of the tablet, and he did not expect it to be read by anyone who did not have the same knowledge; just as many of us make jottings in our diaries which convey a clear message to us, but would be meaningless to a stranger ignorant of the circumstances in which they were written. This problem is still with us, and will always remain; we cannot know all the facts and events of which the tablets are an only partial record. We have to examine them as minutely as we can, to compare them with similar documents elsewhere, to check them against the archaeological evidence.

—John Chadwick, *The Decipherment of Linear B*

Introduction: Cognitive and Physical Contexts as Historical Evidence

The above epigraph—purposefully taken out of context for reasons that will become clear before this introduction is over—is John Chadwick's observation of the contextual factors that had to be accounted for when his colleague Michael Ventris was laboring toward what would become a monumental achievement: the decipherment of one of the earliest forms of Greek, Linear B. It would be tedious to repeat the number of times Ventris and Chadwick remarked on how knowing the context of the writing played a major role in the decipherment of the clay tablets that had puzzled scholars for decades. Of course, "context" is the critical term in fully appreciating the insight of Chadwick's statement, because he meant that accounting for not only the physical but also the cognitive conditions would yield a better understanding of the discourse than would merely attempting to decipher the scratch-marks on the clay tablets alone and in isolation. Knowing the circumstances is no less critical for historians of rhetoric than it is for cryptographers and philologists. Without knowledge of the situation, we too are doomed to make limited observations about the rhetoric of the past. It is reasonable to think, as Ventris and Chadwick did in their own work, that the recent evidence of archaeological findings would be as illuminating to us as historians of rhetoric as it was in their work. To me, this point is so obvious that it hardly bears elaboration. However others in my field disagree, for an abundance of research on rhetoric's history is undertaken with scant (often superficial) attention to the historical context and, in far too many cases, a total disregard for recent archaeological evidence or, for that matter, any evidence whatsoever that falls outside the narrow domain of traditional "literary" sources. The purpose of this essay is not to pour scorn on the textual criticism of rhetoric. Rather, my intent in revealing the inherent limitations that come from traditional research methods in the history of rhetoric is to argue that such methods can be enriched considerably by assimilating such nontraditional resources as archaeological evidence into our research. The focus of this discussion is on my own area of emphasis, classical rhetoric, but the benefits of extending the parameters of our range of primary resources should apply to other periods in rhetoric's history. Without a context, the observations in the epigraph of this essay would be, if not meaningless, a challenge to understand. This principle holds for our approach to historiography as well. The point of archaeological rhetoric is not only to discover and reconstruct physical artifacts that provide insights to the context within which rhetoric took place, but also to reconstruct the mentalities of the culture that produced such discourse. In these two senses, archaeological rhetoric is more than a mere search for observable, empirical evidence; it is also an effort to construct the epistemic processes that invent rhetoric. It is this effort to reconstruct the physical *and* the cognitive that will enhance our current methods of research in classical rhetoric.

One of the primary points of reflection in seeking to evaluate the limitations of conventional scholarly procedures should be a reconsideration of our preference for research methods. Our traditional avenue for knowledge of classical rhetoric has been the descent of manuscripts passed along from antiquity, the Middle Ages, and the Renaissance, and from modern periods of the book tradition. Yet classical rhetoric also is enriched annually by new information that is not from the "book" tradition but from such diverse areas as archaeology, epigraphy, fine arts, cognitive rhetoric, and new media refinements in archival studies. With all of this abundance of potential information, however, we continue to research classical rhetoric from conventional sources and by traditional textual approaches. In fact, many scholars believe that classical rhetoric ought to be studied by classical approaches. Unfortunately, "classical approaches" are not really "classical" at all but rather Victorian; that is, the methods of studying classical rhetoric were based on the methods used in classical studies for the last two centuries. We have, over those two centuries, so strongly associated Victorian philological methods with the study of classical rhetoric that those Victorian methods have been inextricably wedded to (and confused as being) something that grew out of antiquity. As a result of this confusion, the newest, and often the most insightful, theoretical perspectives and innovative historiographical methods are dismissed for no other reason than that they lack (Victorian) tradition. Scholars have so closely associated classical rhetoric with long-outdated Victorian research practices that they are unwilling to risk being "unfaithful" by departing from long-established methods (R. L. Enos, "The Classical Tradition(s) of Rhetoric"). I can, for example, vividly recall in the early 1980s how one reader of a classical journal had technology "issues" and clearly was appalled that a manuscript had been submitted for consideration that had been printed from a "word-processing" computer and not a typewriter! While there is no doubt that well-established research approaches have much to offer, innovative theoretical gains and attendant research heuristics offer fruitful new approaches in the historiography of classical rhetoric that complement long-established research practices.

The Presumptions of Historiographical Research

No arguments need to be advanced (again) that warrant the benefits of historical research in rhetoric. Rhetoric has already been clearly established as a social, political, and educational force in antiquity; in fact, it is now difficult to imagine studying the social history of ancient Greece without accounting for the cultural force of rhetoric. In juxtaposition to this view, we cannot hope to understand rhetoric without understanding the wide-ranging social forces in Hellenic city-states. What does need to be argued are the ways that we try to advance our understanding of the nature and impact of rhetoric within its social context. This issue came to light dramatically some years ago when an active effort began to study women in the history of rhetoric. As was demonstrably pointed out, if we consider rhetoric to be only overtly agonistic acts of persuasion that occur in civic centers, then we constrain our view to only one dimension of rhetoric in social interaction and, by default, exclude women, as well as other marginalized groups who engage in nonsanctioned rhetorical activities. Because women, for example, were normally not given equal access to civic functions, should we presume that they had no "rhetoric" of their own, or that they never used their rhetoric to social ends? This point complements the observations of Cheryl Glenn and Jessica Enoch: "Not surprisingly, feminist theory enabled us (and many others) to resist traditional histories and historiographic practices inside the field as a means to create new kinds of historical inquiry and archival reading practices" ("Drama in the Archives" 333).

Postmodern rhetoric has caused us to reflect not only on our gender preferences but also on our cultural presumptions, cautioning researchers not to exclude "rhetorics" that do not conform to the hegemonic rhetoric of the period and culture being examined. The same myopic constraints that were once held against the study of women in the history of rhetoric could also be applied to self-imposed cultural constraints in classical rhetoric. For example, Athens was a dominant site for rhetoric. So dominant, in fact, that we both tend to generalize Athenian rhetoric as (pan-) Hellenic and to use Athenian rhetoric as a standard for judgment of other contemporary rhetoric(s) of the Hellenic world. Yet current work in ethnography has shown us that every society has rhetoric, but not all of these rhetorics are manifested in a similar fashion; this view is also becoming apparent in current historical research in rhetoric, as is clearly revealed by the edited volume of Carol S. Lipson and Roberta A. Binkley, *Rhetoric Before and Beyond the Greeks*. The relative perspective growing out of ethnographic research in anthropology challenges us to reexamine the traditional, Athenian-dominated perspective on Greek rhetoric. For example, because Athenian and Spartan societies are so dramatically different, a Spartan rhetoric would understandably appear to be far different than an Athenian rhetoric because their respective rhetorics would be fashioned to meet the needs of their own societies and cultures (R. L. Enos, "The Secret Composition Practices of the Ancient Spartans"). In short, if every ancient rhetoric were judged by the standards of Athenian-based rhetoric, each non-Athenian rhetoric would be viewed as both different—because each polis was different—and wanting—because that rhetoric might not attend to features that were important in Athens but not relevant in another city-state in the Hellenic world. Most of us tend to resist new methods and new resources because they disturb the uniformity of conventional, established methods; tend not to venerate the past for its own sake; and may mean that judgments that were once so firmly in place in our minds now need to be reevaluated. Our starting point in doing historical research in classical rhetoric must always be self-reflective; that is, we need always to examine our own preferences with the criterion that our methods and choice of evidence be driven by the belief that they make the most compelling case for convincing our academic community that an interpretation is accurate.

Theory and/as Evidence

The first step in reassessing our methods of doing research in classical rhetoric is to reflect on the theoretical presumptions that drive our work. Can one do historical work in classical rhetoric that is atheoretical? The answer is "yes," but such work would be predicated on a very limited notion of history. Atheoretical historical research is little more than reporting descriptive data—in effect, little more than the chronicling of a story. That is, the task of such "historians" would be to list events and use as their guide a diachronic recording of "when" things happened. Historiography is a narrative activity, but does an atheoretical approach accurately explain the "how" and the "why" of chronicled events? Herodotus is called "The Father of History" because he was the first known Greek historian to advance interpretations *explaining* the outcomes of events that he recorded; that is, Herodotus's *The Persian Wars* accounts for the forces at work that enabled the Athenians to triumph over the Persians. To accomplish his ends, Herodotus travelled outside of Greece to Persia, gathering evidence while seeking to better understand the mentalities of the Persians, so that he could explain their motives and perspective. Such an approach to history requires an interpretation of evidence, but determining what is "evidence" and the perspective taken for interpretation need not be idiosyncratic and personal. In fact, the task of building a theory is driven by both the need to explain and the need to justify not only what is evidence but also the frame of reference to be used to interpret the meaning of what we have discovered. From such a view, it is clear that even the choice and selection of methods must be argued for as the most sensitive heuristics warranting our research-based interpretations. In short, a theory accounts for the facts not only by verifying the accuracy of evidence but also by using the knowledge that we receive from that evidence to advance explanations of the forces at work. The saliency of theories is adjudicated by an audience, a very special audience, who has its own field of argument. Theories must be convincing to this communal audience of disciplinary colleagues. In that sense, each theory is an argument as well as an explanation because it must be judged as valid by those in the community to whom it is addressed. *Theoretical validity is adjudicated based upon the evidence used to warrant the interpretation advanced.*

If we are to consider theory as a force driving research methods of historical rhetoric, and are to believe that the validity of our methods (as well as the theory driving those methods) is adjudicated by our academic community, then the evidence that we use to marshal our "argument" is of paramount importance. Our ability to reason and advance explanations in a manner that makes sense to those who stand in judgment is a critical skill. Traditional research methods in literary studies encourage readers to make "close" or "thick" readings of texts and then to advance observations/interpretations from those texts. Research in historical rhetoric, however, involves more "evidence" than what is printed on a page. Rhetoric, to be sure, may have been recorded on a page, but the rhetoric itself came to life in a real, dynamic situation occurring at a moment in time. Understanding the context that initially prompted the rhetoric is critical if we are to advance meaning beyond what appears on a page. To reproduce the environment within which that piece of discourse was created, we must both gather and create evidence that enables us to attain knowledge of the context: physical and cognitive. To re-create that scene, we must look to any and all artifacts that offer insight to the cultural context of the situation, as well as the rhetoric under examination. This may be seen, in Aristotelian terms, as inartistic proofs and may come in the form of architecture, archaeological artifacts, epigraphy, or any other resource or method that provides evidence about the ethnography and mentality of past rhetoric. These resources, like our rational deliberations, still require interpretative arguments of their relevance and appropriateness.

Physical and Cognitive Contextual Evidence

In Hellenic discourse, artifacts for study are usually considered to be descriptive evidence left in the form of extant orations and manuals of rhetoric. Historical research in rhetoric usually confines itself to deductions and inferences drawn from scribe to scholar over centuries, and observations are often restricted to textual features; in fact, there have even been efforts to dismiss and avoid inquiry into the "artistic impulse" of constructing rhetoric and literature (Gelb 61–66). Without question, scholars of philology have told us much about oral and written discourse in the ancient world based only on the remains of these documents. However, studies that rely on "content analysis" permit only a restricted inquiry into the study of Hellenic discourse and, as I. J. Gelb has revealed, offer little attention to the relationship of writing and language in its living context (64). *In short, considering rhetoric a conceptual, generating process in Hellenic discourse is outside the traditional methodologies used for such historical research.* Yet knowing the epistemological basis and social situations upon which discourse is predicated is essential to understanding contextual meaning—and the process used to help create that shared meaning—of the discourse itself. In brief, archaeological rhetoric gathers physical artifacts but does so not only to better understand the environment of discourse but also as a resource for advancing explanations of cognition and expression that reveal the mentalities driving ancient rhetoric.

If a theory of rhetoric is to capture historical mentalities, then a theory of rhetoric ought to account for all relevant, contextual phenomena—even those that can be classified as "unobservable" notions outside the parameters of content-analytic methodologies but instrumental in the process of language development. Yet as Jerrold Katz wrote, "An assumption about the existence of an unobservable system puts a weight on our credulity that can only be supported by proportionally strong evidence, by evidence strong enough to bear the strain" (18). This sort of "evidence" clearly is not traditional, but neither is it empirical nor even analytical, although both of the latter play a part in its formulation. Rather, as mentioned earlier, it is best understood as a synthesized "argument" for an interpretation of the notions, presumptions, and presuppositions that reveal the conceptual idea that grounds the discourse (Lane 17). Noam Chomsky has been one of the strongest proponents for inquiry into mental processes for the study of language and believes "that a rather convincing argument can be made for the view that certain principles intrinsic to the mind provide invariant structures that are a precondition for linguistic experience" (243). *In other words, in addition to expanding the domain of empirical evidence to include archaeological artifacts beyond the printed page, theories are needed in historical research in rhetoric that provide a sensitive explanation of psychological and epistemological presumptions upon which language constructs are developed and generated.* This explanation cannot come from the traditional methods of philological research indicated above but rather must consider a rhetorical vector, since what is being examined is an epistemic process grounding articulation and expression. In sum, we can improve our contributions to the history of rhetoric—in this instance classical rhetoric—by attending to the relationship between cognition and expression in two respects. First, we should study the rhetoric of the period by grasping the mentality of the time. Reconstructing the mentality of the time can be attained by recognizing that the epistemic nature of thought and its contextual grounding shapes (and is in turn shaped by) a view of reality by the rhetor or by the rhetorician. This notion is akin to studies in anthropology, which goes beyond the text/discourse proper and considers the context of the situation. In historical rhetoric, our attention is to archaeology and the benefits that that discipline offers to this end. That is, an examination of material evidence, much of which has come to light only in the last century, can tell us a great deal about the context of rhetorical discourse and enrich our understanding of the social and cultural factors shaping the mentalities of the time in the rhetors' efforts to create or build upon a shared view of reality with auditors/readers. Understanding the epistemic nature of rhetoric, along with an examination of material artifacts, provide a more thorough accounting for rhetoric's history than conventional research procedures can hope to yield. The role of rhetoric in the structuring of Hellenic discourse will be explained by reviewing a traditional, philological, text-based method of researching Hellenic discourse.

Rethinking Homer: The Homeric Mind and the Homeric Problem

An archaeological approach to classical rhetoric can do more than account for and reconstruct historical artifacts that enrich our knowledge of the physical context. An archaeological approach to rhetoric can also seek to reconstruct the mentalities of the past and, in doing so, better understand the social and cultural context of rhetoric. For example, one of the most prominent efforts in studying Hellenic discourse is Milman Parry's research on Homeric compositional structure (for example, "L'épithéte," "Studies in the Epic Technique," and *The Making of Homeric Verse*). Parry's brilliant pioneering and insightful work concentrates on identifying and isolating formulae, or consistent patterns of work-forms, as a means of determining the nature of Homeric discourse. Parry's research is grounded on the presumption that the formula is *"a group of words which is regularly employed under the same metrical conditions to express a given essential idea"* (*The Making of Homeric Verse* 272; emphasis in original).

Albert B. Lord, Parry's pupil, dissatisfied with his teacher's restrictive methods, created tests for enjambment, formulaic language, and theme in an effort to consider consistency in patterns of syntactic periods and lexical clumps (Peabody 2). Berkley Peabody, in turn, added and refined other tests in order to determine the nature of Homeric discourse: a phonemic test to measure consistency in patterns of language-sounds, a formulaic test to determine consistent patterns of word-forms, an enjambment test to determine consistency in syntactic periods, a thematic test to determine consistency in the patterns of lexical clumps, and a song test to measure consistency in patterns of discourse (3–5). These content-analytic tests are considered valid methods of determining Homeric compositional structure. In the spirit of New Criticism textual analysis, all these "tests" are based on Parry's own unchallenged and unsupported presumption that the development of an empirically formulated measure of quantitative linguistic scales will reveal the "idea" upon which the discourse is formed; that is, the claim that the phenomenon of persistent formularity is in itself the manifestation of the "essential idea." The context of the discourse, the social factors of the circumstances of creation and transmission are not a part of such tests. Because of the dominance of textual close-reading methodology, researchers have observed formulaic patterns but have not advanced cogent interpretations of how and why these patterns were generated—the rhetorical vector of such oral composition is unexplained.

It should be noted that Parry and Lord did do comparative analysis by observing the composition techniques of Yugoslavian bards. This comparison was enlightening, for the similarity of techniques between Yugoslavian bards mapped well with Parry's philological analysis of Homeric composition. Yet this is, in the end, a comparison only and not an archaeological reconstruction of the contexts of Homeric discourse. While observations based on comparison have benefit, there is no substitute for studying the actual event. Some scholars, however, believe such efforts at epistemic reconstruction to be fruitless. J. A. Russo argues that "history has hidden Homer's methods of poetic creation from us, beyond all recovery, and certainly beyond the research of all *ex cathedra* pronouncements about what can be 'proved' from the study of his style" (49–50). In one respect, Russo's views are accurate because the methods of empirical "proof" used to retrieve information on language use and development are too restrictive to yield the desired knowledge. For such claims to be advanced with any degree of saliency, the rhetorical process must be examined. To bring Chomsky's views into the discussion again, "the study of language . . . offers strong empirical evidence that empiricist theories of learning are quite inadequate," and such theories fail because "they are intrinsically incapable of giving rise to the system of rules that underlies the normal use of language" (251).

In brief, the direct opposite of Parry's claim is argued here as a cogent explanation of Hellenic discourse; an understanding of the "essential idea" will account for the discourse generated. The discourse wells up out of its social context and mentality, both of which shape the idea of conceptualization and expression. To accomplish this objective, rhetoric must be seen as a critical process in forming the "essential idea" of the discourse and not merely its final echo in the ear or on the page. Although we know much more about the formal compositional structure of Greek discourse than our Victorian predecessors, we really know no more about the epistemological presumptions based upon a synthesized view of Homer's competency in language use from traditional philological methods. To be sure, such information provides insights as a basis of subsequent inquiry into the notions and presumptions upon which Hellenic discourse is conceptualized. Yet as discussed above, empirical and quantitative textual tests alone can make only limited claims when confined to the analysis of noun-epithet combinations or similar formal measures; in short, proof of "ideas" cannot be empirically verified but must be interpreted and synthesized in cogent argumentative interpretation. The research cited above failed to challenge this presumption by not acknowledging rhetoric in the socially grounded contextual process of language formulation and rhetorical theory as a means of accounting for the development of this process in the history of rhetoric.

In the last several decades, rhetoricians (most notably Robert L. Scott) have argued that epistemic processes can be considered rhetorical both in generating discourse and constructing cognitive processes for the transformation of meaning (Scott, "On Viewing Rhetoric as Epistemic" 9–17; "On Viewing Rhetoric as Epistemic Ten Years Later" 258–66; cf. Cherwitz 207–19). An approach considering the epistemic capacity of discourse to be rhetorical and advancing theories that account for this generative process within its archaeological context, as I have argued, "does not diminish the classical notion of rhetoric as persuasion but rather reveals a deeper structuring of persuasion—as interpretative choice and construction of how one comes to acquire knowledge and view the world" (R. L. Enos, "The Structuring of Rhetorical Theories" 4). In essence, as Chaim Perelman and Lucie Olbrechts-Tyteca posit, it is this fundamental rhetorical process that grounds the "structure to establish a solidarity between accepted judgments and others which one wishes to promote" (261). Thus, if we recognize that thorough explanations of Hellenic discourse necessitate an understanding of the psychological and epistemological structures that "build" Hellenic discourse, and if we recognize the structural process as rhetorical, then we must acknowledge the indispensability of theories that can account for these rhetorical vectors in historical research. Fundamental rhetorical processes have been recognized by scholars in related areas. Henry W. Johnstone Jr., for example, argues that "all philosophical arguments have a necessary and proper rhetorical vector" (61). Moreover, Walter J. Ong explicitly stresses the need for understanding the psychodynamics of discourse in his essay "Literacy and Orality in Our Times": "Speech wells up out of the unconscious, supported by unconsciously organized grammatical structures that even the most ardent structural and transformational grammarians now admit can never all be surfaced entirely into consciousness" (2).

The need for providing rhetorical theory to account for the epistemic processes in historical studies of rhetoric becomes further apparent when one considers the oral tradition that preceded (and was endemic within) Homeric literature. Indo-European historical linguistics spans at least five millennia (Byron 23). Although the Phoenician alphabet may have been introduced to Greece as early as the thirteenth century B.C.E., the oral composition of discourse did not even begin to be replaced by writing until the seventh century B.C.E. When the *Iliad* and the *Odyssey* were composed, Greece was in the waning era of oral literature. Yet we know that for centuries prior to the period, storytellers, called *aoidoi*, orally transmitted heroic adventures similar to those found in Homer. In this respect, and as I have tried to show in earlier work, Homer, an eighth-century B.C.E. *aoidos*, wrote about other *aoidoi*, such as Demodocus and Phemius, who lived during the oral, preliterate period (R. L. Enos, *Greek Rhetoric before Aristotle* 20–42). The discovery procedures of the discourse clearly cannot be limited solely to explanations of empirical observation of literate texts but must account for evolving concepts and generative competency of orality and literacy, that is, the Homeric mentality. In Homeric Greek, for example, there are several words that appear only once (*hapax legomena*): the *Iliad* has 1,097 and the *Odyssey* has 868 such occurrences (Pharr xxvi). One would be hard-pressed to account for these 1,965 "creations" synchronically by the text alone; more importantly, explanatory powers in such a traditional, text-based approach would fail to account for the conceptual creation of these new forms and meanings. Yet by reconstructing the social and cultural milieu, we can also reconstruct the perspective of rhetoric that occurred in the Bronze Age view of reality.

Epistemic processes that assimilate archaeological evidence to supply knowledge of the context within which discourse is generated can be examined in several ways. Homeric Greek, for example, has the dual number for nouns which permits the rhetor to join plural notions within a single word entities with a single notion—such as "two hands" (*cheire*), "two eyes" (*opthalmo*), and "two horses" (*hippo*)—as a normal feature of the language (Pharr 227–28). Perelman and Olbrechts-Tyteca have written extensively to show how the development of such coexistence of two notions in a single expression is a conceptual process revealing how discourse is based upon a presumed structure of reality (327–31). As the dual structure all but passed out of Greek grammar, so, obviously, did the particular structuring of reality through the dual coexistence upon which the form was generated. (Of course, some residue of this form remains to this day; in English we still speak of a *pair* of scissors.) Other comparable examples abound; Greek grammar has five cases: nominative, genitive, dative, accusative, and vocative. Yet there are remnants of three other cases: the locative, instrumental, and ablative (Pharr 228, 232). As any student of Greek grammar knows, the forms of such discourse also indicate a generative, conceptual function in the use of discourse. Essentially, what is being argued is not that we see the discourse as the manifestation of the idea, as Parry and his associates claimed, for that would limit findings solely to textual observation. Rather, the epistemic process upon which the discourse is generated should be understood beyond the text proper. The former perspective confines analysis to observation, the latter to a synthetic interpretation of conceptual processes as an explanatory function of the discourse.

As a beneficiary to this oral tradition, Homer's obsolete or "created" terms (*glossai*) mentioned earlier were most probably conceived during this oral period, but methods of analysis that tolerate only evidence from observable, extant texts would waive any synthesis of the conceptual processes that helped to formulate the evolving discourse. Interestingly, the desire to maintain the "correct" pronunciation of Homer's literature persisted for centuries, despite the influence of dialects and foreign languages (Maas 1; Plato, *Ion* 533c, *det*; Pfeiffer 10–11; Pindar, *Olympian Odes* 2. 83–85). Hellenic rhapsodes became linguistic guardians who synchronically tried to fix and thereby stabilize and preserve ancient phonology. As centuries passed, the evolution of the Greek tongue increasingly distanced the oral characteristics of the contemporary language and made the "correct" pronunciation, intonation, accent, and rhythm of Homeric Greek regressively more difficult (Maas 3–4, 13–15; W. S. Allen 4). Of significance to this work, the rhapsodes and lexicographers had failed to grasp the conceptual processes of Homeric literature and the oral tradition that preceded it; in fact, even Plato, who criticized the rhapsodes in his *Ion*, did not understand the etymology and evolution of the very individuals who transmitted the literature (Plato, *Ion* 533c; R. L. Enos, "Verso"). Consequently, limitations in comprehending the epistemic processes that generated the discourse restricted their knowledge to the observable and oral/aural forms of the literature. Unable to recreate the language epistemically, ancient scholars were reduced to adopting a written system of diacritical notations, or stress symbols, to indicate vocal quality, quantity, and meaning. Such notational systems are a weak substitute for an understanding of the conceptual processes that generated the Homeric tongue and eventually came to be reduced to an artificially fixed form. Ironically, the very inability of rhapsodes to preserve the Homeric tongue through time came because of their inability to reconstruct the conceptual basis of their own language change. Historians of our discipline who ignore "rhetorical" mentalities, and thus fail to account for cognitive processes in theories and attendant methodologies, risk the same fate. The irony is that despite his stringent criticism of writing, Plato's own literate mentality facilitated his ability to abstract thought into discrete ontological concepts, much the same way that doing mathematics orally (that is, without writing or a calculator) makes performing advanced computation exceedingly more difficult if not impossible.

A passage from Isocrates' *Panegyricus* further illustrates this rhetorically epistemic perspective: " *ten men archen eis ton polemon kateste<u>san</u> hos eleutherosontes tous Hellenas, epi de teleutes houto pollous auton ekdotous epoie<u>san</u>, kai, tes men hemeteras poleos tous Ionas apeste<u>san</u>, ex hes apoike<u>san</u> kai di hen pollakis esothe<u>san</u>*" (in the beginning they entered into the war so that they could free the Greeks, but in the end they have betrayed so many of them, and because they [encouraged] the Ionians to revolt from our city, from which they emigrated and were frequently saved) (4. 122). Observation of the text reveals, as indicated by underlining, an empirically verifiable pattern of end-rhyming, which is labeled "*homoioteleuton*" (Smyth 678). Yet much can be advanced beyond observation if epistemic processes are considered. Certainly this discourse is constructed upon the presumption of establishing some sequence or notion of causality, which is evident in the first two verses. In addition, Isocrates apparently presumes that acts are seen as the manifestation of attitudes; for example, "entering into the war" (act) coexists with the manifestation of having been "betrayed" (attitude). The parallel clauses not only demonstrate an observable unity of verse, they also reveal ways that knowledge is conceptualized in both the sequential establishment of reasoning and the coexistence of notions. Such interpretations, since they are not observable in the sense of the figure of speech indicated above, must be argued. Yet a valid interpretation can account for an explanation of the conceptual processes upon which Hellenic discourse was generated, and therefore predicated, once the rhetorical vector of the conceptual process is acknowledged in methodological research. Knowing, for example, that Presocratic philosophers often thought in terms of dissociations (*dissoi logoi*) helps to explain not only their relativistic view of philosophy, but also how they influenced the epistemology of the Sophists who were their students (R. L. Enos, *Greek Rhetoric before Aristotle* 109–42).

Archaeological rhetoric facilitates our understanding of the writings of not only such luminaries as Homer, Plato, and Isocrates, but also mundane, everyday rhetoric as well. That is, recognizing the physical and cognitive contexts of writing tells us a great deal about the functional literate habits of the day in classical Athens or Sparta. For example, over the last century, scholars at the American School of Classical Studies, such as Mabel Lang, have unearthed thousands of inscriptions from excavations in Athens and other environs throughout Greece. Ranging from the middle of the eighth century B.C.E. to the sixth century of our own era, these mundane writings that were never intended for publication nevertheless provide direct evidence of everyday literate habits. From such functional scripts we have learned much about educational practices, political procedures, complex commercial transactions, the writing and reading habits of women and other marginalized groups, and the sophisticated functional writing of labor classes. In addition to insights about education, class, and civic procedures, such graffiti and dipinti record expressive writing that tells us a great deal about attitudes, dispositions, and social practices. In short, such "trivial" archaeological evidence enriches our understanding of the civic context, allows a thicker meaning of what a literate community means, and gives a direct insight to the mentalities of the time.

Conclusion: Contributing to a Study of Thought and Expression

It should be clear that understanding the textual features of formulaic discourse alone does not itself explain the epistemic processes that developed the heuristics used in composition. This latter step has not been fully dealt with in traditional studies of classical rhetoric, and consequently, the larger role of theoretical synthesis in Hellenic discourse has been neglected. *If we take rhetoric to mean a process of choosing and selecting discourse as a means of constructing reality, then rhetorical methods must account for and include archaeological and epigraphical evidence in their research methods if a more sensitive understanding of situated discourse is to be realized than content-analysis alone can yield.*

As a similar feature to the physical counterpart of archaeological rhetoric, rhetorical theory analyzes and synthesizes evidence in order to interpret the epistemology and articulation of Hellenic discourse, discourse that is both situated in time and influenced by the social contexts within which it is involved. The implications of this perspective reveal not only the importance of rhetorical theory driving historical research, but also the methodologies employed in that research. In Homeric literature, to refer to the extended example used here, there is ample evidence to illustrate that eloquence was viewed as a gift from the gods and not a technical skill (for example, Homer, *Iliad* 1. 247–49; 3. 200–224; 9. 433; *Odyssey* 8. 165–85; Hesiod, *Theogonia* 74–103). Moreover, "conviction" is attained by a "persuasion of the heart" of Odysseus, and insight is endowed to Telemachus by such mentors as Athena and referred to as a divine gift (Homer, *Odyssey* 9. 33; 2. 267). Furthermore, to the epic poet Hesiod, Promethus personified the human capacity to create (*techné*) (Pucci 82–101). Yet Promethus's disclosure of divine knowledge to man led directly to Zeus's revenge: Pandora's release of the god's gift to men, including divine eloquence (Hesiod, *Works and Days* 90–105). The loss of this divine power of eloquence led man to a self-conscious *techné* of discourse and a rational approach to language development. Although these mythic notions are grounded in irrationality, and are not revealed by the metrical patterns of formulae, they do reveal some presumptions on the part of Homer and Hesiod about how eloquence was attained and how individuals were persuaded by how they (rhetorically) structured the meaning of reality. As researchers, it is essential to recognize and account for such presumptions if we hope to understand the relationship between thought and expression in ancient Greece.

In like manner, as Presocratic philosophers moved from an accounting of acts via personified forces to such dialectic terms as *logos* and *dissoi logoi*, they revealed a corresponding shift in the presumptions of the acquisition of knowledge and the structuring of reality. In fact, the debate about the nature of rhetoric between Sophists and Socrates is best seen as a debate about epistemological presumptions—that is, the presumptions of what constitutes reality and the grounding of discourse in relativistic or ontological terms. Likewise, when Antiphon employs the notions of "probability," "intent," "presumption," and "motive" in *The Murder of Herodes,* he is revealing an epistemic shift in the notion of what constitutes effective discourse from predominantly emotive utterance to rationalism (R. L. Enos, *Greek Rhetoric before Aristotle* 199–210; Freeman). In brief, rhetorical theories are needed to account for the notions, presumptions, and presuppositions that went into the structuring of such discourse. This position may not seem unreasonable to researchers of contemporary rhetoric or postmodern theoreticians, but it is unknown—or at least unrecognized—to all but a few historians of rhetoric. Among the more standard, long-established works in classical rhetoric, few have dealt with the mentalities of ancient rhetoric. Some of the best of these exceptions include Charles Segal's "Gorgias and the Psychology of the Logos," E. R. Dodds's *The Greeks and the Irrational,* Helen North's *Sophrosyne: Self-Knowledge and Self-Restraint in Greek Literature,* and Eric Havelock's *Preface to Plato.* Many others in the canon of our classical scholarship, however, do not consider the epistemic process or more importantly, recognize its rhetorical nature in their explanations. More recent scholars, however, have begun to depart from Victorian methods and offer new, insightful contributions to the mentalities driving classical rhetoric. Such recent, innovative works include Cheryl Glenn's *Rhetoric Retold: Regendering the Tradition from Antiquity through the Renaissance,* Edward Schiappa's *The Beginnings of Rhetorical Theory in Classical Greece,* Susan C. Jarratt's *Rereading the Sophists: Classical Rhetoric Refigured,* John Poulakos's *Sophistical Rhetoric in Classical Greece,* Jeffrey Walker's *Rhetoric and Poetics in Antiquity,* Ekaterina V. Haskins's *Logos and Power in Isocrates and Aristotle,* Debra Hawhee's *Bodily Arts: Rhetoric and Athletics in Ancient Greece,* and James Fredal's *Rhetorical Action in Ancient Athens: Persuasive*

Artistry from Solon to Demosthenes. All of these current scholars range widely in their topics and orientations, but all share some traits: they all have broadened the range of "evidence" in order to gain new insights to the mentalities creating rhetoric, the context of the environments within which that rhetoric was produced, and the cultural consequences of their historical interpretations. *Accounting for such "evidence" compels researchers to go beyond the drawing of philological inferences from the text and necessitates theoretical inquiry into the epistemic presumptions that structure rhetorical discourse within its historical contexts, physical and cognitive.*

The above discussion has presented concerns about syntactic change (the alteration and evolution of discourse) and philological change (the preservation of sound patterns). It is clear that earlier efforts have emphasized observation and limited study to an examination of textual performance. If the objective is to understand the "idea" of discourse, then emphasis should be placed on the generative competency for the discourse within the circumstances of its utterance. This understanding requires an examination of the epistemic processes of rhetoric that formulate meaning and theories that account for the contextual phenomenon of its performance. The position presented here argues for such a point and that methods of retrieval of such "data" must inevitably turn to rhetoric and, in that sense, reveal its legitimacy and necessity as a tool for the analysis of Hellenic discourse. Inherent in this approach to methodology is the belief that all artifacts of the situation within which that discourse was produced constitute—directly or indirectly—evidence of the context for that discourse. Pottery, epigraphy, architectural remnants, and even the physical topography of the site are all sources for providing a more comprehensive awareness of the rhetorical situation. To be sure, traditional historiographical procedures that draw inferences strictly from textual analysis provide important contributions, but they come with limitations and constraints. These conventional methodologies for research in the history of rhetoric should be viewed as a prologue or means to discover the fundamental processes for the conceptualization of Hellenic discourse. For a thorough understanding of Hellenic rhetoric, epistemic processes also need to be considered, and we must recognize these processes as rhetorical and situated, both mentally and physically. Archaeological rhetoric expands our range of evidence both by assimilating physical artifacts into our analysis of the context of ancient rhetoric, and also by providing theories that account for the mentalities that produce rhetoric. These two dimensions of archaeological rhetoric, the physical and the cognitive, yield "evidence" that helps to advance a richer interpretation of Hellenic discourse than textual analysis alone can hope to provide.

Note

I would like to express my appreciation to Dr. Michelle Ballif for providing me with the opportunity to continue the discussion of my observations on this important topic since the 2009 publication of my chapter in *The SAGE Handbook of Rhetorical Studies* and, more recently, in the 2012 edition of *Greek Rhetoric before Aristotle* (Parlor Press). A supportive and responsible editor, Dr. Ballif made insightful observations with every draft. Wendy Williams and Michelle Iten, Radford Research Associates, also guided me through problems with infinite patience and tact that helped greatly to clarify my views, both for the reader and for myself. As is apparent from the works cited, I have been forming my thoughts on this issue for several years. Many of the ideas that are elaborated in this work first appeared in nascent form in my 1981 essay "Notions, Presumptions, and Presuppositions in Hellenic Discourse." The observations presented here were built off many of those views but modified over time by continuing field work in both Greece and Italy, with exposure to the significant work done by historians of rhetoric, and also postmodern critics of rhetorical historiography. The insights mentioned in the more recent works of such researchers are also referenced in this essay.

All references to classical works appear in the universal, standard form of citation, and all translations, unless otherwise noted, are by the author. Accompanying translations for classical works are available in the Loeb Classical Library Series of the Harvard University Press.

2

ENACTMENT HISTORY, JESUIT PRACTICES, AND RHETORICAL HERMENEUTICS

Steven Mailloux

History exists only from out of a present.
  —Martin Heidegger, *The Phenomenology of Religious Life*

[P]ast events cannot be separated from the living present and
retain meaning. The true starting point of history is always some
present situation with its problems.
  —John Dewey, *Democracy and Education*

Hermeneutics is always about otherness. Hermeneutics theorizes how
otherness is "overcome" through interpretation, the making of sense,
the establishment of meaning. A specifically *rhetorical* hermeneutics claims
that interpretation takes place through tropes, arguments, and narratives
that persuade others to accept a way of sense making about the past, present,
or future. If *text* is defined as any object of interpretation, then rhetorical
hermeneutics theorizes the interpretation of various texts, including past
events, present utterances, or future actions. Within such a perspective,
interpreting the otherness of past practices is analogous to interpreting
otherness in present communication, both understood in relation to some
future action. In other words, we establish meaning for the otherness of the
past in ways similar to understanding others in the present, by relating all
to our own future enactments.

In this essay I will elaborate on the historiographical claims of this first
paragraph in three stages. The first section uses a recent disagreement over
interpreting a text about a fictional future to defend a theoretical account
of interpreting otherness in the actual present. The second section takes
this account as a theoretical frame for doing histories of rhetoric and then
presents a sample rhetorical history. And the third section comments on

this rhetorical history by making some additional historiographical remarks from the perspective of rhetorical hermeneutics.

Appropriating Otherness in the Present

"Shaka when the walls fell." This Tamarian speech act occurs repeatedly throughout the "Darmok" episode of the television series *Star Trek: The Next Generation*. In some of its iterations, the foreign utterance is an assertion that means something like "we have failed to communicate." The interlocutors are Captain Jean-Luc Picard of the Star Ship Enterprise from the United Federation of Planets and Captain Dathon from the Tamarian home world outside the Federation in Stardate year 45047.2 (2368 C.E.). The plot of the episode turns on the captains' repeated attempts to communicate, to make first contact, across the linguistic and broader cultural barriers that separate the two peoples they represent. The Tamarians artificially stage an encounter between the two captains by teleporting them down from their ships to an isolated planet inhabited by a strange Beast that threatens both. Through Dathon's patient tutoring, Picard comes to realize that his fellow captain is not an enemy but actually a potential friend, whose incomprehensible language consists of metaphors taken from Tamarian historical mythology. Once he figures this out, Picard encourages Dathon to tell the relevant story that forms the background for the speech acts the Tamarian is currently performing. Picard is finally able to interpret their current battle against a common enemy as analogically related to the Tamarian story of "Darmok and Jalad at Tanagra." Dathon and Picard then perform similar narrative practices, exchanging stories from their respective cultures. In this way, Picard and Dathon seem to have overcome the otherness of the other and successfully communicated. "Shaka when the walls fell" is replaced by "Sokath, his eyes uncovered!"

This television episode about a fictional future thematizes the fact that ultimately there are no incommensurable cultures: communication is eventually possible, whatever the obstacles, when two interlocutors recognize themselves as interlocutors and don't give up trying to understand each other. But another lesson of the episode is that otherness is always ethnocentrically interpreted in an act of hermeneutic appropriation from within the interpreter's home culture.[1] In *Inessential Solidarity: Rhetoric and Foreigner Relations*, Diane Davis argues against some of these points, or more exactly, she initiates a dialogue trying to persuade me and others that my rhetorical account is significantly incomplete. She suggests that I partially misread the "Darmok" episode and mistakenly advocate only a rhetorical hermeneutics to the exclusion of a nonhermeneutical rhetoric. Calling on Levinas and

Lyotard, Davis claims that rhetorical hermeneutics is a "rhetoric of the said," and only a "rhetoric of the saying" can expose a nonappropriative relation to otherness (*Inessential* 66–85).

Davis's critique pushes me to articulate a rhetorical hermeneutics of otherness. Such a theory relates not only to understanding the other within and across cultures—communication in the present—but also to understanding the otherness and sameness of earlier cultures—doing histories of the past, including histories of rhetoric. Thus, I hope to show how interpreting past practices can be theorized by starting with this present disagreement over interpreting a fictional future focused on the past.

In their volume *Counterpublics and the State*, Robert Asen and Daniel C. Brouwer note that

> counterpublics derive their "counter" status in significant respects from varying degrees of exclusion from prominent channels of political discourse and a corresponding lack of political power. The power frequently denied counterpublics consists not only in the capacity to induce or compel actions from others, but power in the Arendtian sense of that which arises when citizens act jointly. (3)

Like others before them, Asen and Brouwer reference John Dewey's *The Public and Its Problems* in defining the "public." Dewey argues that publics form because individuals recognize that their common interests are affected by consequences of human action. Dewey notes that when persons A and B have a conversation, such a transaction "acquires a public capacity" when its consequences "extend beyond the two directly concerned" and "affect the welfare of others" (*Essays* 244). In a sense, the *Star Trek* captains Picard and Dathon are trying to initiate the formation of a public when they try to communicate and establish a relationship of cooperation. Such communication between alien cultures is not qualitatively different from communication between dominant publics and their counterpublics within the same culture. In both cases, members of different communities interpret the rhetorical actions of those outside their group from within their own (sub)cultures, within their own native networks of beliefs, practices, and desires, which enable and constrain rhetorical agency, identification, and disidentification, as well as successful and unsuccessful communication. Otherness is only recognized as such against a background of commonality. We always make inside sense of the outside.

In her critique of my interpretive theory, Davis wants to supplement this rhetorical hermeneutic model of first contact with a rhetoric of saying that focuses on a "*non*hermeneutical dimension of rhetoric not reducible to meaning making, to offering up signs and symbols for comprehension" (*Inessential* 67). This dimension "counts on a certain reception, but not on the appropriation of meaning. Preceding and exceeding hermeneutic interpretation, it deals not in signified meanings but in the address itself, in the exposure to the other (*autrui*); it deals not in the said (*le dit*) but in the saying (*le dire*)" (68). Davis does not dispute that appropriative interpretation must take place; she just argues that it is dependent upon another, nonappropriative relation to otherness.

Davis's proposed complement to rhetorical hermeneutics strikes me as incisive and helpful. However, significant questions remain: Before a relation of any kind can be established (whether appropriative or nonappropriative), how do we recognize the other as "other" without first interpreting "it" as such? Otherness is always, at a minimum, the result of an interpretation that posits something as different, strange, alien in relation to our usual past experiences, present assumptions, or future expectations.[2] Furthermore, when Davis writes, "The saying names the site of my encounter with and exposure to the other *as* other," I find myself nodding assent; but when she adds, "which by definition leaves my hermeneutic aspirations in the dust" (69), I can't help asking: But for how long? I agree that a site of encounter must precede interpreting within a communicative act, but a nonhermeneutic rhetorical relation cannot be maintained if we are to respond effectively. For even if it were possible to sustain, such a prolonged nonappropriative response would ultimately be empty of any positive ethics or politics.[3] What kind of responsible ethics or effectual politics could possibly be developed from the absolute openness of a nonappropriative, nonhermeneutic encounter?

Perhaps my difficulties with these questions explain why I even disagree with Davis's claim that there are hints of nonhermeneutical responses in the "Darmok" episode itself. She points to Picard's response to Dathon's gift of fire on the planet as an indication of the "other's call" making it through Picard's incessant attempts at interpretive appropriation, his "hyper-hermeneutic disposition." She writes that Picard's "discernable stumble is marked by an instant of silence, a suspension in the interrogation, a shift in countenance, and then: a hoarse 'thank you.' This barely audible expression of gratitude for the present (the fire) is also the gift of a response, a return call, which both affirms and repeats the sharing that 'we' are, prior to any hermeneutic understanding" (77–79). But is it really prior? Picard has appropriately and appropriatively *interpreted* the fire as a gift, not as an attack nor as a subterfuge, and the expression of gratitude is not just a "hoarse 'thank you,'" as Davis claims, but actually includes a repeated assertion of gratitude, "thank *you*," significantly acknowledging an interpretation of the other as an other but only within a context of commonly shared purposes.

Further on, Davis evaluates the outcome of this first contact and notes that at the conclusion of the episode, the two ships simply go their separate ways: "This encounter, then, has led neither to economic gain nor to practical understanding. And yet, there is peace. There is peace without understanding, or better: there is peace despite profound non-understanding" (84). Davis half-convinces me here. Her take on this incident reminds me of a line from another sci-fi series: the *Matrix* trilogy. In *Matrix Reloaded*, we hear the assertion: "Comprehension is not a requisite of cooperation." Interestingly, this statement is made by a member of the Zion Council, who is played by an African American actor, whose day job is professor of philosophy at Princeton University. Cornel West is, among others things, the leading exponent of prophetic pragmatism, a radically historical outlook that looks forward to transformative political praxis.[4]

Anyway, when Davis writes of the "Darmok" encounter, "There is peace without understanding," I nod and think of the *Matrix* line that cooperation does not require comprehension. But then I realize that cooperation does not require *complete* comprehension, but it does require some; and, contra Davis, I think that in achieving peace, there definitely was some "practical understanding" accomplished in the first contact between the two crews in the "Darmok" episode. From my rhetorical-hermeneutic perspective, the episode confirms rather than contradicts the claim that we always make inside sense of the outside. Even when we try to remain open to otherness, we are always in the process of interpretive appropriation. And this is as true of making sense of past utterances, actions, and events (doing history) as it is of the present. Furthermore, the inside sense accomplished in the present is always related purposefully to a future action—in the "Darmok" case, a possible future of productive exchange and mutual cooperation.

But it might be useful now to put aside temporarily the hermeneutic/nonhermeneutic distinction and the opposition between appropriation and nonappropriation. We might instead turn to a thinker both Davis and I depend upon: Martin Heidegger. But Davis quotes the later Heidegger in her critique of rhetorical hermeneutics, while I cite the early: Heidegger of the 1920–21 lecture course in Freiburg on the phenomenology of religion, especially his reading of St. Paul's letters in order to explicate the basic meaning of early Christian lived experience. In his interpretation of Paul's proclamation of the Word, Heidegger uses "factical life experience" to designate both "the experiencing activity" and "that which is experienced through this activity," thus giving the phrase an active and a passive sense

(*Phenomenology* 7). The factical, according to Heidegger, differs from the natural or causal or thing-like; it gains its sense not from the epistemological but the historical. The meaning of this historical life experience is accessible only through enactment or actualization (*Vollzug*); epistemologically oriented "object-historical" method must give way to "enactment-historical" explication (61–63).

Heidegger develops the concept of enactment both critically and meta-critically throughout his Pauline interpretation. Critically, he elaborates Paul's distinction between the called and the perishing as a contrast between those who enact Christian religiosity as temporality and those who miss the enactment. Those who are called grow in faith (2 Thess. 1:3), but the "*pistis* [faith] is not a taking-to-be true, or else the *hyperauxanei* [growing] would have no meaning; the *pistenein* is a complex of enactment that is capable of increase" (*Phenomenology* 76). Paul's Christian facticity must be understood as enactment. Indeed, Heidegger claims, "Paul makes of enactment a theme" (86). Metacritically, Heidegger uses this same concept of enactment to correct past interpretive reductions of Paul's proclamation to its ideational content, its statements of dogma. "It is noticeable *how little* Paul alleges [*vorgibt*] *theoretically or dogmatically*; even in the letter to the Romans" (79). Heidegger argues that "the dogma as detached content of doctrine in an objective, epistemological emphasis could never have been guiding for Christian religiosity. On the contrary, the genesis of dogma can only be understood from out of the enactment of Christian life experience" (79). Thus, in 2 Thessalonians 2:15, when Paul simply advises, "Stand firm and master the tradition that you have experienced," Heidegger comments that "questions of content may not be understood detachedly," separated from the enactment of Christian religiosity (82). The necessity of such enactment is as true for the historian of Paul's letters as it is for his contemporary audience. Heidegger emphasizes the point when he remarks that "object-historical understanding is determination according to the aspect of the relation . . . so that the observer does not come into question"; whereas, in contrast, enactment-history as "phenomenological understanding is determined by the *enactment* of the observer" (57). In these ways, both critically and meta-critically, Heidegger emphasizes the importance of enactment: Heidegger's interpretive enactment explicates Paul's enactment of his proclamation concerning the Thessalonians' enactment of Christian factical life experience.

This notion of enactment can be employed to characterize how a public forms itself and how it relates to others past and present. Picard does not appropriatively interpret or nonappropriatively encounter but rather historically enacts Tamarian otherness. Such enactment then becomes the basis of forming a contemporaneous public. In this alternative description, the contrast between appropriation and nonappropriation tends toward irrelevance.

One additional point before moving on to discuss more explicitly writing histories of rhetoric: Davis's rhetoric of the saying can be seen as both consequentially insignificant and significantly consequential at the same time. It is insignificant insofar as no direct consequences follow from the nonhermeneutical conditions of possibility for the hermeneutical. True, we must have contact before we interpret, but no specific rhetoric, ethics, or politics follows from initial contact as such. But in another sense, if I translate this nonhermeneutic rhetorical stance into an attitude of nonappropriative openness to the other, then it is extremely consequential. For it makes a great deal of difference if my attitude toward the other in conversation entails trying to recognize his, her, or its differences rather than similarities to myself, avoiding the simplistic reproduction of sameness, initially not trying to transform the saying into a said.[5] But I will eventually do so, and then I have interpreted—or, more exactly, I have extended my interpretive recognition already begun. Whether I theoretically characterize the hermeneutic process as an enactment or an appropriation, I still claim that both otherness and openness are what we interpret them to be and that no absolute otherness or openness is possible. The familiar and the other, similarity and difference, make up a person's hermeneutic being-in-the-world, in which he or she can never be free from enabling presuppositions, assumptions, prejudices, desires, interests, and so on. Thus, I am back to a rhetorical hermeneutics, claiming that we can only make inside sense of the outside. Which is what I have been doing again and again throughout this section.

Doing Histories of the Past

Now let's turn directly to how rhetorical hermeneutics deals with doing histories. Writing about otherness in the past involves some of the same theoretical considerations as interpreting otherness in the present. In this section, my extended historical example is the otherness characterizing past rhetorical practices and theories, specifically those of a religious order founded in the sixteenth century, the Society of Jesus. What does it mean to do a history of early Jesuit rhetoric? I will answer this question by doing a rhetorical history and then return in my conclusion to the theoretical issues about such doing.

My history begins with a Greek word in a Latin text by the French Jesuit Nicolas Caussin, the seventeenth-century confessor to King Louis XIII and opponent of Cardinal Richelieu. In his 1619 *Of Sacred and Profane Eloquence*, Caussin retells the story of Paul's trial before Antonius Felix, the Roman procurator of Judea, as recorded in chapter 24 of Acts of the Apostles. After three missionary journeys, Paul had been arrested in Jerusalem and sent before Felix in Caesarea, where he was attacked by the prosecuting advocate, the rhetorician Tertullus. Paul skillfully defends himself, and Caussin describes the result: "In this incident appears how weak and meager is human eloquence, compared with the divine; here the θεορήτωρ [theorhetor] Paul demolished the machinations of that rhetorician with a crushing blow of the spirit" (*Eloquentia* 6).[6]

For Caussin, a theorhetor is someone who speaks to others for or about God, the ultimate other. Caussin's celebration of Paul's theorhetoric follows the Jesuit tradition of emphasizing the power of eloquence in educational theory and cultural practice. During the Catholic Counter-Reformation, Caussin's compatriots in the Society of Jesus developed and advocated their own brand of theorhetoric. Through interpreting and following the rhetorical examples of Jesus Christ, his disciples, and especially the missionary Paul, Jesuits updated these models in response to the exigencies of the Renaissance and Reformation. Jesuit theorhetoric concerned itself with how the relations among oral, scribal, and print media could be managed in rhetorical practice and theory, especially when turned toward theological topics and when addressed to foreign audiences.

A historical practice attending to rhetoric's relation to interpretation can capture something of this complex rhetorical ecology. We can define *rhetoric* here as the use of language in a context to have effects, both linguistic effects on an audience through argumentative persuasion and language's effects on itself through figuration. Assuming that we establish the meaning of anything (past, present, or future) through rhetoric's suasive and tropological effects, a rhetorical hermeneutics does histories of rhetoric by concentrating on past performances of interpretation and rhetoric within cultural politics. More specifically, the term *rhetorical hermeneutics* can refer to both a historical way of talking (a method) and a historical text talked about (a subject matter).[7] For example, as a method, it uses rhetoric to practice theory by doing history. The previous section illustrated how rhetoric could be used to practice hermeneutic theory by giving a brief account of a recent interpretive disagreement. The present section uses theorhetoric to practice a bit of media theory by doing some Reformation and Counter-Reformation history. But *rhetorical hermeneutics* can also refer to the subject matter being discussed. For instance, Augustine's *De Doctrina Christiana* presents its own rhetorical hermeneutics. The first three books provide a theory of Biblical interpretation that forms the basis for the concluding book on Christian preaching. I have, of course, not chosen Augustine's text at random. It was the most important Christian rhetoric throughout the Western Middle Ages and into the Renaissance, doing significant cultural work in serving as a model for Christianizing classical rhetoric and, with other Augustinian texts, reconfiguring the relations among emotions, reason, and religious faith.[8]

A rhetorical-hermeneutic approach to the theorhetoric of Augustine, Luther, and the Jesuits tracks the rhetorical paths of theological thought through these authors' texts and their receptions. That is, rhetorical hermeneutics focuses on the use of theorhetoric (particular tropes, arguments, and narratives) and the theorizing of that use; or, again, it interprets the rhetoric of theological thinking and theological thinking about rhetoric. In what follows, I bring this rhetorical-hermeneutic perspective to a history of Jesuit rhetoric, describing how Christian theology (embodied in theorhetoric) served as one condition of possibility for the print revolution in the early modern period of Europe. This theorhetoric of the Reformation and Counter-Reformation functioned as a kind of media theory to promote and justify the use of a new communication technology, and this technological innovation then affected the development of a distinctive Jesuit rhetoric.[9] My history moves from Luther's theorhetoric around 1520 to that of the Society of Jesus founded in 1540.

The media revolution of the early modern period has been variously characterized by cultural and intellectual historians. In *The Printing Press as an Agent of Change*, Elizabeth Eisenstein argues that the transformation was not from an oral to a written culture but rather from one kind of written literate culture (scribal) to another (print). Manfred Schneider suggests a more conflicted revolution pitting a Protestant hot print media of concentrated individual Bible reading against a more diffuse Catholic cold multimedia of Church ritual and priestly interpretive mediation of scripture through preaching. Both accounts help us understand the rhetorical and hermeneutic effects of printing when compared to earlier oral and scribal media technologies. With the adoption and spread of the printing press, typographical fixity encouraged textual preservation and standardization. These new possibilities, combined with an enthusiasm for classical philology, promoted a more intense concern with textual purification and authorship among a learned elite. Also, the printing press enabled wider textual dissemination over space and time. On the one hand, this wider dissemination of standardized texts reinforced uniformity or secured publicity for the same textually transmitted controversial opinions and news events. On the other hand, more rapid production and circulation made more books and pamphlets available to individual readers; these printed texts could be compared, synthesized, and diversified into new ways of thinking or used to reinforce and revivify old ways of thinking—rhetorical effects that were far more divisive than unifying.

The media effect most often noted, of course, is the popular availability of vernacular translations of the Bible. As many historians have argued, a Protestant theology "stressed Bible-reading as necessary for salvation," and this doctrine generated "unusual pressures toward literacy"; while a Catholic theology of mediation and authority resulted in a "refusal after [the Council of] Trent to authorize alternatives to the Latin Vulgate" and "worked in the opposite direction" against widespread literacy, defending the Church as authoritative mediator between God and his lay children (Eisenstein 333). Paulus Bachmann, a German Cistercian abbot, stated the Catholic argument in 1527: "The written word of God, as the Lutherans call the Gospel, cannot always be productively presented to the simple folk according to its bare words or literal meaning but rather requires interpretation and the addition of commentary" (qtd. in M. Edwards 81). Such a position not only expressed Catholic Church doctrine but supported priestly privilege and ecclesiastical authority.

A very different political theology of print appeared in the writings of Martin Luther, who famously referred to the relatively new medium as "God's highest and extremest act of grace, whereby the business of the Gospel is driven forward" (qtd. in Black 432).[10] Lutheran theorhetoric enthusiastically embraced the disseminating and publicity powers of print. But for Luther, this dissemination and publicity served most importantly, not the circulation of his theological proclamations and controversial pamphlets, but the promotion of individuals reading the vernacular Bible for themselves. In September 1522, Luther published arguably his most influential piece of theorhetoric, his German translation of the New Testament. *Sola scriptura* interpreted as "with scripture alone": this was the theological doctrine at the center of Lutheran thought. Through reading the vernacular Bible, individual believers could have direct, unmediated access to God's Word. Luther figured this direct access in an explicitly rhetorical way in his scriptural theology. For example, in his commentary on Psalm 121, he describes the Holy Spirit as being rhetorized (*rhetoricatur*) within the hearer of the Word.[11]

The theology of Lutheran Reformers supported the expansion of print culture as much as printing supported the success of Reformation theology, promoting the view that the laity and not the clergy alone should have direct access to scripture and debates about interpretive authority.[12] When the Catholics responded to Luther with their own printed pamphlets in the vernacular, they were obviously caught in a paradox: They argued that the debate over reform should not take place in public before the easily misguided laity, yet they made their own cases before that same audience through vernacular pamphlets. But the media paradoxes were not just on the side of the Catholics. Though Luther claimed "Scripture interprets itself," he provided a plethora of hermeneutic guides instructing readers on how to read scriptural passages as he read them. Despite vigorously criticizing the established church and its clergy for improperly insisting on a mediated scripture, Luther in his turn mediated God's message through his Biblical glosses, prefaces, and independent commentaries.[13]

I'd now like to turn more directly to the theorhetoric of the Catholic Counter-Reformation, in particular the tradition of Jesuit rhetoric. Founded by Ignatius Loyola and his companions in 1540, by 1615 the Society of Jesus had established 372 colleges throughout Europe and the rest of the world and had sent missionaries to India, China, Japan, and the Americas (T. Campbell 343). What constitutes a specific tradition of Jesuit theorhetoric? We find a clue by turning to the Jesuit *Formula* used to establish the society through the papal bull of Paul III in 1540.[14] The Jesuit *Formula* names the multiple practices that the new order recognized as ministries for achieving its stated goals of defending and propagating faith and of fostering the progress of souls in Christian life and doctrine. These practices include performing and guiding the *Spiritual Exercises*; spreading popular education; administering confession and other sacraments; doing works of charity; and preaching, lecturing, and performing other ministries of the Word. A certain Jesuit rhetoric of thinking permeated all of these practices and was accompanied by an explicit Jesuit thinking about rhetoric.

Ignatius's *Spiritual Exercises* promotes a specific rhetorical hermeneutics of potent affects and vivid imagining throughout its program of daily contemplative exercises. The faculties directed for use include imagination, memory, intellect, and will, and the sequence of practices have a particular rhetorical arrangement, what Ignatius calls an "order of procedure." This order includes first the "Preparatory Prayer," a framing supplication and statement of the general goal of all the exercises, followed by up to three "Preludes," including one called a "composition of place," a preparatory imagining that dramatically envisions the scene of the topic chosen for the exercise, and a second, more specific supplication, asking God for a desired gift (for example, a specific attitude or feeling) to result from the exercise. The preludes are followed by several "Points," operational practices of meditation or contemplation using memory to recall, intellect to understand, and will to move toward the desired goal of the exercise; and finally there is the "Colloquy," an imaginary conversation on the exercise topic, reinforcing the result of the operational practices. This brief description illustrates the Ignatian emphases on vivid imagination and embodied feeling, on concrete images and spiritualized emotions, which make up the core of the *Spiritual Exercises* as theorhetoric.

The centrality of rhetoric more generally within the Jesuit paideia can be seen in the *Ratio Studiorum* of 1599, an outline of the different levels of Jesuit education written collectively over three decades.[15] Several professorships are described for grammar, humanities, rhetoric, philosophy, and theology. In the first paragraph under "Rules for Professors of Rhetoric," we read that the goal of the class in rhetoric is *eloquentia perfecta*: to instruct the students to perfect eloquence. The class should include the arts of oratory and poetry, with oratory being given preference. The purpose of the pedagogy should be both practical utility and cultural enrichment, meaning that perfect eloquence includes skill in the language arts and development of erudition. Erudition should come from the study of history and ethnology, the study of *moribus gentium* (the customs or morals of nations or peoples). Erudition should derive from scholarly authority and from all Church doctrine ("*Ratio*" 208–9). But such learning must be adjusted to the capacities of the students. Here we see an indication of Jesuit accommodationism: rhetorical attention to the nature of specific audiences and adjustments of one's rhetoric to those audiences. This rhetorical accommodationism was part of everything Jesuit, from their confession manual instructions concerning individual sinners to their missionary policies toward whole native populations.[16]

Regarding the preferred rhetorical theory and practice, the rules of the *Ratio* were quite specific: precepts should come primarily from Cicero, Quintilian, and Aristotle, and "style is to be learned only from Cicero" ("*Ratio*" 208). For a rhetorical textbook, the *Ratio* recommends that of the Jesuit Cyprian Soarez, his *Three Books on the Art of Rhetoric Taken Especially from Aristotle, Cicero, and Quintilian*, a volume revised and reprinted in different versions more than two hundred times from its first publication in 1562 through the late eighteenth century.[17] Soarez calls eloquence "nothing else but wisdom speaking fully" (Flynn 428–29), but he also warns that eloquence must be purified by moral (in his case, Christian) teaching (Flynn 113). With Cicero, he describes the "restraint and wisdom of the perfect orator" and declares that eloquence must be joined "with integrity and utter discretion. If we were to teach the ability to speak to people who lack these virtues, we would certainly not be training orators but would be providing mad men with weapons" (Flynn 119–20). For Soarez and others in the Jesuit rhetorical tradition, ideal rhetoric combines eloquence, wisdom, and virtue. Jesuit *eloquentia perfecta* thus becomes a particular kind of Christian rhetoric, a specific development of the Ciceronian and Quintilian ideal orator: the good person writing and speaking well for the public good. This Jesuit rhetoric holds that the teaching of eloquence should always be combined with critical thinking, moral discernment, and social responsibility.

Soarez's textbook on profane rhetoric and later Jesuit sacred and general rhetorics, such as Caussin's in 1619, included a distinctive emphasis on the spiritualized emotions and concrete imagery promoted in Ignatius's *Spiritual Exercises*. Most Renaissance sacred rhetorics shared a similar focus on passionate rhetoric and religious persuasion (Shuger 55–110). But for the Jesuits, such an emphasis played an especially significant role in a rhetorical ecology of the ministries they practiced, as outlined in their founding formula: their rhetorical ministries of the Word were embedded in other Jesuit practices of administering the sacraments, especially confession, educating students in colleges, and guiding individuals in the *Spiritual Exercises*.

In the theorhetorics of both the Reformation and the Counter-Reformation, we see versions of a rhetorical hermeneutics that in different ways attempt to persuade believers and mediate scriptural interpretation through uses of available media. For the Jesuits, this meant developing and promoting a rhetoric of talking for and about God by paying close attention to writing and reading, as well as speaking and listening. Such a theorhetoric embodied both oral and written media, the spoken and printed word in both private and public spaces. Indeed, in Schneider's McLuhanesque terms, the Jesuits maximized the potential of rhetoric as a cool medium. "Rhetoric is the epitome of cool medial communication. Through the combination of different linguistic, bodily, vocal techniques, it traps the listener and binds him to a cultural code" (212). If, as Schneider suggests, "rhetoric designates the ability to produce effective speeches, whereas theology names the amplification effect of true speech" (212), then Jesuit theorhetoric purports to be effective mediation and amplification of the Logos, performed through multiple ministries of the Divine Word, including sermons, lectures, conversations, and confessions, as well as confession manuals, pedagogical textbooks, and theological treatises.

I began this section with the Jesuit Caussin calling Paul a theorhetor in his treatise on sacred and profane rhetoric. Earlier he describes Paul as one of the practitioners of a "divine eloquence," which "has made men into subjects, inflaming their deepest feelings by means of a kind of divine fire," an eloquence that "has tamed kings, and . . . enticed cities, provinces, and finally the entire world to accept the yoke of Christ" ("From *On Sacred*" 274–75). Caussin compares this divine eloquence to another kind he calls

"heroic," which is "a conflation of the human and the divine," combining
learned art and natural ability (275). It is the Jesuit version of this eloquence
that Marc Fumaroli describes so eloquently himself in the following passage:
"Jesuit rhetoric . . . was at bottom a theorhetoric, a deciphering and a tuning
of the dialogue between human nature and God's love encompassing the
inward and the outward, religion and science, personal salvation and the
welfare of the political body." In contrast, Fumaroli continues,

> the Lutheran and Calvinist Reformations and the lay Enlightenment
> made a different choice: they connected human welfare, along with
> science and philosophy, to the secular state and therefore placed it
> in the political sphere; they reserved the dialogue with God's Word
> for the private sphere. ("The Fertility" 101; see also Fumaroli, *L'Age of
> l'eloquence*).

We don't have to agree completely with Fumaroli's stark contrasts here,
but they do foreground the role of theorhetoric's political theology both for
interpreting the media culture of the early modern period and for understanding that of our own. Moreover, Fumaroli's summary comment provides
a fitting end to my brief history of early Jesuit rhetoric.

Rhetorical Hermeneutic Historiography

In this conclusion, I will resume the theoretical questioning of the first
section by discussing the rhetorical history presented in the second. How
do the differing theoretical accounts of interpretation as appropriation and
enactment relate to my history of Jesuit rhetoric? Viewed as appropriation,
my historical interpretation places early Jesuit rhetoric into a framework of
rhetorical-hermeneutic practices and metapractices. Jesuit praxis included
spiritual exercises as hermeneutic technologies of the self and pedagogical
theories as accommodationist accounts of otherness.[18] Viewed as enactment,
this rhetorical history actualizes an exegesis of Jesuit life as embodied in
rhetorical-hermeneutic experiences, both inner (spiritual exercises and con-
fessional practices) and outer (preaching, teaching, and missionary work).

To develop this rhetorical historiography further, we can adapt the methodological distinction from early Heidegger alluded to in the first section
and tentatively contrast an "object-historical" interpretation with an "enactment-historical" explication. Object-historical method interprets the past in
terms of some framework of "objects" (ideas, concepts, theories, practices);
the "object-historical attitude" fits the chosen object of study (Paul, Augustine, Jesuits) into "a historical complex" of ordered objects (Heidegger,
Phenomenology 120–21). This object-historical interpretation appropriates

the otherness of the past into a present-day, object-filled framework for sense making. In contrast, enactment-historical method attempts to actualize the other's past experience in the dimensions of its own sense making; that is, the enactment-historical explicates the lived experience (Paul's proclamation, Augustine's confession, Jesuits' rhetoric) as meaningfully actualized in its historical situation. (From a rhetorical-hermeneutic perspective, we might be tempted to say that object-historical method results in an appropriative interpretation of the past, while enactment-historical method performs an explication of a past interpretation—a present appropriation of a past appropriation.) In prefacing his phenomenological explication of Paul's First Letter to the Thessalonians, Heidegger illustrates an objective-historical interpretation by placing the letter writing in the context of Paul's first missionary trip right after his arrival in Corinth, having earlier been forced to leave Thessalonica by Jewish opposition and after having been minimally successful in his teaching at Athens. But enactment-historical explication of the same letter, according to Heidegger, "write[s] the letter along with Paul," asking such questions as: "How does Paul, in the situation of a letter-writer, stand to the Thessalonians? How are they experienced by him? How is his *communal world* given to him in the situation of writing the letter?" (61).

Whatever one thinks of this methodological distinction between object-historical and enactment-historical, it is helpful in drawing out two different ways of viewing and extending my history of Jesuit rhetoric in the previous section. By suggesting that early Jesuit rhetoric consists of certain interrelated rhetorical practices and theories, this history describes a particular historical configuration that could serve the purposes of doing either object-historical or enactment-historical interpretations. The object-historical aspects are most apparent in the placement of rhetorical practices in an objectified historical context of rhetorical and nonrhetorical practices of the Renaissance and Counter-Reformation. The enactment-historical possibilities of the history reside in the lived rhetorical experience of the Jesuits in performing those practices. The early Jesuits lived their rhetorical experiences partly through performing the *Spiritual Exercises*, during which act they engaged in particular rhetorical practices, including specifically spiritual exercises that, in turn, shaped and embodied their lived experiences.[19]

In the preceding paragraphs, we moved from hermeneutic models to interpretive methods. I transformed two different theoretical accounts of what historical interpretation is (appropriation versus enactment) into two practical strategies for how to do rhetorical histories (object-historical vs. enactment-historical). Rhetorical hermeneutics embodies this contrast between historiography as explanatory hermeneutic theory (a description of doing history) and historiography as practical interpretive guide (a prescription for doing histories). Thus, rhetorical hermeneutics *as historiography* becomes still another way of using rhetoric to practice theory by doing history.

Notes

1. See Mailloux, "Making Comparisons."

2. For a Levinasian counter-argument, see Davis, *Inessential* 170n10, 182n22.

3. In contrast, see Davis, chap. 5, "Judgment."

4. See West, *American Evasion* 228, 237; and *Cornel West Reader* 133, 186.

5. Cf. Muckelbauer; Davis 180n18. I am grateful to Diane Davis for our ongoing dialogue, including her comments on an earlier version of this section.

6. My translation. I thank Daniel Gross for leading me to Caussin's text; see Gross, "Caussin's Passion."

7. See Mailloux, *Disciplinary* 9–66; Mailloux, *Reception* 43–71.

8. See J. Murphy, *Rhetoric* 56–64; Shuger 41–50; R. L. Enos and Thompson.

9. I am grateful to Christopher Wild and Uli Strasser for providing the initial impetus for this media perspective on early Jesuit theorhetoric. In their invitation letter to participate in a December 2009 conference, "Theology as Media Theory," at the William Andrews Clark Memorial Library, they described the conference as taking "the historiographical commonplace 'no Reformation without print'" and proceeding "from its chiastic inversion 'no print without the Reformation' to highlight the importance of theology to the fortunes of print and, more broadly, to the formation of media cultures throughout the early modern period" (letter of 27 April 2009).

10. See also Eisenstein 304.

11. Dockhorn, 164, quoting Martin Luther, *In XV Psalmos graduum. Weimer Ausgabe*, XL, 13 (59).

12. See Scribner; J. Newman.

13. See M. Edwards 115.

14. De Aldama; J. O'Malley 35–36.

15. See A. Farrell.

16. On Jesuit rhetoric and accommodationism, see Maryks.

17. "*Ratio*" 202, 217; Flynn 257.

18. On technologies of the self, see Foucault, *The Hermeneutics of the Subject*; Martin, Gutman, and Hutton.

19. Cf. Hadot; Rabbow.

3

WRITING THE OTHER INTO HISTORIES OF RHETORICS: THEORIZING THE ART OF RECONTEXTUALIZATION

LuMing Mao

> The Master said, "Even when walking in the company of two other men, I am bound to be able to learn from them. The good points of one I copy; the bad points of the other I correct in myself."
>
> —Confucius

> Goodness consists in taking up a position in being such that the Other counts more than myself.
>
> —Levinas, *Totality and Infinity*

In the past few decades, rhetoric and composition scholars have showed a collective interest in crossing borders and in studying other discursive traditions and practices. This discursive turn in part reflects a growing realization that our existing accounts of rhetorics remain partial, incomplete, and in want of expansion and revision. To broaden and rewrite histories of rhetorics, these scholars have been making a greater effort to give much-needed voice to those discursive practices that have long been neglected, silenced, or altogether forgotten. Thus far we have seen impressive growth and development in work on indigenous rhetorics (Baca; Baca and Villanueva; Powell; Stromberg), on Latino/a rhetorics (Kells, et al.; Ramírez), on ancient non-Greek rhetorics (Lipson and Binkley, *Rhetoric Before and Beyond the Greeks* and *Ancient Non-Greek Rhetorics*), and on ancient and contemporary Chinese rhetorics (Lu; Lyon "Confucian," "Rhetorical Authority," and "Why Do the Rulers"; Mao "Reflective Encounters," "Studying the Chinese Rhetorical Tradition," and "Searching for the Way"; Wang; Wu; You). Collectively these endeavors not only have transformed and enriched our understanding of these other rhetorical practices but also are reshaping some deeply held assumptions about our own disciplinary identity and methodological beliefs. They have further illustrated how power dynamics and issues of location and authenticity directly influence and complicate the ways in which these other discursive practices and traditions are being recognized and represented.

As rhetoric and composition scholars continue to bring to light more and more indigenous, non-Western discursive practices and traditions, the issue of methodology has become front and center for all those involved. What right, for example, do scholars have to represent this or that particular culture and its rhetorics? From what vantage point do they position themselves, and how does their position in turn shape and influence the outcomes of their studies? Why do we often encounter, in the accounts of the other, the privileging of facts over experiences or of logic over other modes of thinking? Our responses to these questions and the methodologies we develop will have significant epistemological consequences because they directly impact how we write the other into histories of rhetorics and how we develop a new discursive order where the modus operandi is not to establish provenance and dominance but to valorize experience and interdependence.

In this chapter, I develop my response to these questions and to the issue of methodology by undertaking three specific tasks. First, I discuss a few methodological approaches of the recent past to identify the major challenges we face. Second, I move to propose what may be called "the art of recontextualization" in order to develop a framework that will allow us to critically interrogate, for example, the areas of representation we choose, the kinds of methodologies we deploy, and the strategic and ideological positions we take. Third, I apply the art of recontextualization to a reading of the *Daodejing*, a Chinese classic that has recently garnered a lot of attention among rhetoric and composition scholars. Finally, I conclude by briefly reflecting on the two epigraphs with which I begin this chapter and on a few more implications for writing the other into histories of rhetorics.

Methodological Challenges in Representing the Other

The tendency to rely on Western rhetorics or their basic concepts as the starting and/or end point to represent the other has remained strong and persistent. For example, scholars in our field have deployed an Aristotelian or a Burkean rhetoric in their study of the other, and other studies have appealed to Western logic and epistemology as their undergirding frame of reference. Any such approach in and of itself should not be necessarily subject to criticism. Serious problems do arise when one fails to examine, among other issues, the constructed nature of one's starting point and the inherent power dynamics attending each and every form of representation. For George Kennedy, the use of Greco-Roman rhetorical models and concepts aims to help us understand non-Western discursive practices and traditions. He is equally interested in testing and determining the applicability of his Aristotelian rhetoric so that he can use it to develop his "General Theory of Rhetoric." Since the major problems stemming from this approach have been discussed in the past (Hum and Lyon; Garrett; Mao, "Reflective"), I am not going to rehearse them here. This much perhaps bears repeating: While Kennedy has no stated intention to impose his Aristotelian rhetoric upon all other non-Western rhetorics, he has created a rhetorical hierarchy where the Aristotelian rhetoric is perched at the top and the rest of world rhetorics are being grouped below, looking up and gravitating toward the very top.

Other scholars have done it differently, though. Drawing upon a Burkean rhetoric as one of her starting points, Krista Ratcliffe proposes a listening rhetoric to help locate commonalities and differences with others and interrogate one's own cultural logics. For Ratcliffe, rhetorical listening serves as a code of cross-cultural conduct that promotes "a stance of openness" in relation to any person, text, or culture and that seeks conscious identification leading to productive communication (*Rhetorical Listening* 25). In advocating openness predicated on rhetorical listening, she challenges Western disciplinary and cultural biases that have displaced listening and recuperates it as a trope for interpretive invention and as an integral part of an undivided *logos* (one that both speaks and listens) (25–27). Similarly, Arabella Lyon uses Anglo-American ordinary language philosophy to read the writing of Han Fei (circa 289–233 B.C.E.), one of the foremost Legalists in ancient China. Lyon shows how the relationship between speaker and audience, individual subjects and the state, and speech and act was differently conceptualized in Han Fei's writing and how such a reading can in turn help critically reflect on and complicate speech act theory and our understanding of rhetoric in general ("Rhetorical").

Then there is the effort to hypercorrect or overcompensate the past ills seen in the accounts of the other. Having realized the past failures to represent others on their own terms, scholars can become so anxious to see others in their otherness that they may end up representing them beyond their otherness either by overemphasizing their differences to the exclusion of commonalities with Western rhetorics or by projecting them as an idealized other to past and present problems in Western rhetorics. Let me take Confucian rhetoric as an example.

Confucian rhetoric has been extensively mined and appropriated in the recent past both inside and outside of China. Confucian ideology, which saw its fortune fall more than once in modern China, has made a triumphant comeback since the 1990s—not only to fill an ideological vacuum but also to help promote cultural nationalism (Liu 172–77). Chinese political leaders have appealed to the Confucian concepts of *zhengming* (rectification of names) and *hexie* (harmony) to help prescribe and implement a new set of social norms and practices (Lu and Simons 266–69). Similarly, on this side of the Pacific, Lyon has suggested that Confucian rhetoric possesses the potential for democratic deliberations because of its distinctive strategies of silence and remonstration ("Confucian"). And Xiaoye You has proposed that Confucian rhetoric should be understood not in terms of verbal persuasion but through the framework of ritualization informed by work in the West on social functions of ritual in symbolic anthropology and sociology.

While I have no quarrel with the intent or even some of the specificities of these arguments or appropriations, I have grown increasingly concerned about taking Confucian rhetoric, or any other non-Western rhetorical practice for that matter, out of its own political and social context and about the increasingly blurred distinction between the level of importance we want to attribute to Confucian rhetoric because of our own present needs or wants and the level of importance that accrued to Confucian rhetoric because of its own context and its own terms. Not that we should necessarily find fault for either justification, but it would become our fault indeed should we fail to distinguish one from the other.

As Mary Garrett first noted in 1999 and as I further elaborated in 2003, we rhetoric and composition scholars face a methodological paradox. That is, we have to start somewhere when studying the other—and most likely with concepts or points of reference familiar to us only. We thus risk imposing them on the other, either forcing an unwanted fit at the expense of subtle but real differences or espousing a radical divide or incommensurability where similarities and affinities may very well lurk not far behind. To counter this methodological paradox, we must cultivate and indeed demand an intersubjective, interdependent ethos so that our own historically privileged dispositions can be consistently challenged and made manifest throughout the entire process of representation.

In the Face of the Methodological Paradox: The Art of Recontextualization

To respond to this methodological paradox, I want to promote a different approach that would enable us to traverse the traditional boundaries and to redraw the line between, for example, self and other, past and present, and essence and experience. To begin with, since not every single discursive practice by or about the other can be studied, we must be deliberate in what we include or exclude and explicit about whether the work at hand is more important to the players then and there or to us scholars here and now. Equally important, we must foreground how our representation reveals our own experience and affiliation and speaks to our own authority and legitimacy. We must ask, too: How can we represent these other discursive practices free of ethnocentrism, since many of them have hitherto been ruled as anything but rhetoric? In what ways can they be made familiar to us like a neighbor without a predetermined context or principle? In other words, is there some standard or heuristic out there that can somehow stand outside, or stand up to, this perennial urge to appeal to one's own value or worldview?

Similarly, we should not underestimate or overlook how the conditions of the present influence what we represent and how we represent. For example, how do the material and sociocultural conditions of our time shape the act of representation? How do our ongoing dialogues and entanglements across national, political, and linguistic boundaries inflect and influence our engagements with other discursive practices and traditions? Do the conditions of the global necessarily impinge upon the effort to write for and about the other that is closely tied to the local ways of doing and being? How can the production of such a history further help effect a new set of relationships and a new paradigm of cross-cultural dialogue that in turn can transform the conditions of the present?

In her much cited "The Problem of Speaking for Others," Linda Alcoff identifies the major challenges scholars face and must address in speaking for and about others.[1] Among them are how to recognize and interrogate the epistemological impact of a speaker's location on the construction of subject positions and what, if anything, one can do to transcend one's location and to avoid the possibility of misrepresentation or misappropriation. She proposes a four-step strategy to help meet these challenges and to reject both "a general retreat from speaking for" and "a return to an unselfconscious appropriation of the other" (24). The four-step strategy consists of: analyzing and questioning the impetus to speak; interrogating the bearing of one's location and context on one's representation; holding oneself accountable to what one says; and recognizing and examining the consequences of one's claims or representations on the discursive and material context (24–27). What stands out in Alcoff's strategy is an unmistakable ethical commitment to the cause of speaking for and about others.

To use Alcoff's ethical commitment as a source of inspiration, I propose that we practice the art of recontextualization. I want to use this approach to engage the methodological paradox so far outlined, to negotiate the dynamics and complexities involving the subject under study and the subject position taken for that study, and to recognize and, better still, transform the specific conditions of the present that directly influence the ways in which knowledge is being produced, circulated, and consumed.

In proposing the art of recontextualization for writing for and about the other, I am in part invoking the work of the comparative philosopher David Hall and the sinologist Roger Ames. In their effort to describe Chinese correlative ordering on its own terms, they have developed a focus/field perspective and the art of contextualization. First, any item as focal resides in its immediate context in such a way that it shapes, and is being shaped by, that context as field. Second, this focus/field perspective must be understood in terms of the art of contextualization. By that they mean a "this-that," rather than a "one-many," model where individuals as focal seek out, and actualize themselves in, "this" or "that" family relation or sociological order, which they help to name and constitute, and which in turn constitutes and shapes them. Third, these kinds of "this-that" relationships, never fixed or determinant or self-contained, constitute this correlative ordering, which appeals to functional similarity and meaningful disposition and rejects any overarching context to be used to determine the shape of other contexts. It allows the mutual interdependence of all things in Chinese culture to be assessed in terms of particular contexts defined by social roles and functions (the fields), which are in turn constituted by individuals and their distinctive experiences (the *foci*) (Hall and Ames 273–75).

Drawing upon this emphasis on openness and interdependence, the art of recontextualization rejects any external principle or overarching context to determine the context of the other and relies on terms of interdependence and interconnectivity to constitute and regulate representation of all discursive practices. This kind of engagement enables scholars to bring both their own context and that of the other into critical view. Perhaps more important, by substituting "recontextualization" for "contextualization," I want to inject a necessary sense of dialogism into the act of contextualization. That is to say, any act of contextualization always remains incomplete and open-ended, and it calls for and indeed begets a new one, and ad infinitum. To appropriate M. M. Bakhtin, each act of contextualization represents a response to preceding acts of contextualization and further anticipates a response from similar future acts. Filled with other echoes and reverberations, each act responds, rejoins, realigns, and reaffirms (91–92). While no single algorithm is available to determine or specify their meaning or order, such acts command their own logic and authority as meaning-making links in the chain of representation.

So, how does the art of recontextualization address this methodological paradox? That is, how can one write for and about others on their own terms unencumbered by one's own ideological baggage? Now a link in the chain of representation, every act of contextualization is necessarily an act of recontextualization. As a result, scholars will have to interrogate their own, often historically privileged, context and examine how their own "rituals of writing"—discursive practices of speaking or writing involving both the utterance and its position within a sociocultural order including participating individuals (Alcoff 12)—exert influence on those they are representing and on how they represent them. Moreover, the act of recontextualization must be extended to the context of the other, too. Namely, as scholars look to the local context for terms of contact and modes of representation, they must also examine its political, economic, and sociocultural underpinnings. In other words, the turn to the local, motivated by the desire to escape the shadow, if not tyranny, of one's own context, does not entitle scholars to take the context of the other at its face value. Nor should they equate the other with one unified or homogeneous entity always speaking in one voice. On the contrary, scholars are now required to investigate how the other's own heterogeneity inhabits its space and how it inexorably influences the other's own multiplicity. This kind of interrogation, though no panacea for resolving all the challenges present in writing for and about others, constitutes the first step toward responsible, ethical representation.

Predicated upon the belief that real understanding can happen only through a dialogic process, the act of recontextualization insists on developing terms of interdependence and interconnectivity, aiming not merely to reverse our evaluation of the self/other binary or any other binary for that matter, but to recalibrate it and to replace it. In the process, we neither project the self onto the other nor erase the self with the other's alterity (Zhang 53), and we stop conferring more power and legitimacy upon ourselves when we actually need or deserve them the least. We further engage in an open dialogue where self and other work together to eliminate the use of any overarching context to determine the context of the other and to yield continuous moments of what may be called "togetherness-in-difference" (Mao, Reading).

Practicing the art of recontextualization is more than bringing both self and other into critical view. It further calls on us to recontextualize the contingencies of the present. By that I mean recognizing how the conditions of the present can influence the act of representation and even perpetuate the existing power imbalances. By that I also mean cultivating a processual model of representation—where we continuously trouble our own modes of thinking and learn to listen to the voice and claim of the other, so that we can celebrate experiences just as readily as we do facts and promote relations of interdependence just as comfortably as we do structures of sameness or difference. A corollary to this model, then, is a strong ethical imperative—the moral responsibility for the other by acknowledging the existence of its discourses and by holding oneself accountable to the act of representation.

Given the global condition of our time, practicing the art of recontextualization also entails recontextualizing the other against the imaginary of today's global contact zones. It means we do not yoke the other with the global in the name of achieving harmony at the likely expense of uprooting the other from its own native environment. Nor does it mean that we remain uncritically tethered to the other's local milieu for the sake of "going native." Rather, practicing the art of recontextualization in today's world means negotiating between developing a localized narrative and searching for its new and broader significance within and outside its own tradition; between looking for rhetoric where it has been categorically ruled nonexistent and rejecting a concomitant temptation to reduce rhetorical experiences into facts and equate heterogeneous resonance with either sameness or difference; and between using the other for transformative agendas and resisting methods and logic that continue to silence or make invisible the same other. In so doing, practicing the art of recontextualization redraws the boundary between the global and the other, possibly shifting the global and the other into a new alignment where the global may very well aid the less dominant in opposition to the dominant *within* the other.

Finally, a disclaimer is perhaps in order. By proposing the art of recontextualization as a new way of writing the other into histories of rhetorics, I am certainly not being idealistic. That is, I am not suggesting that the art of recontextualization is the silver bullet for all the challenges that writing for and about presents, nor am I suggesting it can guarantee responsible, ethical representation in all instances. What I am proposing, and indeed hope to practice, is a critical apparatus that would enable us to extricate ourselves from the aforementioned methodological paradox and to cultivate an inter-subjective process where self and other engage in a cross-cultural dialogue with an abiding sense of self-reflection, interdependence, and accountability.

Enacting the Rhetoric of the *Dao*

Lately I have been drawn to the rhetoric of the *Dao* (導 Way) as part of my effort to contribute to the ongoing dialogue among rhetoric and composition scholars in the US on classical Chinese rhetorics in general and on the rhetoric of Daoism (Taoism) in particular (Combs; Lu; Lyon, "Why Do the Rulers"): not only because the school of Daoism emerged as a direct challenge to Confucianism and Legalism of its time, but also because the Daoist sensibilities have permeated Chinese culture and its thought patterns (Lu 228), even demonstrating unexpected affinities with postmodern views regarding, for example, language, truth, and rationality (Combs 3–4; Graham 227–29).

The Chinese classic *Daodejing* (*Classic of the Way and Virtue*), consisting of eighty-one chapters, can be characterized as a kind of proverbial wisdom literature (Ames and Hall, Historical 5). The text has often been credited to the legendary Laozi ("The Old Master") who was believed to be a slightly older contemporary of Confucius (551–479 B.C.E.). Others have also contested his authorship, arguing that it was compiled by many individuals over a period of time culminating in the early or mid-fourth century B.C.E. (Ames and Hall, Historical 2; Yu 165–66). While this is no place to engage in the *Daodejing*'s textual history, it is perhaps safe to state that the concept of the *Dao* circulated and acquired its core meanings over a span of several hundred years during the Spring Autumn and Warring States eras (722–221 B.C.E.) (Lu 228–29).[2]

What is, then, the rhetoric of the *Dao*? That is, how does it shape and guide human conduct? How does it articulate its ontological and epistemological functions? What strategies, if any, does it offer to translate the *Dao* into bringing about effective, benevolent government? More important, how can we represent the rhetoric of the *Dao* to transform the conditions of the present and the relationship between the local and the global without beholding to our own value or worldview? To help address these questions, I focus on a few key terms and concepts in the *Daodejing,* and on how they cluster around to form their own discursive field.[3]

I begin with the central word *dao,* which has often been translated as a noun in English, such as: "way," "path," or "effective method." However, its primary meaning is actually more verb-like, conveying the idea of "moving ahead in the world," of "forging a way forward," or of "speaking"—hence Ames and Hall have translated *dao* as "way-making" (Glossary 57–59). The word *dao* appears seventy-three times in the *Daodejing*. Although there are variations and even ambiguities in these instances (Yu 170; G. Chen 35), one meaning remains constant and central: *dao* is the mother of everything in the universe and it never ceases its own movement. So Laozi tells us:

> Way-making (*dao*) gives rise to continuity,
> Continuity gives rise to difference,
> Difference gives rise to plurality,
> And plurality gives rise to the manifold of everything that is happening (*wanwu*).   (chap. 42)

Elsewhere *dao* is described as "the predecessor of everything that is happening (*wanwu*)" (chap. 4) or as "giving things their life" so much so that
"all things (*wanwu*) honor way-making" (chap. 51) and "it does not suffer
alteration" (chap. 25).

Meanwhile, we may still not recognize *dao*'s form, hear its sound, or
feel its shape:

> Looking and yet not seeing it
> We thus call it "elusive."
> Listening and yet not hearing it
> We thus call it "inaudible."
> Groping and yet not getting it
> We thus call it "intangible." (chap. 14)

Nor can we name it. Laozi tells us that *dao* that can be named or put into
words is not constant *dao* (chap. 1), or *dao* is "so profuse as to be nameless
(*wuming*)" (chap. 41). He actually admits that he does not know its name, and
if forced to give it a name, he would call it "grand" (chap. 25).

How do we then fully appreciate this nameless and invisible *dao* if we
do not want to fall into the trap of dismissing it as an example of mysticism
and irrationality or attributing it to the author's mistrust and rejection of
language? I suggest we turn to a few related terms in the *Daodejing*—terms
that help both to realize *dao*'s potency and potential as the *Dao* and to form
the discursive field of *dao*.

First is the term *ziran* (自然, "spontaneously so"), which literally means
"self-so-ing." It refers to a spontaneous, unimpeded state or course of action that is embodied by its own (self) movement and process. It is the most
fundamental of all specific expressions of order (Ames and Hall, Glossary
68). So, we read:

> Human beings emulate the earth,
> The earth emulates the heavens,
> The Heavens emulate way-making,
> And way-making emulates what is spontaneously
> so (*ziran*). (chap. 24)

Here *dao* emulates *ziran*; that is, *dao* manifests itself when all things (*wanwu*)
act in accordance with their own conditions and potential without co-
erced action or external intervention. In fact, it is this kind of spontaneity
that helps express *dao*'s very existence and movement in particular situations as the *Dao*. So the sages help all things follow their own course
without imposing their will or desire (chap. 64), and excellent rulers stop

excessive legislating and interfering so that their subjects can feel free and spontaneous (chap. 17).

Second, and very much related, is *wuwei* (無爲). While it literally could mean "no action" or "nonaction," *wuwei* in the *Daodejing* actually means (performing) an action that conforms to *ziran* and that transcends all external rules, principles, or standards. Paradoxically, *wuwei* provides *dao* with a discursive agency to engage the world noncoercively. Thus Laozi tells us that "It is simply in doing things noncoercively (*wuwei*) / That everything is governed properly" (chap. 3). Repeating the same theme, Laozi describes *dao* this way in chapter 37: "Way-making really does things noncoercively, yet everything gets done." On the other hand, what *wuwei* objects to are reckless, excessive actions by those rulers who filled their stomachs with exquisite food and dressed themselves with colorful and embroidered clothes while leaving granaries empty and farm fields overgrown with weeds (chap. 53), or the kinds of actions that are slavishly bound to or severely compromised by conventions, regulations, and restrictions. By contrast, for those sage rulers who do things noncoercively (*wuwei*) and who choose not to interfere, their people will prosper and follow the right, spontaneous course by themselves (chap. 57).

Closely related to *wuwei* in both form and meaning are several other *wu*-terms. Chief among them are *wuzhi* (無知) and *wuyu* (無欲). Once again, *wuzhi* is not so much about "(having) no knowledge" as about rejecting the kind of knowledge that is conventional and based on or drawn from ritualized conduct or prescribed conventions. Likewise, *wuyu* does not mean "having no desire"; rather it means desiring not to own, to contend, and to consume, but to follow *ziran* and to celebrate things in accordance with their own nature. Or as Laozi tells us, we should emulate sages to "act on behalf of things but do not lay any claim to them" (chap. 2) or to act without contending (chap. 81; see also chaps. 9, 34). Therefore, *wuzhi* and *wuyu* provide *dao* with an additional set of discursive means to guide humans to conduct themselves appropriately. It follows that if *ziran* can be characterized as helping constitute *dao*'s existence, imbuing all things (*wanwu*) with experience and potential, then *wuwei*, *wuzhi*, and *wuyu* provide *dao* with the necessary means to realize and internalize such experience and potential and to challenge conventions, stereotypes, or any other kinds of contrived moral standards. When humans succeed in carrying out these *wu*-activities, they exemplify virtue or excellence (*de* 德), to which I now turn.

De is often translated as "virtue," "power," or "excellence." *De* is central here because it embodies a symbiotic relationship with *dao*. That is, if *dao* encodes the spontaneous way all things are at the metaphysical level, *de* manifests *dao* at the day-to-day level as an expression of character, potency, or efficacy. So, for Laozi, if *dao* gives life to all things, *de* or its particular efficacy nurtures them (chap. 51; see also chap. 10). Further commenting on their symbiotic relationship, Laozi elsewhere observes,

> Thus, those who are committed to way mak-
>   ing (*dao*) in what they do are on their way.
> Those who are committed to character (*de*) in what they do
> Achieve this character;
> While those who lose it
> Are themselves lost.
> Way-making is moreover enhanced by those who express character,
> Just as it is diminished by those who themselves have lost
>   it. (chap. 23)

Seen in this light, *dao* and *de* are inseparable—hence the expression *daode*. If *dao* is the source of all things in the universe, *de* is its myriad manifestations through particular efficacious performances within each and every specific communicative context.

To ground our representation in the evidence required for enacting the art of recontextualization, we must look further. We must include the polysemous *fan*. *Fan* (反 or 返) can be translated as "returning," which Laozi uses to characterize *dao*'s movement: "'Returning' is how way-making (*dao*) moves" (chap. 40). Moreover, *fan* also means *xiangfan* (相反)—that is, "being opposite (of each other)." The deployment of *fan*, as a result, cannot help but convey these two related meanings. According to Laozi, all things grow in accordance with their own particular laws of *ziran*, culminating in their full maturation. The moment they start this journey toward maturation, they already begin the process of their anticipated decline, "returning" (返) to where they originated and to their very "opposites" (相反) or roots (see chap. 16), which would in turn signify the beginning of a new cycle, a new returning. Otherwise stated, every constituent in the universe has its own opposing counterpart, and both are mutually dependent on, and entailing of, each other. They constitute a dynamic, cyclical process, enabling all things to grow in fullness only to "return" as "opposites" for another new cycle. For Laozi, then,

> As soon as everyone in the world knows
>   that the beautiful are beautiful,
> There is already ugliness.

As soon as everyone knows the able,
There is ineptness.
Determinacy (*you*) and indeterminacy (*wu*) give rise to each other,

Difficult and easy complement each other,
Long and short set each other off,
High and low complete each other,
Refined notes and raw sounds harmonize (*he*) with each other,
And before and after lend sequence to each other—
This is really how it all works.

(chap. 2; see also chaps. 22, 24, 25, 42, 58, 76)

So, beautiful is "beautiful-returning-to-ugly" and the able is "the able-re-turning-to-ineptness," for example.

There is more. In the *Daodejing, fan* performs the act of "reversing," too, because returning to the opposite may also be a reversal. By way of *fan*, Laozi regularly reverses the opposites and champions what is convention-ally, linguistically, or habitually considered the "lesser" of the binary. For example, Laozi tells us, "The softest things in the world ride roughshod over the hardest things. / Only the least substantial thing can penetrate the seam-less" (chap. 43). Or: "The soft and weak vanquish the hard and strong" (chap. 36). This kind of deliberate reversal, a common trope in the *Daodejing*, jolts its readers out of their conventional habit of mind. We experience another similar jolt in chapter 45:

What is truest seems crooked;
What is most skillful seems bungling;
What is most prosperous seems wanting;
What is most eloquent seems halting.   (see also chaps. 20, 81)

In short, *fan*, by returning and being opposite of each other and by further reversing the value system that informs conventional categories or expres-sions of order, helps illustrate the *Dao*'s yin-yang dynamic—the contrastive qualities that express "the mutuality, interdependence, diversity, and creative efficacy of the dynamic relationships" (Hall and Ames 261).

To summarize: The discursive field of *dao* consists of *dao*, which is the mother of all things in the universe. To translate it into securing benevolent government and efficacious conduct as the *Dao*, one must first adhere to a course of action that is spontaneous and free of external interference (*ziran*). To do so, one engages the world noncoercively (*wuwei*), rejecting the kind of knowing that is predicated upon transcendental presence (*wuzhi*) and exercising the kind of desire that celebrates, rather than possesses, things (*wuyu*). Further, the *Dao* will be fully experienced only when one is able to both embody and induce character, efficacy, and potential for one's individual experiences (*de*), and when one is able to appreciate how all things undergo a perpetual process of transformation through returning, renewing, and reversing (*fan*).

By constructing the discursive field of *dao,* I aim to put the art of recontextualization to work and to find a way back to the time and context where ancient Chinese dealt with the questions and problems they were actually concerned with. I want to find out what work such a discursive field does and what sense it is expected to make. Or to adapt a famous expression of Lévi-Strauss, how is this discursive field of *dao* good for ancient Chinese to think with (Lloyd, *Adversaries and Authorities* 122)?

Simply put, the discursive field of *dao* gives rise to the rhetoric of the *Dao.* By championing *ziran* and *fan*, the rhetoric of the *Dao* creates a different discursive order, which not only recognizes the limits in linguistic and social conventions but also promotes and enacts a dynamic, transformative cycle. By privileging *de* and *wuwei*, the rhetoric of the *Dao* enables humans to noncoercively embody and produce character and potency within particularizing contexts. These outcomes challenge and subvert Confucian ideology, which stresses conformity to and reverence for social rituals and contrived moral precepts. They challenge and subvert the ideology of Legalism, too, in that they wrest agency and authority away from the realm of law and punishment and reinstall them in *daode*—in this symbiotic relationship where *de* expresses the *Dao* through each and every individual experience.

As I have suggested above, the art of recontextualization calls on us to recognize and value the other's own heterogeneity and its own balances and counterbalances. The rhetoric of the *Dao* provides a compelling example of the other's own heterogeneity. Because of this symbiotic relationship between *de* and *dao*, the rhetoric of the *Dao* embodies a keen understanding of the dialectic of interdependent binaries in nature and in the human world, nurturing a perpetual tension between cultivating this creative and processual dimension at the individual level and elevating one of many competing *Daos* to the status of one and the only *Dao* at the community, state, and cosmic level. That is, as individuals realize and celebrate their own *Daos* in their dealings with one another and with their immediate surroundings, the social and political pressure to codify one of them as *the Dao* for everyone else to follow will become ever more intense. For example, during the Warring States era (481–221 B.C.E.) and through the emergence of a centralized Han empire in the subsequent four hundred years or so, politicians, counselors, and other masters of thought were far more interested in promoting their *Dao* as the only *Dao*. They further argued that they knew how to translate their *Dao* into effecting a good life and a prosperous state. This collective move, driven by the rhetorical exigencies of the time and spurred on by political ambition, ended up equating the *Dao* "with the new unified, centralized empire and its foundations in the cosmic order" (Lloyd and Sivin 201). The need to stake an exclusive claim for one and the only *Dao* in fact became an indispensable part of all succeeding dynasties because it represented the Mandate of Heaven (*tianming*).

How can we, then, bring the rhetoric of the *Dao* to bear on, or speak meaningfully to, the conditions of the present? Let me offer one brief example here. The recent rise of the discourse of cultural nationalism—a discursive hybrid made of Confucianism, global capitalism, and Chinese Marxism—continues the centuries-old tradition of searching for and codifying one and the only *Dao* against other competing *Daos*. As the discourse of cultural nationalism rallies the Chinese people to help build a harmonious society, the concomitant effort to talk down and even silence these other competing *Daos* intensifies. However, any effort to anoint and reify one and the only *Dao* cannot help but fly in the face of the rhetoric of the *Dao*. As I have just illustrated, the rhetoric of the *Dao* demands that we recognize and mediate the inherent tension between the need to enable individuals to experience and embody their own *Daos* and the social and political imperative to elevate one to the status of *the Dao* (read as the state ideology or the law of the land). Our failure to recognize such a tension and to openly engage the *Dao's* own spatial-temporal contingency or experiential particularity takes the discourse of cultural nationalism out of its own context and out of its own dynamics. We thus deny the discourse of cultural nationalism any chance to search for and establish an equilibrium between the state's imperative to create a unified, harmonious nation and the individual's desire to exercise his or her own creative energy. Without such equilibrium and without proper understanding of the dialectic of the *Dao* and other *Daos*, the discourse of cultural nationalism may not survive the challenges posed by other *Daos* on the ground. In other words, opposition, difference, and even dissent (read as other *Daos*) should not be viewed as a destabilizing force to the discourse of cultural nationalism or to any other emergent or dominant discourse for that matter. Rather, they are an integral part of a transformative process that accompanies each and every communicative experience, and they are the stuff the rhetoric of the *Dao* is made of.[4]

Conclusion: From the View of the Other to
the Lens of Interconnectivity

I started this chapter with two epigraphs, one from Confucius and the other from Levinas. Living more than two thousand years apart, both Confucius and Levinas have shown a remarkable affinity in their attitude toward the other. Both advocate the need and sensitivity to engage in dialogue with the other and to be attentive to the other's voice and claim. For Confucius, such an engagement reflects his commitment to studying the other's strengths and weaknesses and to reform and improve upon one's self accordingly. For Levinas, such an engagement is based on and further mobilized by the realization that the other counts more than the self and that it is the self's moral responsibility to adopt a stance of openness and to practice a logic of accountability (Alcoff; Ratcliffe, *Rhetorical Listening* 31–32). In turn, the self becomes more aware of its own historical givens. Confucius arrives at this commitment by way of appealing to models or exemplars the other provides, whereas Levinas seems to have reached the same conclusion by defining what the other objectively means to the self.

My turn to the rhetoric of the *Dao* has been equally mobilized by my own commitment to the other. By writing for and about the *Daodejing* and the rhetoric of the *Dao*, I have aimed to take my audience to a different time and space. I have wanted to identify a particular discursive field in the *Daodejing* and to articulate the rhetoric of the *Dao* on its own terms. I have argued that the rhetoric of the *Dao* rises to contest other rival rhetorics for social and political dominance by putting forth a new discursive order and by empowering its practitioners to translate such an order into efficacious conduct and virtuous governance.

Representing the rhetoric of the *Dao* constitutes my effort to write Chinese rhetorics into our histories of rhetorics on their own terms and to resist writing or insinuating Western or other external assumptions and categories into such accounts. The writing of the rhetoric of the *Dao* also aims to promote a process sensibility that emphasizes relational and integrated experience and sees the world through the lens of interdependent binaries. No less important, though, is my desire to use the rhetoric of the *Dao* as a countervailing force to any ongoing effort to anoint the existing or emergent discourse with the role of *the One* because the perennial tension that undergirds one's search for the single *Dao* must be recognized and respected and because the *Dao* cannot help but be realized through each and every particularizing experience.

As we continue to represent the other beyond our own space and time and within an increasingly global environment, we must make it clear that the other is neither homogeneous nor unified. As Longxi Zhang rightly reminds us, "there is no such thing as *the* other, only a multiplicity of others, and there is no one unified voice but a diversity of voices, all engaged in a 'dialogized heteroglossia'" (83). Further, as we renew our moral commitment to the other, we must resist the temptation to see the other as *other* to Western rhetorics and as the latter's very opposite, be it imagined or idealized. Once again, I think that the rhetoric of the *Dao* may provide a corrective to this kind of false dichotomy and that it may help usher in a new paradigm for cross-cultural dialogue and understanding. Ironically, however, by appealing to exemplars or individual experiences and by shying away from objective connotations, the rhetoric of the *Dao*, which poses a direct challenge to Confucian rhetoric, turns out in this instance to be more Confucian than Levinasian.

Notes

1. Alcoff acknowledges the difficulty in distinguishing speaking *about* from speaking *for*, both because speaking *for* others may have to involve "simultaneously conferring information *about* them" and because speaking *about* others may be no different from "speaking in place of them, that is, speaking for them" (9; emphasis added; see also 30n7). I agree because I see them as interconnected and parasitic upon each other.

2. For ease of exposition, I will, for the remainder of this essay, use Laozi as the "author" of, or "speaker" in, the *Daodejing*.

3. For more on the concept of discursive fields and its application, see Mao ("Studying" 223–25).

4. In some interesting ways, this creative tension between *Daos* and the *Dao* has also been addressed by John Ramage, who describes rhetoric or the way of rhetoric as "a dynamic of 'recurrence,'" as perpetually negotiating "between constant flux and permanent stasis" (20).

4

RELEASING HOLD: FEMINIST HISTORIOGRAPHY
WITHOUT THE TRADITION

Jessica Enoch

To challenge and revise the rhetorical tradition—this phrase captures
the prevailing exigencies for feminist historiography in rhetoric. The
pervasiveness of this scholarly agenda becomes evident in a quick survey
of the initial and groundbreaking work in this area, where metaphors of
disruption and revision abound. For example, while Andrea Lunsford writes
that the goal of feminist historiography is to "interrupt the seamless narrative" of the rhetorical tradition ("On Reclaiming" 6), Cheryl Glenn calls for
"re-mapping" the familiar rhetorical landscape (*Rhetoric Retold* 4). Working toward a similar aim, Susan C. Jarratt encourages feminist scholars to
"burs[t] into the male study, tak[e] books off the shelf, and fli[p] irreverently
through them, rearranging the furniture of *the* history of rhetoric" ("Performing" 2). These calls for radical revision to the rhetorical tradition make
perfect sense. For more than two thousand years, conventional rhetorical
history has recorded the work of elite male rhetors and rhetoricians as well
as masculine forms of rhetorical practice, inscribing it as agonistic, com-
petitive, public, and linear. In so doing, rhetorical history has ignored not
only women's rhetorical production but also alternative ways of theorizing
and practicing rhetoric. Given the rhetorical history feminist scholars have
received, altering the rhetorical tradition becomes the most obvious and
important mode of scholarly production.

As numbers of scholars have observed, feminist historians have worked
to achieve the goal of revising rhetorical history by creating scholarship
that falls into two dynamic and robust categories: (1) histories that recover
the work of female rhetors and rhetoricians, and (2) histories that reread
the rhetorical tradition through the lens of gender theory. Recent surveys
of feminist research substantiate this claim. For instance, in their review
of more than sixty works of scholarship, Elizabeth Tasker and Frances B.
Holt-Underwood assess that the "paradigms" of recovery and rereading

have "shaped the purposes, methods, and goals of feminist historical research" (55). Kathleen J. Ryan's study of major edited collections dedicated
to feminist historiography finds that "recovery and gender critique are two
general research methods feminists have brought to rhetorical studies to
challenge the ways patriarchal oppression has shaped its study and textual
tradition" (23). And in describing the canonization process in feminist
rhetorical scholarship, K. J. Rawson explains that the "two primary methodologies" of recovery and gendered analysis "guide" the majority of work
inside the "feminist rhetorical canon" ("Queering Feminist" 40). While the
efficacy of both historiographic modes has certainly been reflected upon
and debated,[1] the explicit naming of these categories as well as the effusive
production of these two types of scholarship suggests what it means to
write a feminist history of rhetoric: the objective is to revise the rhetorical
tradition, and the means of achieving that objective is by either recovering
historical figures or rereading canonical texts, knowledge, and practices.[2]

My project in this chapter is not to challenge these claims about the
means and ends of feminist historiography. After reviewing more than 125
articles published in the past fifteen years, I too found recovery and gendered analysis to be the dominant modes of practice that work toward the
ultimate goal of destabilizing the rhetorical tradition.[3] And while naming
these taxonomies and their overarching project certainly has the potential
to diminish the range and vibrancy of scholarship that falls inside these
categories, it is safe to say that recovery, gendered analysis, and revision
serve as key methodological terms in this field of study.

Rather than interrogating these dominant terms and working within
these categories, I am interested in exploring what is left out of the dominant
narrative told about feminist historiography. For while recovery, rereading,
and revision are the most prevalent ways to write feminist rhetorical history, they are not the only modes of and goals for historiographic production that scholars engage and identify. My interest in this chapter, then, is
to investigate historiographic "outliers"—that is, feminist scholarship that
pushes beyond these categories of analysis—as a means of examining what
this kind of work is doing, how it's doing it, and how it might speak back to
the larger project of feminist historiography.

To pursue this investigation, I highlight two strands of scholarship that
offer different theoretical approaches to feminist historiography than recovery and gender analysis. The two strands of scholarship I consider here
are investigative trajectories that explore the rhetorical practice of remembering and the rhetorical process of gendering. While I certainly see these
two projects to be motivated by different historiographic concerns than

recovery and gender analysis, I do not view them as operating completely outside the two more recognized categories of work. Instead, I see the rhetorical practice of remembering as working within while expanding the boundaries of historiographic recovery, and I understand the rhetorical process of gendering as an extension of and elaboration on gender analysis. In other words, I view these alternative historiographic approaches as ones that continue to engage concerns at the heart of dominant practice but approach traditional concerns from different angles and pursue familiar lines of inquiry in different ways. In studying these four methodologies together, however, I have observed a noticeable and important difference between the conventional and alternative historiographic modes. This difference is in the way these alternative modes identify the "end game" for their work. Scholarship that engages the rhetorical practice of remembering and the rhetorical process of gendering releases hold of the prevailing exigencies of feminist historiography. Rather than working toward canonical revision, these methodologies envision a broader historiographic end: interrogating the dynamic relationships among rhetoric, gender, and history.

My work in this chapter is to consider how the two "outlier" modes of historiography might help scholars develop new scholarly projects. In particular, I'm interested in considering the ways the two "outliers" enable us to think beyond (or at least put pressure on) both the dominant modes of practice as well as the overarching goal of feminist scholarship. It is important to note that in looking beyond recovery and gender analysis I am in no way discounting these historiographic methodologies, for I see them making tremendous contributions to the work of troubling disciplinary assumptions and expanding understandings of rhetorical theory, history, and practice. My interest here is to build on this work by considering how we might continue to expand the feminist historiographic repertoire. In each of the two sections that follow, I begin by articulating the relationship between dominant and alternative practices, identifying connections and disconnections between the historiographic pursuits of both recovery and remembering as well as gender analysis and the rhetorical process of gendering. I then identify scholarship that takes up questions of remembering and gendering, and I use these works as both models of inquiry and heuristics for invention that enable us to elaborate on their historiographic potential.

Remembering Women

> ... someone in some future time
> will think of us.
>
> —Sappho

Feminist scholars of rhetoric can and have interpreted Sappho's poem as an exigence for their work, reading it as a prompt to recover forgotten women rhetors and "think of" their words. In fact, Joy Ritchie and Kate Ronald use this poem to open their anthology of women's rhetorics, setting out that Sappho's "hopeful boast captures the impetus behind our efforts here: gathering women's rhetorics together in order to remember that the rhetorical tradition indeed includes women" (xv). But inclusion, of course, is not the primary goal of recovery. Instead of inserting women's rheto-rics into the establishment of rhetorical history, feminist scholars such as Ritchie and Ronald have celebrated the ways that recovery enables (and often compels) them to challenge the rhetorical tradition and compose new understandings of canonical theories, knowledge, and terms.[4] Indeed, in recovering the rhetorical practices of an ever-increasing range of raced, classed, and cultured women from Aspasia and Ida B. Wells to Lu Yin and Hermila Galindo,[5] feminist historiographers have reanimated an astound-ing array of seemingly conventional topics, including the role of the rhetor (Wang; Ray; Tonn), rhetorical canons (Jarratt, "Sappho's"; Ede, Glenn, and Lunsford), rhetorical appeals and tropes (Engbers; C. Ramírez; Skinner), rhetorical agency (Logan; Sharer, *Vote*; Zaeske), and rhetorical education (Donawerth; Enoch, *Refiguring*; Kates).

Lindal Buchanan's excellent study of eighteenth-century actress Sarah Siddons illustrates the work that recovery can do. In her essay "Sarah Sid-dons and Her Place in Rhetorical History," Buchanan recovers Siddons, the "foremost tragedian of the late eighteenth century" (413), whose deliv-ery practices were included in prestigious rhetorical manuals of her day as "model[s] of delivery" (415). Buchanan points out that even though Siddons was once celebrated in such canonical texts, she is now a "forgotten figure" in the rhetorical tradition (416). Buchanan's work, however, is not to return attention to Siddons as a rhetor who meets traditional criteria for exem-plary delivery. Rather, Buchanan investigates how Siddons's "negotiations of feminine forms and display of pregnancy on stage" offer opportunities for scholars to consider how questions of gender complicate understandings of the canon of delivery (416). Elaborating on the article's title, then, Buchanan makes clear that when Siddons finds her place in rhetorical history, she does so by revising that history and its traditions in the process.

If we see Buchanan's essay as illustrative of feminist historiographic re-covery, we understand the dominant methodological questions to be "How have women practiced rhetoric, and how might their practices challenge traditional rhetorical scholarship and history?" There is a group of scholars, however, who take a different approach to this recovery project. Continuing to engage questions of recovery, these scholars release hold of the ultimate end of feminist historiography in rhetoric in that they do not (re)turn to the rhetorical tradition to engage in canonical revision. Rather, they shift their attention to the rhetorical work of recovery writ large, investigating the rhetorical work that goes into remembering women and, consequently, examining how women's memories are composed, leveraged, forgotten, and erased in various contexts and situations. Pursuing this line of inquiry, these scholars ask, "How have women been remembered, and to what rhetorical purpose has their memory been put?" To address this question, feminist historians have extended their interests to scholarship on public memory, an area of study only a select few feminist scholars have engaged. Before delving into feminist explorations of rhetorical remembering, it's important first to offer a brief sketch of public memory theory and scholarship.

According to scholars such as Carole Blair, Kendall Phillips, Bradford Vivian, and Barbie Zelizer, public memory is a vernacular presentation of the past composed specifically for the purposes of the present. Given this definition, it is no surprise that such scholars understand the creation of public memory as a "highly rhetorical process" (K. Phillips 2) in that people compose public memories not so much to remember with precision the way things were, but to formulate the past in ways that confirm or disturb ideas about the way things are and should be. As "willed creations" (Morrison 385), constructions of public memory hold a powerful constitutive function: these visions of the past work in the present to define identities, shape communities, and inform interpretations of the world. And while it is certainly true that articulations of public memory are multiple and varied, because these memories hold such import in terms of group identity formation and political activism, they are subject to and reflective of the relations of power that circulate in the publics of interest. As Blair notes, "struggle over symbolism in the past is just as surely a struggle over power in the present" ("Communication" 57). Thus, there are dominant public memories that fortify the status quo, and there are counterpublic memories that disrupt visions of life as it was, is, and will be.

With these understandings of public memory in mind, rhetoric scholars explore the strategies for and effects of remembrance, many times working toward the ultimate goal of gaining a fuller sense of the interanimation of power, persuasion, and memory formation. Subjects of study in this case are often what Pierre Nora has called "sites of memory," or those material places such as museums, memorials, and monuments where the past presents itself in everyday life. To make their analyses, scholars approach sites of memory with such concerns as "why historical actors constructed their memories in a particular way at a particular time" (Zelizer 217); "why one construction [of public memory] has more staying power than its rivals" (217); and "how [public] memories are erased, forgotten, or willed absent" (220). Because public memory scholarship interrogates the relationship among remembrance, rhetoric, and power, a small group of feminist scholars have recognized an opportunity to consider how questions of gender might be brought to bear on this discussion. These scholars refigure feminist historiographic concerns by considering not how recovery allows for canonical revision but how the recovery (and remembrance) of women is itself a rhetorical practice that has critical importance for feminist studies. Kristy Maddux, Rosalyn Collings Eves, and Carol Mattingly are three scholars who have pursued this opportunity, as their work considers the rhetoricity of remembering as well as the operations of power and the possibilities for resistance in creating and sustaining women's presence in public memory.[6]

In her article "Winning the Right to Vote in 2004," Maddux investigates the rhetorical effects of producing public memories about women. Here, she analyzes *Iron Jawed Angels,* an HBO feature film that portrays the US women's suffrage movement and considers how the film remembers—and persuades its viewers to remember—the first-wave feminist movement. Working from the theoretical perspective of "retrospective framing," Maddux examines the ways present-day ideas about feminism inform the memorialization of the suffrage movement, creating a situation in which "contemporary sensibilities . . . selec[t] and deflec[t] the elements" of first-wave feminism that are "most and least intelligible in contemporary terms" (75).

Maddux makes clear, however, that it is not enough to state that understandings of the present shape understandings of the past. Her focus is on the implications of the selecting and deflecting process inherent in the process of memory making. Interrogating this concern, Maddux argues that because the film interprets the first-wave feminist movement through third-wave principles that celebrate individual agency, it "closes down possibilities" for contemporary audiences to remember, identify with, and possibly even practice "collective [feminist] action" (90). Maddux's analysis confirms and adds nuance to the claim that "memory ignites the process of invention" (Ede et al. 410), for in the case of *Iron Jawed Angels,* memories of the suffrage movement are seen as constraining inventive possibilities for contemporary feminist activism. Thus, Maddux's work interrogates the rhetorical nature of women's memorialization by examining its heuristic potential to function as argument, proof, and model for practice at the moment of memory construction.

Maddux's work offers one example of scholarship that studies the rhetorical effects of women's memorialization. Extending and complicating this line of thinking, other scholars focus attention on an earlier stage in the memory production process to investigate the ways that power and patriarchy inform the most basic (and crucial) decisions about who should and should not be remembered in the first place. Especially in examining prominent sites of memory, scholars have found that, similar to rhetorical history, women are often not present. Blair's assessment of memorial space in Washington, DC bears out this claim: she writes that "male bodies" are the primary "kinds of bodies [that] have been deemed 'appropriate' or acceptable markers of national history and identity" ("Reflections" 276). The relative dearth of prominent memorials dedicated to women has not entirely checked opportunities for feminist investigation, however. Negotiating this constraint, scholars have looked beyond the national monument to search for and analyze alternative sites of memorialization, as Eves does in "A Recipe for Remembrance."

In this essay, Eves studies a series of cookbooks produced by the National Council of Negro Women and identifies them as alternative sites of memory that commemorate the famous and not-so-famous African American women who shaped their communities. Eves argues that by working from the premise that food triggers memory, the cookbook writers use recipes as well as the reminiscences about black female community members woven throughout the texts to prompt readers to replace "flawed dominant cultural memories of African American women" with the more positive iterations of black female leadership, love, and nurturance (281). Eves's methodological approach to women's remembrance explores how alternative modes of memory production have the potential to offer alternative ideas about women's identities as well as their involvement in community life, past and present.

As feminist scholars such as Eves turn their attention to alternative sites of remembering, they also interrogate dominant criteria for memorial production *and* maintenance to better understand the lack of representation of women on the landscape. Carol Mattingly addresses this concern in an essay that investigates memorials produced by the Women's Christian Temperance Union (WCTU) at the turn of the twentieth century. In this piece, Mattingly explores the "massive effort" of WCTU activists to "establish a powerful place in public memory for women" by funding a building (the Woman's Temple) and public fountains that paid tribute to women's temperance activism ("Women's" 133, 134). Her focus, however, is not on the rhetoricity of the monuments themselves or the ways the WCTU women argued for a place on the public landscape, although these would certainly be valuable pursuits for feminist scholars. Instead, Mattingly attends to the "difficulties" of maintaining public memorial space dedicated to women over time and "amid the efforts of more powerful forces" (134).

In the case of the WCTU memorials, Mattingly interrogates what Blair would see as the "durability and vulnerability" of these material structures ("Contemporary" 37). Pointing to emerging militarist discourse of the early twentieth century as well as changing architectural investments, Mattingly argues that these forces led to the monuments' demise in that they contributed to the lack of interest in and attention to the WCTU memorials—factors that eventually resulted in the demolition of these monuments and the subsequent erasure of WCTU achievements from the landscape. Thus, Mattingly's essay attends to the varied constraints and conditions that influence public remembrance of women, as her study contemplates the difficulties faced by those who intend to remember women: they must not only persuade the public of the figure's or group's importance at the time of construction, but they must also find ways to sustain that interest as years pass on.

The scholarship of Maddux, Eves, and Mattingly recasts the feminist historiographic practice of recovery. Disconnecting the act of recovery from the goal of revising rhetoric's history, these scholars turn their attention to the rhetorical practice of remembering women. From this kind of work emerges historiographic practices that examine the ways women's pasts have been leveraged and the rhetorical ends these remembrances served; that analyze the dominant and alternative modes of production groups have used to remember women; and that investigate the constraints groups have faced and the negotiations they have made in their attempts to commemorate women.

Even as we tease apart the distinctions between this scholarship and conventional methodologies of historiographic recovery, we can (happily) hear echoes between the two, for these investigations of remembering may ultimately be seen as a return to and revision of the canon of memory. However, a close examination of these studies reveals a departure from this project. The scholarship here does not primarily represent memory as one of the five canons by understanding it as a "storage facilit[y]" for information or even a "structured heuristic system" that works at the service of the invention of argument (Crowley, "Modern" 35). Rather, the emphasis is on the construction of memory on its own terms. Memory here is seen as a rhetorical act in and of itself. Thus, the concern is not so much to revise the canon of memory but to explore how rhetors remember and to what uses these memories are put. In pursuing this project, then, we can imagine at least two more possibilities for historiographic exploration.

First, this kind of work has the potential to reorient scholarly approaches to archives. Recently, feminist scholars have dedicated a great deal of attention to archival research methods, a move that makes sense given the fact that the historiographic recovery of women rhetors has depended on the revision of traditional ideas regarding archival practice as well as the identification of evidence.[7] Considering the archive from the perspective of memory studies, however, changes feminist historiographic concerns and priorities. Rather than using the archive to recover women, a feminist memory studies approach to the archive prompts scholars to see it as a site that creates and shapes public memories for and about women. In this case, then, feminist scholars would not just approach archival sites such as the Lesbian Herstory Archives (New York) and the Women's Archives (later Schlesinger Library, Cambridge, Massachusetts) as places only to retrieve information. Rather the work would be to study these archives in and of themselves as rhetorical producers of public memory about women. The goal of such investigations would be to explore both how these archives were initiated and conceived as creators of public memory and how they have variously taken up the work of women's commemoration. In many ways, then, this project would work in concert with the one articulated by Morris and Rawson in this volume in that both studies would acknowledge, explore, and approach archives as "sites of rhetorical invention " (page 78 [of this volume]) that "function variously as rhetorical resources, political engagement, constructionist historiography, and collective memory" (page 79 [of this volume]).

Second, as this line of inquiry engages strategies for remembering women, it also calls attention to strategies for forgetting them. Vivian writes that forgetting should not always be seen as an innocent process in which something or someone falls out of use or into oblivion (169). Rather, forgetting can be seen as a more strategic practice of erasure, a purposeful act of striking from public memory that often occurs by "substituting one memory for another" (Zelizer 220). Forgetting in this sense is a "rhetorical phenomenon," a "communicative, discursive, or symbolic activity fashioned to achieve a persuasive effect" (Vivian 169). Such an understanding of forgetting has great potential for feminist historiographic work as it prompts scholars to consider not just the strategies for remembering women like Siddons but also the rhetorical work that went into forgetting her.

Studies rooted in questions of remembering (and forgetting) women offer different kinds of historiographic possibilities to feminist scholars than those rooted in recovery. It is true that in taking up the work of remembering, scholars would move away from the widely accepted project of feminist historiography, which, as Bonnie Dow reminds us, is to "intervene in a rhetorical tradition dominated by the study of elite, white males" (106). But even though explorations of memory turn attention toward different concerns, they ultimately pursue another, equally important, feminist project also articulated by Dow: "to use the intellectual resources of feminism to understand and to valorize the contributions of women to public life, specifically public discourse, and to critique the ways in which these contributions have been and continue to be marginalized" (106). Feminist historiographic practice works toward this end by recovering the ways women throughout history have used rhetoric to participate in public life. But so too does scholarship that investigates the rhetorical process of remembering as it explores how memories of women have been constructed, revised, and erased in and through public discourse.

Gender and Rhetorical History

Transformation comes not only from women finding women authors but also from a gendered rereading of that masculine rhetoric.

—Susan C. Jarratt, "Performing
Feminisms, Histories, Rhetorics"

The second major paradigm of feminist historiography is often recognized as gendered rereading or gender analysis.[8] A gendered rereading of masculine rhetoric means that rather than identifying and analyzing the work of recovered women rhetors, scholars leverage gender theory to interrogate the relations of power operating inside the tradition that defines and naturalizes legitimate (masculine) and illegitimate (feminine) rhetorical theory, practice, and knowledge. In critiquing the hierarchical categories that undergird the rhetorical tradition, scholars consider how these hierarchies have maintained critical attention to a particular set of rhetorical topics; they investigate the effects of these hierarchies on women and marginalized groups throughout history; and they explore the theoretical and practical possibilities that productively emerge from their gender critique. Like historiographic recovery, the scholarly endeavor of rereading also points to radical revision as its goal: the project, Jarratt explains, is to "shake up disciplinary concepts" at the heart of the rhetorical tradition ("Speaking" 193).

Roxanne Mountford is one scholar who has effectively taken up this work by analyzing a specific rhetorical concept: the rhetorical space of the pulpit.[9] In *The Gendered Pulpit*, Mountford interrogates how the prized rhetorical space of the pulpit was constituted and reconstituted as an authoritative, sacred, separate, powerful, and, therefore, masculine space. These modifiers,

Mountford argues, ultimately helped to define the pulpit as a space built for men and, in the process, created a situation in which the presence of the woman preacher at the pulpit became "metonymically problematic" (26). Mountford's work, though, does not end with these understandings. Rather, she goes on to explore how women preachers have negotiated the pulpit by composing new rhetorical spaces for themselves and consequently cultivating new preaching styles.[10]

As Mountford's study shows, when feminist scholars enact gender analysis, they do the important work of investigating how gendered hierarchies have shaped rhetorical history. In so doing, they revise the tradition by disturbing conventional understandings of what is valuable and what is not and attending to those theories, practices, and understandings deemed inadequate or even invisible through the gendering process. While this approach is certainly a dominant mode of feminist historiography, a group of scholars have reinterpreted the project of analyzing how rhetorical principles have been engendered. I highlight here scholarship by Jordynn Jack, myself, and Catherine Palczewski as work that explores, instead, the rhetorical process of gendering.

Like scholarship that interrogates the rhetorical practice of remembering, these scholars' analyses of the rhetorical process of gendering also release hold of the rhetorical tradition. Their project is not to place canonical knowledge at the center of their interrogations. Rather, their work is predicated on the idea that the process of gendering is deeply rhetorical in that it relies on discursive, material, and embodied articulations and performances that create and disturb gendered distinctions, social categories, and asymmetrical power relationships. Of course, the human body is a primary site for this kind of performance, but in taking a cue from such exemplary work as Mountford's, this scholarship also acknowledges that the body is not the only entity that is gendered. Gendered designations can be mapped onto a host of historical subjects, spaces, and activities. Thus, the historiographic methodology articulated here enables scholars to consider how the rhetorical process of gendering participates in the "concrete and symbolic organization of all social life" (J. Scott 45). In so doing, this kind of historiography explores the specific rhetorical strategies used to constitute, sustain, disrupt, and redefine gendered categories. It analyzes the rhetorical contexts in which gendered definitions and redefinitions are deployed, and it investigates how particular gendered designations create, shape, and bar opportunities for historical actors.

Jack takes up this work when she examines the rhetorical strategies that stabilized gendered categories in a particular time of stress, a time when the fiction of "true" gendered distinctions had the potential to be exposed. In "Acts of Institution," Jack investigates the World War II rhetorics that strived to retain understandings of the white, middle-class female body as delicate, domestic, and fragile even as these women entered the wartime factory to engage in what could have been seen as "hard" (masculine) labor. Her examination brings together rhetorics of the body, time, space, and dress to survey how the confluence of these discourses ensured that woman's factory work was in no way altering traditional ideas about her femininity. Rhetorics of time, for example, called for workday adjustments to account for the female workers' supposed susceptibility to fatigue, while rhetorics of the body suggested women were especially fit for certain jobs because of their "nimble fingers" and their ability to work with "intricate objects" (291). Such rhetorics, Jack ultimately contends, created a sense of gendered continuity before, during, and after the war years; since once the war ended, these discourses set the foundation for arguments that women workers should return to the home and their "normal" childrearing responsibilities. Jack's historiographic methodology, then, takes as its subject the varied rhetorical strategies that constituted and reconstituted gendered difference at a moment when these differences had the potential to be challenged and even transformed.

While historiographic examinations into the rhetorical process of gendering may certainly assess discourses that stabilize normative gendered categories, they might also investigate those that enabled gendered change. My study of the early-nineteenth-century New England schoolhouse engages such rhetorics as it considers how this physical space transitioned from a place where the schoolmaster ruled over his students with corporeal punishment to one where the schoolmarm nurtured her students with feminine virtues (Enoch, "Woman's"). I argue that this transformation happened through the rhetorical regendering of the schoolhouse. During this period, educational leaders such as Horace Mann and Henry Barnard renovated this site through both discursive and material means not only by advocating for teaching practices based on feminine virtues of compassion and love but also by making physical changes to the schoolhouse itself, transforming it from a public, vulgar, dirty, and masculine space to a private, clean, decorative, and feminine space, one replete with beautiful draperies and flowers on the mantel.

Thus, this study interrogates how the rhetorical process of gendering functioned to transform a masculine space into a feminine one. It sees the schoolhouse as a rhetorical performance that, like other gendered entities, is capable of being "constituted and, hence, capable of being constituted differently" (J. Butler, "Performative" 402). This project also articulates the consequences that proceed from gendered (re-)constitution. Surely, the feminization of the school created opportunities for mainly white, Northern women to leave the home and enter the classroom, but the newly gendered classroom also shaped expectations for the pedagogical work that could happen inside it: the female teacher was not a scholar or community leader, but rather a mother figure who "simply" cared for and nurtured her students.

As Jack's and my work suggest, this type of historiographic inquiry examines how gendered rhetorics call for and create categorical consistency and change. But there are other intriguing possibilities that allow scholars to work within and beyond these two poles. In "The Male Madonna and the Feminine Uncle Sam," Catherine Palczewski investigates how the specter of gendered categories in crisis or the possibility of gendered revision can also function as a logical appeal. Here, Palczewski examines turn-of-the-century antisuffrage postcards, asserting that the visual rhetorics of these texts delivered arguments regarding the gendered consequences of suffrage on both women and men. Palczewski points out that while some postcards showed suffragettes adopting "masculine" practices such as smoking, others implied that the vote would engender women with a less favorable kind of femininity. These postcards depicted suffragettes as "public" or sexualized women who "showed their ankles and sport[ed] low cut bodices" (378). Palczewski also analyzes postcards that foretold the gendered consequences of women's suffrage on men, as these texts envisaged the public and enfranchised man becoming the emasculated father (or rather male mother) who would bear the responsibility of childrearing and caring for the home. Palczewski's examination underscores how historical agents have enthymematically leveraged the anticipation of gendered change; in this case, arguing that if women get the vote, then men will become feminized. Her study also, though, reveals the contextual nature and the multiple definitions of masculinities and femininities, prompting other scholars to continue to interrogate the rhetorical deployment of varied gendered understandings.

All three of these studies hold a generative function for scholars, encouraging them to imagine an array of historiographic pursuits that start from the premise that all gendered entities exist as both rhetorical process and product. Although we may have known this fact for years now, by historicizing this claim and analyzing the rhetorical practices that create gendered product(ion)s, feminist scholars can provide greater insight to the specific rhetorical work that goes into engendering and regendering. Thus, the scholarship discussed here provides a framework for feminist inquiry that examines the ways gendered norms are grafted onto bodies, spaces, activities, and even ideas; explores how these norms are destabilized and disturbed; investigates the varying referents for what is deemed masculine and feminine; and analyzes the consequences of gendered categories, definitions, and revisions. Moreover, these studies remind us that gendered distinctions are not always consistent. They do not call up the same referents across both time and space. This variability and rhetoricity underscores the importance of investigating the rhetorical process of gendering, reminding us that we should not assume we already know what this gendering process does, whom it effects, where it takes place, and how it shapes the world.

Another productive line of inquiry here is to explore how such examinations could bring together the investments of feminist historiography with those of queer and transgender rhetorics. While there is not space to adequately define these two burgeoning areas of study, a brief description of each reveals the resonance with the feminist rhetorical work described above. Building from the scholarship of Judith Halberstam, David Halperin, and Michael Warner, queer rhetorics can be seen as those discourses that both expose the constructed nature of and protest against heteronormative behaviors and ways of life, articulating instead "nonnormative logics and organizations of community, sexual identity, embodiment in space and time" (Halberstam 6). Meanwhile, transgender rhetorics, as defined by Jonathan Alexander, are rhetorics that "create cracks in the monolithic structure of gender identification to search for wiggle room in what William Pollack has aptly termed the 'gender straightjacket'" (53). Bringing these rhetorical imperatives into dialogue with the iteration of feminist historiography discussed here underscores the need for inquiry not just into the rhetorical process through which gendered norms are established but also into the rhetorical means necessary to protest them.

Furthermore, by examining how the rhetorical process of gendering has proceeded throughout history, feminist scholars could invigorate their historiographic efforts in the way K. J. Rawson calls for in "Queering Feminist Rhetorical Canonization." In this essay, Rawson argues that feminist scholars must "address the problem of gender normativity" by conducting "recovery efforts [that] focus on figures who have engaged in gender advocacy or on work that supports free expression and embodiment for an infinite range of genders, supporting true freedom of gender expression" (47). Historiographic explorations into the rhetorical process of gendering can support and invigorate such recovery efforts. Combining these two historiographic imperatives would enable scholars not only to draw attention to how gendered categories are mapped onto the body and beyond, but also to recover rhetors who have attempted to undo the binds of what William Pollack calls the "gender straightjacket."

Finally, it is important to consider how this methodological approach has the potential to elide or ignore other categories of constitution such as race, culture, class, physical ability, and sexuality. For instance, it would be remiss not to note that the rhetorical gendering in World War II factories and nineteenth-century schools functioned under the assumption of whiteness in that the referent for "woman" in these cases was a white woman. Investigations into rhetorical gendering, however, can open up rather than close down inquiry into these overlapping and mutually informing categories. That is, this kind of study can and should create opportunities for scholars to consider how categories of race, class, physical ability, and sexuality complicate and enhance understandings of the rhetorical process of gendering and vice versa. Furthermore, scholars could take it as their project to explore the effects and consequences that specific gendering processes have on bodies that are not white, middle class, heterosexual, or able bodied. Thus, the prospects for this historiographic methodology are wide ranging, as it prompts scholars to consider the numerous possibilities that emerge when the historiographic concern becomes the history of rhetorical gendering rather than gendered rereading of the rhetorical tradition.

Releasing Hold

This chapter offers two alternatives to the feminist historiographic paradigms of recovery and rereading. In underscoring and elaborating on scholarship that investigates the rhetorical practice of remembering and the rhetorical process of gendering, my goal is not to discount the innovative accomplishments of feminist scholars who pursue established lines of inquiry. Rather, my aim in this chapter has been to consider other ways to imagine the practice and product of feminist historiography in rhetoric. The feminist scholarship I identify here releases hold of the rhetorical tradition to consider what *else* a feminist historiography might do if it does not work towards canonical revision as its ultimate goal. Releasing hold in this way may indeed make some of us feel unmoored, as it might prompt us to ask uncomfortable questions about how our work engages rhetorical studies writ large and how it speaks back to scholars with other intellectual and political investments. But it also might free us to turn our attention to different rhetorical problems and to see a more broadly conceived *telos* for feminist scholarship: historiographic research that interrogates the complicated imbrication of rhetoric, gender, and history.

Notes

Special thanks goes to Pamela VanHaitsma, whose expert research skills supported my work in this essay.

1. See K. Campbell ("Biesecker," "Consciousness-Raising"); Biesecker ("Coming to Terms" and "Remembering"); Bizzell ("Opportunities"); Jarratt ("Performing" and "Speaking"); Rawson ("Queering Feminist"); Wu; and Kirsch and Royster.

2. While scholars have indeed placed these two historiographic projects in opposition to each other, a great deal of scholarship brings the two projects together. See Ryan's essay for a more detailed discussion of this point.

3. My survey reviewed feminist scholarship published from 1994 to 2010 in such journals as *Quarterly Journal of Speech, Rhetoric Society Quarterly, Rhetorica, Rhetoric Review, College English*, and *College Composition and Communication*. I also consulted edited collections such as *Reclaiming Rhetorica* (Lunsford), *Listening to their Voices* (Wertheimer), *and Rhetorical Women* (Miller and Bowles) as well as journals such as *Women's Studies in Communication, Feminist Media Studies*, and *American Studies*, reviewing articles written by feminist historiographers of rhetoric.

4. Scholars also extend and revise the rhetorical tradition by recovering women rhetorical theorists and by composing new rhetorical theories based on the work of recovered women rhetors. See J. Campbell; Donawerth, *Rhetorical*; Glenn, *Rhetoric Retold* and *Unspoken*; and Ratcliffe, *Anglo-American Feminist Challenges to the Rhetorical Traditions*.

5. See Glenn (*Rhetoric Retold*),; Royster; Wang ("Breaking"); and C. Ramirez.

6. See also Bessette, Biesecker ("Remembering"); Borda; Stormer; and Enoch and Jack.

7. See R. L. Enos ("Archeology of Women"); Glenn ("Truth"); Glenn and Enoch ("Drama"); Hogg; Kirsch and Rohan; Kirsch and Royster; Mattingly ("Telling"); Jarratt ("Rhetoric"); and Ramsey et al.

8. Gender analysis was initially developed as a critique of historiographic recovery. See Ballif ("Re/Dressing"); Biesecker ("Coming to Terms"); and Jarratt ("Performing" and "Speaking").

9. For additional studies in which scholars take up gender analysis to examine rhetorical principles and precepts, see Brody; Enders; N. Johnson; and Shaver.

10. Another approach to gendered analysis is to reread canonical texts through the lens of gender theory. See Bizzell ("Praise"); Lyon ("Sources"); and Swearingen ("Plato's").

5

QUEER ARCHIVES/ARCHIVAL QUEERS

Charles E. Morris III and K. J. Rawson

In 2006, Charles E. Morris III lamented that "the archive itself . . . has yet to be subjected to sustained critical-rhetorical reflection by scholars in this discipline" ("Archival Turn" 113). Recently, however, the figure of the archive has been looming increasingly large in rhetorical studies, including a number of essays published that same year in Morris's guest-edited forum in *Rhetoric and Public Affairs*; Gesa E. Kirsch and Liz Rohan's 2008 edited collection, *Beyond the Archives: Research as a Lived Process*; and Alexis E. Ramsey et al.'s 2010 collection, *Working in the Archives: Practical Research Methods for Rhetoric and Composition*, as well as a number of other recent publications on archiving (Glenn and Enoch; L'Eplattenier; Ranney; Rawson, "Accessing Transgender"). Although archival work has a long history, "the archive itself" is increasingly becoming a recognized and concentrated site of critical and theoretical regard in rhetorical studies. Despite this critical attention, however, rhetorical scholars have been much slower in responding to the "queer turn," despite a decade of visible scholarship in this field and twenty-five years' worth of influential scholarship in the academy writ large (Morris, Introduction; Alexander and Rhodes; Alexander and Wallace). We believe that one useful means of addressing this ongoing disciplinary heteronormative neglect and omission, and contributing to the project of rhetorical historiography, is to chart and mobilize queer archives and archival queers. In other words, we aim to make good on Michelle Ballif's claim that "what is at stake, then, in re/dressing histories is the production of new narratives, new discourses, new idioms" ("Re/Dressing" 96).

Our collective attention to archives has developed out of the lineage of revisionist rhetorical historiography, with its critical shift from historical subjects to historical production itself. More recently in this lineage of "Archivists with Attitude" came the significant realization and revelation that the archive is a key site of that historical production, materially and ideologically constitutive and thus consequential. As Wendy Sharer has argued, rhetorical historiography should always (re)consider what an archive is and does, how it means and matters, and for whom:

> Researchers should consider both the materiality of the objects from which we might derive "new" knowledge, and the physical construction of collections containing these bodies of knowledge. We cannot afford to ignore the various material processes—acquisition, appraisal, collection management, description, indexing, preservation, oxidation, and deaccession—that affect the corpus of historical records on which we may be able to construct diverse and subversive narratives to challenge previous, exclusionary accounts of rhetoric. ("Disintegrating" 124)

Cara A. Finnegan punctuates this repositioning of the archive by asserting that all rhetorical scholars, before they can engage its contents, "need to critically engage the archive itself" (118). Where we encounter rhetorical history and how it is embodied—the archival manifest—are inseparable from the tales and "truths" that comprise it. In this spirit we offer our theoretical and critical exploration of queer archives and archival queers.

Queer Archives

"Queer" does not simply signify a nonheterosexual *identity*. Queer, as we invoke it throughout this essay,

> challenge[s] the normalizing mechanisms of state power to name its sexual subjects: male or female, married or single, heterosexual or homosexual, natural or perverse. Given its commitment to interrogating the social processes that not only produced and recognized but also normalized and sustained identity, the political promise of the term reside[s] specifically in its broad critique of multiple social antagonisms, including race, gender, class, nationality, and religion, in addition to sexuality. (Eng et al. 1)

Thus queer is not interchangeable with lesbian, gay, or homosexual; instead, queer implies a broad critique of normativity along many different axes of identity, community, and power. At times, queer even functions to destabilize various strains of homonormativity (Duggan; Stryker), one variation of which is the resonant critique that LGBT (Lesbian, Gay, Bisexual, Transgender) scholarship regularly fails to attend to race (C. Cohen; E. P. Johnson, "'Quare' Studies"; McBride). Queer as a continuing and capacious challenge to normativity, without ever displacing the lives of actually existing LGBT people, is what makes the term useful for our purposes here in regard to rhetorical historiography.

As an extension of this definition, what we refer to as a "queer archive" includes but is not synonymous with the LGBT materials that may be collected in any given archive. Intentional collecting of LGBT materials began in the United States in the first half of the twentieth century as a politically motivated response to their longstanding omission from the archives. When Jim Kepner failed to find "objective information about homosexuality" in the San Francisco Public Library in the early 1940s, he began collecting materials to counteract the oppressive normativity that dictated what would and wouldn't be preserved and made publicly available ("The 1940s"). Of course LGBT materials have always, often unwittingly, appeared in public collections, but without official sanction or mainstream acknowledgement, and they may have been deliberately excluded if they were deemed too "pornographic" or "immoral." Queer archives, then, in their very existence, critique and challenge the normativizing collecting and circulating practices of other institutions. In response to James O'Toole's question, "When is the act of recordmaking more important than the record that is made?" (51), we offer queer archives as an answer. Our distinction between LGBT materials and queer archives indicates a recognition that archives as a whole can function outside of or beyond the specific materials collected within them.

Since the 1940s, the cultural landscape for collecting LGBT materials in the United States has seismically shifted. Joan Nestle, cofounder of the Lesbian Herstory Archives and another early pioneer of queer archiving, described in 1998 just how much had changed:

> When the New York Public Library opened its gay and lesbian history exhibit last year in a cocktail party atmosphere, I knew our pioneering days were over. As I toured the exhibit[,] . . . I thought of all the years the library had been part of the problem—its card catalog a journey in self-hatred for a curious "homosexual." Our history . . . is hot stuff now, capable of pulling in much-needed revenue, and it is true that these institutions have the staff and often the space for which grassroots archives have to beg. My heart lies with the lesbian and gay grassroots history projects and archives that risked all when the establishment would not go near queer material except as examples of pathology, but these are new times. (235)

It has been more than a decade since Nestle made these observations, and LGBT materials have only continued to gain popularity. Given the vast number of US libraries and archives that now inttentionally collect LGBT materials, to merely collect LGBT materials is vital although no longer inherently queer.

While these cultural shifts to embrace LGBT collecting may be partly credited to the queer archival activism of individuals such as Kepner and Nestle, there has also been a theoretical shift relevant for scholars in rhetorical historiography, namely *queering* archives. Let's start with two interwoven questions: What are archives, and what do they do? The Society of American Archivists offers the following definition of "archives," which seems consistent with popular understandings: "Archives are the non-current records of individuals, groups, institutions, and governments that contain information of enduring value" ("So You Want"). The ambiguity of "enduring value" implicitly suggests that archiving can never be a neutral or objective practice because value is always political and subjective (the category of "enduring value" would be a useful rubric for analyzing which LGBT materials are routinely collected and why).

For queer archival projects, what is of enduring value seems to be closely tied to that which evidences the queer past, which means that queer archives often function as bodies of evidence. Such holdings register a fundamental revelation, indeed a declaration, that "we" were here. Within longstanding and ongoing contexts of erasure, these revelations and declarations remain profound and necessary, even as one recognizes in light of various queer historical critiques Judith Halberstam's premise that such an archive is "a complex record of queer activity" (170). Who "we" were/are, in other words, cannot be understood as given or stable or uncomplicated; however, the queer archive always functions, simply by being, as an assertion that "queers have been here" and thus constitutes an intervention against (hetero/homo) normativity's retrospective governance and discipline.

This evidentiary claim is of course precarious. As José Esteban Muñoz observes,

> Queerness has an especially vexed relationship to evidence. Historically, evidence of queerness has been used to penalize and discipline queer desires, connections, and acts. When the historian of queer experience attempts to document a queer past, there is often a gatekeeper, representing a straight present, who will labor to invalidate the historical fact of queer lives—present, past, and future. Queerness is rarely complemented by evidence, or at least by traditional understandings of the term. (*Cruising Utopia* 65; Morris "Hard Evidence"; Butt; Boyd and Ramírez)

We share Muñoz's perspective. We can also imagine—especially within an epistemic economy in which positivism within historiography, public history, and public memory, however illusory, continues to hold sway—the queer archive as a powerful reversal of "state's evidence." That is, queer exhibits ground a prosecutorial case against the state and other institutional regimes for crimes, past and present, of homophobia and heteronormativity.

Within queer studies, Elizabeth Freeman argues that "many of [the new queer historians] have championed eclectic, idiosyncratic, and transient archives including performances, gossip, found objects, and methods (or anti-methods) that rely on counterintuitive juxtapositions of events or materials" (Introduction 162). The queer archive, then, necessarily includes ephemera, the "trace, the remains, the things that are left, hanging in the air like a rumor" (Muñoz, *Cruising Utopia* 65), extending beyond those traditional sites and the objects housed in them. Muñoz is not alone in que(e)rying these potentialities, accumulating and exhibiting a diverse and perverse array of found objects, gestures, movement, emotions, talk, and repertoires that reconfigure the what and where of the archive (Butt; Cvetkovich; Fox; Halberstam; John Howard; E. P. Johnson; H. Ramírez; Rawson, "Archive This!"; D. Taylor). Such efforts not only enlarge and usefully fragment and transmogrify perceptible materializations and representations and structures of feeling but also unsettle any notion of the traditional archive, even valuable LGBT archives, as an unadulterated boon.

At the same time, we resist any permanent departure from those spaces and collections traditionally understood as the archive. We find both accurate and troubling Ann Stoler's assessment that

> one could argue that "the archive" for historians and "the Archive" for rcultural theorists have been wholly different analytic objects: for the former, a body of documents and the institutions that house them, for the latter a metaphoric invocation for any corpus of selective collections and the longings that the acquisitive quests for the primary, originary, and untouched entail. (45)

This unfortunate binary involves not only theoretical differences but material consequences regarding the resources and rhetorical potentialities of queer pasts, their resonance and utility. In response, we advocate an ongoing dynamic engagement with "archive" in its multiplicity, extrapolating Diana Taylor's observation that "the archive and the repertoire exist in a constant state of interaction" (21), as a call to engage queer holdings and embodiments wherever they might be found and in their relationality.

One key dimension of relationality is that of queer archives as sites of rhetorical invention. Even before any specific manifestation of how queer archives function as such, it is significant that they induce or deepen a will to the past and its presence (now and in the future). As Muñoz posits, "These ephemeral traces, flickering illuminations from other times and places, are sites that . . . assist those of us who wish to follow queerness's promise, its still unrealized potential, to see something else" (*Cruising Utopia* 28). The archival encounter—even granting multifarious and diverse archival sites and movements—that would generate such an impulse or will is not guaranteed, thus requiring the rhetorical invention requisite to produce it. In other words, among the multiple ways that queer archives are rhetorically constructed, invention creates the conditions of possibility for what Carolyn Dinshaw has called a "queer historical impulse, an impulse toward making connections across time between, on the one hand, lives, texts, and other cultural phenomena left out of sexual categories back then and, on the other, those left out of current sexual categories now" (1). That queer will to the past having been fomented, archives then function variously as rhetorical resources of cultural production, political engagement, constructionist historiography, and collective memory, that is, the wellspring of queer world making (Biesecker, "Of Historicity, Rhetoric"; Morris, "Archival Queer"). The queer archive, therefore, provides the conditions and resources for becoming archival queers.

Archival Queers

In contemplating and advocating possibilities for queer world making, we argue that archival relationality is indispensable, requiring of us a heightened and dynamic consciousness of that fact, as well as its attendant commitment and enactment. Our understanding of being archival queers, in other words, derives its premises from Laura Doane and Sarah Waters's theory that "retrospection is a condition of homosexual agency" (qtd. in Rohy 343), and Faedra Chatard Carpenter's conclusion, in recognizing the performativity of "historicized imaginations and imagined histories," that "history is fashioned and its documentation is inevitably filtered through the lens of the archivist, who—unwittingly or consciously—impresses himself on the record" (188). Carpenter's call to "que(e)rying history," it should be emphasized, reverberates not only through the academy but throughout zones of cultural production, wherever we might witness and encourage "homosexual agency" (or, even more expansively, queer agency). We are all potentially archival queers.

The significance of being archival queers is deepened further when we acknowledge the stakes in recognizing, engaging, accumulating, and speaking these traces, these holdings, these embodiments of queer pasts for self and communities, for transformation. Horacio Ramírez envisions this agency as a mode of testifying: "to connect the past to the present, to make of history a collective process of human signification where all of us become agents for its production" (119). Such a testament is crucial because "for marginalized communities constantly involved in struggles for visibility, political identity, and space . . . *testimonios* about their existence are critical acts of documentation" (116). Put otherwise, archival queers' sense and embodiment of agency emanates from what Roger Hallas calls an "archival imperative": "The question of the archive is thus in the end not whether it succeeds in preserving the past from oblivion but how the past that eventually emerges from it can potentially produce a revelatory historical consciousness of the present" (435). Archival queers' historical consciousness also centrally embraces futurity, queerness not-yet-here and yet-to-be, Muñoz's queer utopian vision that "a posterior glance at different moments, objects, and spaces might offer us an anticipatory illumination of queerness" (*Cruising Utopia* 22).

In elaborating the modalities of archival queers, let's consider in greater detail identification and disidentification, critique of the "amnesia archive," and infrastructural rhetorics of "mnemonic socialization." To begin, we might productively imagine archival queers as those who develop queer relationships with the past, what Dinshaw refers to as "affective relations across time" (142). Just as Ann Cvetkovich describes the Lesbian Herstory Archives (LHA) as an archive that "aims to provide an emotional rather than a narrowly intellectual experience" (241), becoming an archival queer involves a willingness, indeed an imperative, to resist the archive as a purely intellectual space and to seek out affective relations with the past. While some archives, like the LHA, are developed specifically to facilitate emotional experiences, affective encounters happen in any and all archives. To approach archives expecting affective encounters with the past is to cede power to the archive as "a technology of identity" (Rohy 354), as a place where our identities can be built, shifted, deconstructed, intensified, and queered. In common queer historiographical parlance, such affective relationships with the past are often accounted for in terms of identification and disidentification.

For many contemporary LGBT people, history offers rich potential for identification—to find oneself and gain affirmation that LGBT people have always existed and will always continue to exist. To relate to history as an archival queer may therefore involve an intentional quest for affirmative identity formation, to read queer triumphant history as a positive genealogy of queer identity when the realities of lived queerness may not seem so successful or so glamorous. For example, *Transgender Warriors* details Leslie Feinberg's personal quest for affirmative transgender history: "I realized that I am part of a vast movement of people who have been shamed and threatened and beaten and arrested because of the way we define our sex or express our gender. And many of us have emerged stronger and prouder" (64). To be part of a vast movement is comforting, even when that movement shares experiences of profound injustices and oppression, because there is a shared strength and pride in facing and overcoming injustice.

David Halperin and Valerie Traub both rightly point out that within a historical framework, "identification is desire" (Halperin, *How to Do the History* 15), and as a consequence, figures from the past should not be understood as "subject *to* our identifications, but as objects *of* our desire" (Traub, *Renaissance of Lesbianism* 354). This shift of historical figures from subjecthood to objecthood importantly marks the historian's power and our contemporary ability to control representations of the past. Yet despite our ability to control these representations, there will always be elements of the past that refuse affirmative identification. Rather than seeing history as constituted by willing objects of our desire, Heather Love argues that there are

> texts that resist our advances. Texts or figures that refuse to be redeemed disrupt not only the progress narrative of queer history but also our sense of queer identity in the present. We find ourselves deeply unsettled by our identifications with these figures: the history of queer damage retains its capacity to do harm in the present. (8–9)

For Love, identification is a painful process of shared shame and abjection because "the experience of queer historical subjects is not at a safe distance from contemporary experience; rather, the social marginality and abjection mirror our own" (32). Identification for the archival queer is therefore not necessarily a singularly redemptive experience but may produce negative affects as well (Halperin and Traub).

These processes of queer historical identification are based on a fundamental alignment with the past; even when the past is not receptive to our advances, we still imagine ourselves as part of a coherent lineage of queer history. Muñoz, in his earlier work on disidentification, complicates this model by suggesting that we often relate to people or objects when we are coded precisely *not* to be aligned with them. He explains,

> To disidentify is to read oneself and one's own life narrative in a moment, object, or subject that is not culturally coded to "connect" with the disidentifying subject. It is not to pick and choose what one takes out of an identification. It is not to willfully evacuate the politically dubious or shameful components within an identificatory locus. Rather, it is the reworking of those energies that do not elide the "harmful" or contradictory components of any identity. It is an acceptance of the necessary interjection that has occurred in such situations. (*Disidentifications* 12)

Navigating the singularly affirmative or shameful identifications discussed above, disidentification is a way of relating to an object or subject that engages and reworks harmful or shameful elements. Unlike depictions of historical identification that seem to focus exclusively on the contemporary person, the one identifying with the past, disidentification is a reciprocal process that deeply influences both. To put this into a historical context is an invitation to see how, through the process of disidentification, we might alter the energies of historical materials and engage in a transhistorical relationship of "call-and-response" (Muñoz, *Disidentifications* 62; Alexander and Rhodes).

A community art project supported by the San Francisco Public Library (SFPL) titled "Reversing Vandalism" captures well archival queers' spirit of identification and disidentification. In 2001, more than six hundred books, mostly on LGBT topics, HIV/AIDS, and women's health, were vandalized in the SFPL ("Project History"). After the perpetrator was caught and the books were returned to the library, program manager Jim Van Buskirk and SFPL staff faced an archive of "ruined" texts. However, to simply throw the books away "would only complete the vandal's crime" because they would be eliminated from circulation and the painful history they memorialize would be elided ("Project History"). Instead, artists from around the world were invited to transform the damaged books into art, an invitation that effectively conjured hundreds of archival queers. Not a simple act of reclamation, many of the participating artists extended the damage done to the books as part of the project, creating something new, but often something very far removed from a book. Through this form of "critical recycling," artists became aligned with the vandal, enacting a form of disidentification as they "work[ed] to retain the problematic object and tap into the energies that are produced by contradictions and ambivalences" (Muñoz, *Disidentifications* 58, 71).

In a piece titled *The Best Medicine*, for example, artist Cedar Marie transformed one of the ruined books, *AIDS and HIV in Perspective: A Guide to Understanding the Virus and Its Consequences*, by shredding the book, filling gel capsules with the shreds, and putting the capsules into a glass bottle. As Marie explains, "enclosing the shreds in gel capsules, which could represent vitamins or medicine, creates an impossible paradox that could apply both to AIDS, which has no known cure, and to the book itself, which cannot be repaired." By relating the vandalized books to queer experience, *The Best Medicine* highlights the appropriative potential inherent in this project. This illustrates the "'accidental' positive identity-affirming effect" (Muñoz, *Disidentifications* 69) of such disidentifications in that despite the vandal's homophobic intentions, the artists served as archival queers as they used the vandalized objects as sources for identity-building and affirmation through reclamation.

The Best Medicine, by Cedar Marie (2003). Photo by Tom McInvaille; courtesy of Cedar Marie.

An archival queer might take a similar approach by forging connections with historical materials that seem unavailable to identification, materials not "culturally coded to connect with the disidentifying subject" (Muñoz, *Disidentifications* 12). This approach would prompt a more expansive engagement with the past that develops not only from affirmative identifications but also from discomforting and unpleasant archival encounters. If, as Love asserts, "queer critics and historians have often found themselves at a loss about what to do with the sad old queens and long-suffering dykes who haunt the historical record" (32), perhaps the strategy of an archival queer would involve intentional, direct, and affective engagement with precisely those figures that haunt us the most. The resulting relationships with the past could include a call-and-response-style dialectic that serves to change both the contemporary person and the historical object.

It should be emphasized that the processes of identification and disidentification cannot be taken for granted. Even if we are bequeathed pasts, even if we inadvertently function as vehicles of transmission, archival queers must be constituted by our activated agency, exertion in relation to potentiality, which requires rhetorical labor. One key mode entails exposure and critique of heteronormativity and homophobia in relation to what Lauren Berlant and Michael Warner have called the "amnesia archive," which they describe as "the part of collective memory sanctified not by nostalgia but by mass aversion. . . . The motto above the door is Memory Is the Amnesia You Like" (549). In the broadest sense, the amnesia archive would include, which is to say erase, the whole of queer pasts, any and all traces or taint, engendering Christopher Castiglia and Christopher Reed's observation that "assaults on memory—on particular memories and on the value of memory itself—therefore threaten not only our knowledge of the past, but our ability to imagine, reshape, and make claims for identifications in the present and future as well" ("'Ah Yes'" 158). Archival queers must therefore directly expose and confront such mnemonicide (Morris, "My Old Kentucky Homo"), and other homophobic versions of history's machinations (Meyer; Vogel; Burton; Castiglia and Reed, *If Memory Serves*). Moreover, archival queers must be relentless not only in the operation but also the discourse of preservation and proliferation, a mobilizing discourse that inculcates a functional and committed relationship to the past. Such discourse is propaedeutic to archival will and action, a queer historical "fighting spirit" if you will, as well as generative of "living historiographical intervention" (H. Ramírez 113), countermemories (Bravmann; Castiglia; Chisholm; Dunn; Herring), conjuring of "ghosts" (Muñoz, *Cruising Utopia* 33–48), "queer archive activism" (Juhasz), and "retroactivism" (Hilderbrand) among other modes of historical resistance (Chauncey, "'What Gay Studies Taught the Court'").

It is also important to recognize that queers, too, bequeath and enact such erasures in the amnesia archive. As a pressing case, consider Christopher Castiglia's powerful critique of "counternostalgia," those "attempts to authorize sexual conservatism by normalizing gay memory . . . a look back with fury at the sexual 'excesses' of the immature, pathological, and diseased pre-AIDS generation" (Castiglia and Reed, *If Memory Serves* 160). Equally powerful is Susan Stryker's critique of "homonormative disciplinarity," "the micropolitical practices through which the radical implications of transgender knowledges can become marginalized" (153). Stryker's analysis of the 1966 Compton's Cafeteria riot exposes this "homonormative gaze" as operative among queer theorists as much as among gay cultural producers, obscuring not only trans history such as the Compton's legacy but also the "critical role of embodied difference in the practice of archival research" (153). Such embodied difference makes a difference in every act of memory and can become consequentially reified as the common ground of a marginalized "community," as Scott Bravmann's analysis of Stonewall reveals:

> Queer fictions of Stonewall create various versions of "us" by defining and refining the past. The powerful "common-sense" fiction that "we" share at least some of the common goals—goals that are symbolically represented by the resistance during the riots—is one centrally problematic way Stonewall erases and creates historical memory, in regard to relations between gay men and lesbians as well as racial and political differences. (85)

Academic and cultural rhetorics challenging the amnesia archive, however, are necessary but not sufficient. Archival queers must also address vexing issues of audience. We suspect that many of those who champion and theorize and assemble queer archives, histories, and memories dangerously presume audiences' receptivity, recognition, and response. Put differently, we are not confident that LGBTQ communities, especially of the current generation, are inclined to be interested or invested in queer archives, history, or memory, because mnemonic infrastructure and discourse do not exist sufficiently to render it a quotidian, resonant, and relevant articulation or political mainstay. In noting George Chauncey's observation that gay history has been "almost entirely forgotten in popular memory" (*Gay New York* 1), John Howard queries: "How can we account for this social amnesia? Is it possible to speak of a queer collective memory? If so, how did it fail us? Or did it? And who are among the 'us' to which I refer? For whom are acts of reclamation important today?" (146). In partial response to Howard's questions, we argue that if issues of relevance and resonance aren't addressed, then the work of archival queers may not *matter*. Being archival queers, in other words, must be understood and enacted as a matter of inducement, and thus also a matter of infrastructural rhetorics that might seek to (re) create, however imperfectly, "milieux de memoire" (Nora).

Underdeveloped, in our judgment, is what Eviatar Zerubavel calls "mnemonic socialization"—that is, communal "norms of remembrance" and the conditions and practices that instill and perpetuate them (5). Consonant with Zerubavel's conceptualization, Michael Warner argues that "one reason we have not learned more from this history is that queers do not have the institutions for common memory and generational transmission around which straight culture is built" (*Trouble with Normal* 51–52). The substantial challenge of queer mnemonic socialization, then, is rhetorical, a matter of invention. George Chauncey has argued that

> we need to invent—and constantly reinvent—a tradition on the basis of innumerable individual and idiosyncratic readings of [queer] texts[,] . . . embed its transmission in the day-to-day social organization of [our] world . . . passed on in bars and at cocktail parties, from friend to friend, from lover to lover, from older . . . serving as mentors to younger . . . just beginning to identify themselves as gay. (*Gay New York* 283)

This impulse also reverberates through Lucas Hilderbrand's meditation on the first generation of AIDS activism as conveyed in archival footage on ACT UP documentary videos such as James Wentzy's *Fight Back, Fight AIDS*. Hilderbrand advocates "retroactivism" through "intergenerational nostalgia," a form of cultural memory that "accounts for generative historical fascination, of imagining, feeling, and drawing from history" (Morris, "Forum" 308; Morris, *Remembering*).

Absent the prospects of any substantive or reliable queer transformation of curricula in US education or other mainstream institutions, archival queers must rhetorically induce and construct queer mnemonic socialization in alternative contact zones and counterpublic sites and subcultural spaces. Judith Halberstam, drawing on Elizabeth Freeman's concept of "temporal drag," assesses one such effort at the 2002 Queer Arts Festival in San Francisco, which featured intergenerational pairings of dyke performers. In these performances and onstage interview segments, archives of women's music and lesbian culture were both transmitted and destabilized (in terms of race, gender, and class). The artist Ferron, in particular, "created an interesting relay of sentiment and affect between herself and the young audience," exemplifying Halberstam's idea that "older performers create an affective vortex by pulling new audiences to a place they neither remember nor know through history, and by simultaneously taking older audiences back to that place between the time of lesbian and the time of queer" (183, 185–86).

In Halberstam's example of intergenerational performance pairing we find a core element in a project of mnemonic socialization: queer matchmaking. Notwithstanding claims that this generation lives in a "retroculture" (Hilderbrand 307), we argue that especially queer "affective relations across time" need a helping hand, perhaps even a little meddling, within a context of mnemonic infrastructural deficit. We favor the notion of queer matchmaking because it suggests desire and agency but does not presuppose (in the way that a term like "cruising" might, for example) homogeneity in affiliation or what these conditions of possibility will produce. This is not a variation on Match.com. As Victoria Gannon describes it, "A match is not a set of identical objects or people, but of complementary ones. A match is a dialogue. Think tennis or chess, in which one player's move determines the other player's next move. Back and forth, back and forth. Finally, a match is an object of ignition, an inert stick with the potential to make fire."

Queer matchmaking constitutes arranged or incited archival encounters, which is to say brushes and happenings that manifest the past in space, document, object, body, gesture, performance. We are inspired in this imagining by Alexander Chee's recollection of the moment he recognized, in an unexpected archival encounter, an existing relationship among time, space, self, community, past, and present:

> There on a blanket [on a sidewalk in the Castro during a time when "there was no way to find the Castro on any maps"] stood a pair of black leather steel-toed boots, twelve-hole lace ups. . . . As I approached them, feeling the pull of the hill, I drew up short to examine the rest of the sidewalk sale. Some old albums, Queen and Sylvester, three pairs of jeans; two leather wristbands; a box of old T-shirts; a worn watch, the hands still moving; a pressed-leather belt, Western style; and cowboy boots, the same size as the steel-toes. I tried the steel-toes and took a long look at the salesman as I stood up, to feel at that moment that they were exactly my size. This man was thin. He was thin in a way that was immediately familiar. Hollowing from the inside out. His skin reddened, and his brown eyes looked over me as if lightning might fall on me out of that clear afternoon sky. And I knew then, as I paid twenty dollars for the boots, that they'd been recently emptied. That he was watching me walk off in the shoes of the new dead. And that all of this had been happening for some time now. (22–23)

Such encounters need not happen in San Francisco, nor are their embodiments prescribed. Scott Herring in his "queer anti-urbanism" project assembled an "eclectic archive . . . that spans almost one hundred years of metronormativity," including Confederate portraits of working-class white males, African American bulldagga performances, and Alison Bechdel's graphic memoir *Fun Home*, "that readers can make use of, and, if they like, remodel for the micropolitics through which the radical implications of transgender knowledges can become marginalized further ends" (24). Sally Newman traveled from Australia to Colby College in search of an elusive pressed white rose apparently tucked in an envelope among a sheath of letters shared by two women in 1887–88 (51–52). For some, (mis)recognition occurs in a vintage photograph found in a flea market, yard sale, or on eBay (Ibson; *Other People's Pictures*). For others, entering or traversing places and spaces generate sparks and scenes of memory and history (Sember; Halberstam, esp. 22–46; John Howard; Chisholm). What matters are the inducements such queer encounters, juxtapositions, hauntings might produce.

One noteworthy archival queer promoting mnemonic socialization is E. G. Crighton, first artist-in-residence at the grassroots GLBT Historical Society in San Francisco. In 2009, Crighton's project and exhibition *Lineage: Matchmaking in the Archive* brought artists, composers, writers, filmmakers, and performers, ten in all, into contact with boxes of archival materials— documents as well as ephemera. Each participant was paired with a queer past life embodied in those archival traces and asked to create something in response to them (Roberts). As Crighton explained it,

> My job is to create metaphorical conversations between the living and the dead. These relationships create fertile ground for art to bring our history off the archive shelf in unexpected ways. For people whose collective and individual traces have been erased, taking charge of our community memory is still a radical act. It is a kind of lineage that resides outside of bloodlines, the kind that has nurtured us for a long time. (qtd. in Wessels)

Responses included a poem, an aria, a monologue, written conversation, a letter, a short film, sculptural installations, and an interactive computer work. Some works expressed gratitude to forebears; others derived from the archive a theme or mood for a piece that lacked entirely direct reference to the life remembered. Tina Takemoto's *Gay Bachelor's Japanese American Internment Camp Survival Kit* was mailed back through the decades to Jiro Onuma:

> The kit included handmade objects such as exercise devices, playing cards, cuff links, and recreations of the erotic male exercise magazines. By intervening within the archive of someone whose sexuality and racial identity was rendered invisible and threatening during his lifetime, Takemoto grants Onuma a visibility and credits his survival to a queer imagination. (Roberts)

Through these archival experiences, across sexuality, gender, race, and class, participants "themselves become reflections of their archives, as queer texts constitute the reading subject in their own image," Rohy argues. "In the process of discursive identity-formation, what appears as a moment of discovery is really a moment of invention, which retroactively creates the subject as having always been inverted, gay, deviant, queer, Uranian, trans, lesbian, or homosexual" (355). *Lineage: Matchmaking in the Archive* suggests that archival queers promote encounters with the queer past that are individually meaningful but occur in conjunction with others, thus deepening mnemonic socialization. To extrapolate from Barry Schwartz: "There can be no community . . . that is not a 'community of memory,' and there can be no community of memory without the retelling of 'constitutive narratives'" (67).

Whatever modality we as archival queers enact and urge, ultimately our hope is that we will embed the impulse, deepen the will, and induce the vigorous engagement of remembrance of queers past, and pasts queerly remembered. We would do well to imagine "queer archive activism" as Alexandra Juhasz does AIDS images of the past, to "not merely to get stuck in remembering . . . but rather to relodge those frozen memories in contemporary contexts so that they, and perhaps we, can be reanimated" (320). Such queer archival reanimation could continue to fuel the momentum of the archival turn, and deepen our commitment to the queer turn, in rhetorical studies.

6

PAN-HISTORIOGRAPHY: THE CHALLENGES OF WRITING HISTORY ACROSS TIME AND SPACE

Debra Hawhee and Christa J. Olson

What does it mean to practice "pan-historiography"? We pose this question as historians of rhetoric, each of us in the thick of researching and writing histories that spread across a vast expanse of time—one an examination of how *topoi* of indigeneity helped shape national identity in Ecuador over more than a century (Olson); the other a consideration of animals in the history of rhetoric that spans the multicentury, multinational, and multicurricular life of the *progymnasmata* (Hawhee). Our respective projects have attuned us to the intricacies of what we term "pan-historiography": writing histories whose temporal scope extends well beyond the span of individual generations. Pan-historiography can also refer to studies that leap across geographic space, tracking important activities, terms, movements, or practices as they travel with trade, with global expansion, or with religious zealotry.

Though neither of us embarked on our current studies with the specific goal of pursuing pan-historiography, the process of shaping them has convinced us that wide-ranging histories, in their very expansiveness, make unique contributions to rhetorical studies and, as such, merit specific methodological reflection. Our move to theorize pan-historiography is all the more pressing since, in the course of mapping out our own pan-historiographies, we have noticed that such expansive histories run counter to a disciplinary trend. That is, histories in rhetorical studies seem to be moving away from broad-based ones, like George A. Kennedy's many historical bird's-eye views (for example, *Classical Rhetoric and Its Christian and Secular Tradition from Ancient to Modern Times, A New History of Classical Rhetoric*, and *Comparative Rhetoric*) or Jeffrey Walker's *Rhetoric and Poetics in Antiquity*, and toward more restricted or focused histories.[1] It is far more common these days to see book-length rhetorical histories bound tightly by a short span of dates or by the lives of particular figures than to encounter texts that explain or explore the rhetorical histories of a concept or cultural group.[2] And yet even scholars who focus on one or two decades might well skate across a continent, even an ocean or two, in the course of their history telling; similarly, claiming larger relevance for specific histories often requires drawing parallels across time and place.[3] Our field's histories have a tendency to spread.

The move to restrictive, specialized histories may well reflect rhetoric's coming-of-age as a discipline. Historians of rhetoric have begun to move away from disciplinary histories and have access to a number of more-or-less comprehensive histories of Western rhetoric. They are thus free to detail the contours and textures of a particular moment or place. The move toward narrow rhetorical histories also—perhaps relatedly—corresponds with a spike in historiographic scholarship, much of which, of late, focuses on archives.[4] Or, more accurately, on "the archive," a methodological and theoretical focus that lends itself to specific histories and carefully targeted scopes.

We open with this broad sketch of the state of history and historiography in the field to situate our own sense of the lingering usefulness of those histories that sprawl across long stretches of time and/or space and multiple archives, and the concomitant need to share methods and cautionary tales pertinent to writing such histories, to take preliminary steps toward a pan-historiography. From here, we would like to consider the rationale for pan-historiography, examining what expansive histories might have to offer rhetorical studies today. We do not wish to consider the merits of pan-historiography over and against more focused histories; rather, we believe the two work in tandem to provide comprehensiveness as well as depth. Indeed, a guiding assumption of our reflections is this: the expansion of the wide-ranging histories we are working on necessitates the contraction of more focused histories, and vice versa. In this way, disciplinarity breathes and moves through its histories, by turns zooming and hovering, simultaneously posing big-picture questions and fine-grained ones.

We suggest, therefore, that this moment of contraction toward predominantly close-range histories is a perfect time to consider the possibilities of expansion while also tapping into the insights of the narrow history, particularly the deeply textured contributions of archival work. We will assert the usefulness of sprawling histories by examining two central theoretical and methodological complications posed by pan-historiography and the potential dividends yielded by dwelling with those complications. After a brief section laying out justifications for the choice to span, we will consider, first, the risk of ahistoric skating across time and culture that thematically organized studies can pose, and second, the challenge of working with multiple archives of varying scales and types of materials. We will close with reflections on how the strategies of pan-historiography can allow diverse archival materials to, in a sense, move. That is, by taking a wide scope, both of us strive to attend to that which is necessarily absent from or barely present in archival, documentary materials: bodies, habits, activities, or what performance theorist Diana Taylor calls "repertoires." Underlying our discussion of widely flung histories, then, is a broader question: How can pan-historiography meet its own challenges *and* enliven its materials to create animated histories, histories that bear down even as they expand? A robust treatment of these questions and complications is, anyway, our goal. Our discussion, therefore, will meld theoretical and methodological inclinations: we will share our concrete approaches to and justifications for expansive histories and examine the conceptual orientations underlying and emerging from those historiographic practices.

Choosing to Span

Most frequently the advice to history writers is to "go small," to eschew the unmanageable. But it might be better to pause and wonder about the function of a particular history before making this choice. What is the history's central motivating question? What materials will help answer that question? Do the answers change across time, and if so, is there a particular time period that provides more insight than others, or is diachronic change itself of interest? Would understandings of the history at hand be better if slices of time were presented next to each other?

Both of us are working on questions not yet broached by scholars in our discipline, and we have each settled on a time-slicing approach for what it can reveal about the issues we are addressing *across* time. The particular contributions that our projects will make to understandings of rhetorical theory and practice are tied to questions of persistence and change which, therefore, take center stage in our analyses. As we discuss in the remainder of this section, the choice to take such an expansive, thematic approach is, at heart, a disciplinary move. The decision to span depends on and responds to the aspects of rhetorical history or theory that the study hopes to illuminate and the contributions a rhetorical perspective might make to clarifying the broad themes (in our cases, of nation formation, and of human/animal relations) under consideration.

The choice to span also recalibrates the distinction between diachronic and synchronic history that is the legacy of structuralism and poststructuralism (most notably de Saussure and Foucault).[5] The distinction is drawn from de Saussure, who argued for both approaches to language and history—the synchronic to attend to political and cultural specificities in a particular moment, and the diachronic to attend to long-view history. Foucault himself favors synchronic studies, which examine structures at a particular moment in time (with time), whereas the diachronic approach is more broadly historical (through time).[6] A diachronic approach has too often been dismissed as what Jana Evans Braziel, a scholar of transnational literature, calls "a monolithic and homogeneous stretch of knowledge across time, across history" (105). We share in Braziel's rejoinder to such criticisms and her view that synchrony and diachrony ought to be brought into balance, for as she puts it, "constructs (or signifiers) also attain and accrue meaning historically" (106). Together, both synchronic and diachronic approaches can offer a productive "historical reservoir of meaning . . . synchronically constructed and diachronically residual" (Braziel 106). In other words, contrary to the assumption that underwrites the command to "go small"—that short, synchronic histories are the only way depth can be achieved—the diachrony central to pan-historiography, with its attention to residual accumulation of *topoi*, beliefs, and strategic practices, brings its own kind of depth.

Hawhee's study of animals in the history of rhetoric, for example, might be the first book-length, historical consideration of philosophical questions about animals and rhetoric. On the one hand, it might make sense to start small and build from there. But on the other hand, the story—or at least the story she will tell—promises to hew tightly to the school exercises known as the *progymnasmata*, in which animals feature prominently, and which persisted in rhetorical education practices for at least fourteen centuries. That is, the permutations—and surprising persistence—of animals in the history of rhetoric make a good deal of sense when followed in light of the *progymnasmata*. While the *progymnasmata* are not the exclusive object of the study (these exercises exhibited a remarkable consistency over such a long time span, and others have studied them in depth), they nevertheless form the unifying backdrop for what is turning out to be a bundled set of in-depth studies that together move across time. The study is therefore book-ended by two key progymnasmatic figures—Aesop, whose loric invention of the fable helped place animals at the fore of ancient rhetorical education, and Erasmus, whose early-sixteenth-century theories of *copia* and writings on animals bear the stamp of the *progymnasmata*. Such book-endings, believe it or not, provide a way to limit the study to pre- and early-modern rhetorics.

The modern counterpart to this history would also be fascinating, but the discourses of Enlightenment and evolution and their twin devotions to science would no doubt take the investigation in a completely different direction, one that would be more appropriate for a separate volume. Selecting pre-Enlightenment figures, texts, and practices opts for a stretch in which rhetoric's tendrils wended their way into cultural beliefs and practices. Furthermore, in the pre- and early-modern eras, nonhumans for the most part inhabit the domain of rhetoric in a lively, communicative, action-based way, whereas the dissection and evolutionary theory of the modern era tends to hold animals a bit more still. With such a selection, then, the prevailing logic is somewhat similar to that put forth by Jeffrey Walker in *Rhetoric and Poetics in Antiquity*, where he writes that he initially "cheerfully imagined" that his investigation would span both antiquity *and* modernity, "and soon discovered how impossibly large that subject really was, and is" (viii). He continues, "I have accordingly confined myself to rhetoric and poetics in antiquity, which already is a subject more than large enough, and indeed even here I have found it necessary to make selections" (viii).

It is worth noting here that even the most expansive histories still work within set parameters (historical, thematic, or, more usually, both): historiography always involves making selections. With more expansive histories, those selections slice up time, selecting representative figures or movements in order to create a larger narrative arc. In any event, the resulting book on animals in the history of rhetoric will hopefully function, much as Walker's *Rhetoric and Poetics in Antiquity* does, as both a commentary and a resource, a suasive starting point for those interested in the questions it engages. In this instance, the guiding question centers on the roles nonhuman animals have played—culturally, politically, historically—in the shaping of rhetoric, a decidedly human (and humanist) art. The story promises to be one of both surprising thematic durability and contextual, cultural mutation.

That emphasis on thematic durability and contextual mutation across time has been a shared interest for us. In sketching the contours of Ecuadorian national identity as it developed from independence through the present, Olson was struck by an apparent contradiction between the visibility of indigenous people in images of the nation and their exclusion from equal participation in the republic. Her analytical approach therefore emphasizes the work those recurring images of indigenous people did for the artists who made them and for the Ecuadorians who purchased and circulated them. It aims to uncover the connections between indigenous visibility and indigenous marginality. In that context, focusing on a single period or organizing the study around period case studies would limit its ability to treat nationalism as a sustained and sustaining rhetorical process. A thematic approach that lays slices of time alongside one another better reveals patterns of continuity and rupture in depictions of indigenous people and indigenous political agency. The study thus emphasizes what Michael Warner calls the "concatenation of texts through time" ("Publics" 62) that, in this case, created and sustained the idea of the Ecuadorian nation and convened a national public. It traces accumulations of rhetorical artifacts around a handful of themes that have been used to invoke the nation even in distinctly changed contexts. Examining those themes as rhetorical *topoi*, the study focuses on the common sense force that repeated, resilient images acquire over time and allows insight into the particularly rhetorical nature of national identity. As we will discuss below, that turn to *topoi* also lends methodological coherence to the temporal and archival span.

Examining shifting common sense over time allowed Olson's study to engage disciplinary understandings of publicity and rhetorical constitution. It demonstrates that rhetorical theories of identification and publics formation must pay close attention to both stability and fluidity, both momentary actions and accumulated sensibilities. Such a focus keeps in mind Jeremy Adelman's argument that studies concerned with continuity must also "contend with the indeterminacies of life if they are to mean anything historically" (12). It also situates the creation and maintenance of national identity as a process of rhetorical constitution that brings a nation into awareness of itself through repeated, accumulated narratives. The study examines how both political Constitutions and the wide array of artifacts that Kenneth Burke calls "constitutions-behind-the-Constitution" undergird common-sense arguments about who and what the nation is (*Grammar* 362). Expansive pan-historiography makes sense for studies of national identity formation, then, because it brings attention to the consistencies and ruptures that characterize nationalisms as they develop diachronically and function on multiple planes of symbolic action. A widely flung approach makes space for the overlapping and contradictory forces that nationalisms wield. This expansive history, then, is able to uncover some of the macro-level rhetorical workings of national publicity but also pay attention to how local conflicts and subaltern resistance contest, shape, and appropriate those overarching narratives of the nation.

As the previous pages have suggested, both our studies turn toward the expansive for a combination of conceptual, theoretical, and practical reasons. Our guiding questions bring us face-to-face with issues of continuity and change, and we could not pursue them in the narrow frame. Similarly, our disciplinary interest in bringing rhetorical insights to bear on topics such as national identity and human-animal relations pulls us toward the expansive history. Understanding how each of our objects of study engages a range of communicative actions in the effort to "make things matter" (T. Farrell 1) requires looking at processes and accumulations of artifacts and actions through time. For each of our topics, the making of meaning and of influence is an expansive project, one whose contours and complexities would be lost if pursued only in the scope of a few years or a single figure.

Avoiding the Sweep

Because of their orientation toward continuities and developments, expansive histories always run the risk of slipping from wide-angle views of indeterminacy to totalizing narratives. Their very strengths, the ability to account for change over time and demonstrate the cumulative nature of rhetorical practice, can put them at risk. "The sweep," that tendency to homogenize whole eras, places, and controversies into manageable and misleadingly coherent terms, must be counterbalanced by theoretical, methodological, and structural practices designed to keep texture and complexity in the foreground. Expansive rhetorical histories cannot merely acknowledge that change happens or that the rhetorical situation of one moment is distinct from that of another; they must have theoretical and methodological orientations that make those evolutions and breaks integral to the analyses they forward.

The "time-slicing" strategy that we reference in the previous section is one approach to that task. By selecting key historical-cultural moments to anchor individual chapters or fix the exploration of themes, we attempt to prevent the kind of ahistoric skating that all historians want to avoid. Those slices, chosen to reveal "continuity in . . . dialectical terms—as the products of interaction, even conflict" (Adelman 2), give our pan-historiography texture. Pairing fine-grained analysis of the complexities in those slices with comparisons across slices helps ensure that our claims, though broad, are grounded.

For one of us (Olson), that orientation toward change takes theoretical form in explorations of rhetorical *topoi*. Looking at how *topoi* cultivate and sustain national common sense and how such common sense invokes publics and counterpublics lends a dynamic orientation to her expansive history, helping avoid the traps of homogeneity and teleology that might otherwise plague a study of national identity. Wide-ranging archival research, in turn, lends that theoretical orientation methodological heft and structural complexity.

Evidence of the commonplaces of national identity circulating across visual and textual forms appears in an array of Ecuadorian archives. Moving among archives, like moving among periods, uncovered both consistencies over time and conflicts within particular moments. In particular, the accumulations of texts and performances generated across archives and eras pointed toward the myriad ways that elites and subalterns all participated in calling national identity into being and wielding it for rhetorical advantage.

Similarly, research in different archives demonstrated that many of the *topoi* under consideration worked simultaneously in rhetorical contexts eventful (that is, intentionally constitutive paintings, speeches, and texts) and everyday (that is, quotidian administrative missives, petitions, and sketches). Without a theoretical orientation toward change and a methodological commitment to encountering archival contradictions, the resulting history of Ecuadorian national identity could have easily fallen into a deceptively coherent narrative of white-*mestizo* dominance and one-dimensional nation building. Theoretical and methodological orientations toward change, however, kept in the foreground those indeterminacies that underlie the appearance of continuity, persistence, and development over time.

While Olson's study demands attention to multiple voices, Hawhee's time-slicing technique arises from the markedly different contexts in which animals and rhetoric meet across time and place. How does one decide where to make these slices? The question is difficult to answer separate from a particular project, but it does involve looking askew at existing disciplinary narratives. Hawhee decided on each chapter's focus by first noticing mentions of nonhuman animals in rhetoric's traditional texts while teaching a survey titled "The Rhetorical Tradition," and then by later taking an inquisitive view of rhetoric's existing histories, from which animals are largely absent. She discovered not only that animals are used as literary stand-ins for difference in school exercises, and teachable metaphors in theoretical treatises and philosophical dialogues, but also that actual animals and depictions of them reach prominence in trends and practices that barely receive mention in rhetorical studies. For example, much has been written in legal studies about the medieval practice of bringing animals—pigs, locusts, dogs, and rats—to trial in ecclesiastical and secular courts, and yet no one has examined remaining accounts of and testimonies in these trials. The trials, which provide the focus of a chapter in the middle of the book, read quite differently when situated in relation to the longstanding practice of featuring animals in fable and encomia (two of the *progymnasmata* exercises), and school declamations or practice speeches, where students regularly ascribe to animals the twin qualities of agency and culpability, at times even speech.

While teaching a seminar on Aristotle's *Rhetoric* and attending to that text's manuscript tradition, Hawhee noticed that late manuscripts and early print editions of the treatise are elaborately decorated with animals, especially scorpions, and so she is now planning a chapter that will examine rhetoric's emblems. The chapters mentioned here take as their focus a wide range of objects and cultures—from lighthearted schoolroom arguments praising flies and parrots, to religious and legal arguments premised on nonhuman accountability, to emblems and book culture. Each one is planted in a different historical and cultural context and contains its own set of specific argumentative roots. When examined from the perspective of rhetorical history, they help provide a long view of rhetoric's shape-shifting, migratory, nonhuman participants, but it is a long view that is held in check by careful attention to the particular conditions of the objects/practice/ movements under scrutiny. All the chapters are guided by versions of the questions: How did images of/arguments about animals take hold? What do they achieve rhetorically, and what can they tell us about rhetoric's history and the rhetorical theories we have inherited? About human and animal relations in that particular cultural context? About identity and difference? Symbols and strategies?

In each of our manuscripts, a set of coherent, open-ended questions helps to rein in and unify a study in which the objects—and their answers—can be wildly incongruous. The net effect can be a study that both ranges and slices, a study, that is, composed of miniature studies, each making its own point that contributes to, even as it complicates, the longer view. This ranging and slicing brings together the diachronic and synchronic movements discussed earlier. Combining synchronic slices in a diachronic narrative effectively temporalizes the perspectivalism favored by the likes of Friedrich Nietzsche and Kenneth Burke. As Burke puts it, "the universe would appear to be something like a cheese; it can be sliced in an infinite number of ways" (*Permanence and Change* 103). Pan-historiography, as we envision it, emphasizes deliberate slicing—and a piecing together of slices—even as it resists beginning or ending with anything like a whole cheese.

Rethinking "The Archive"

As hinted at in the above discussion, pan-historiography brings with it the necessity of consulting multiple archives. For the past decade or so, scholars in rhetorical studies trained in both English and communication departments have begun examining "the archive," and noting the need for more thorough and rigorous training in archival methods.[7] While we are proponents of both archival research and greater emphasis on research pedagogies, we wish to use this discussion of pan-historiography to reconsider the tendency in rhetorical studies to speak of "the archive." Cheryl Glenn and Jessica Enoch, despite a titular reference to "archives" ("Drama") and discussions of their and others' need to work in multiple archives ("Invigorating" 13; "Drama" 326–28), still use "archive" in the singular (328, 333). The editors of two recent collections about archival research (*Working in the Archives* and *Beyond the Archives*) similarly title their books in the plural, but the essays tend again toward writing about "the archive" in the singular (Ramsey et al.; Kirsch and Rohan). Likewise, contributors to the 2006 forum in *Rhetoric and Public Affairs* on archival research speak almost uniformly about "the archive" ("Forum"). C. Brereton writes of "our archive," suggesting that the discipline (in this case, of rhetoric and composition) uses a select set of materials, but one that "has been expanding dramatically" of late (574). It is difficult to determine the guiding rationale for the use of "the archive" in the singular, but it seems to arise when authors are at their most theoretical, at which point "the archive" tends to recede a notch from material spaces. We prefer to follow Linda Ferreira-Buckley in speaking of archives in the plural ("Rescuing"), but for perhaps different reasons.[8]

Moving from the plural buildings and rooms in which we conduct research to the singular conceptual realm of available resources—from archives to "the archive"—encourages, or at least allows, a homogenization troublingly similar to "the sweep" we discuss above. We don't wish to belabor the grammatical point, but our experiences researching and writing pan-historiographies have made clear to us that archives, especially those chronicling different times and places, are most productively approached in the plural. This is not just because writers of expansive history must consult multiple archives—writers of more tightly bound histories often do the same. Rather, our need to discuss archives in the plural stems from our encounters with one of the major challenges posed by pan-historiography: the challenge of what we call archival incongruity. Archival incongruity names the dissonance that can result from working with the media and material available in different periods and locations. As media preferences shift and change across decades or centuries, so do the materials found in (and outside of) archives. We have found, in other words, that even archives treating the same discrete topic, if they are spatially or temporally expansive, do not cohere either materially or conceptually into a single conceptual archive. They are resolutely plural.

We first noticed this when one of us (Olson) was researching and organizing her dissertation. Her interest in visual culture, in particular, brought the incongruous nature of archives and archival materials across time starkly to light. Even putting aside the different realities of print culture in the late nineteenth and mid-twentieth centuries, the technologies available to authors and artists meant that understanding and describing "what is seen" (Roeder 275) posed a serious challenge. How might she talk about the pervasive presence of images of indigenous people when comparing hand-produced and copied watercolor paintings with mass-reproduced photographs and prints? Her solution lay in elaborations of the same strategies for pan-historiography that we have invoked already: focusing her analysis on the circulation of *topoi* rather than the circulation of specific images or artifacts, she is able to account for changes in archival practices, technical capabilities, and reporting systems over time. Thus, her emphasis on *topoi* gathered from the concatenations of disparate artifacts allows her to advance an archives-based history of the conceptual resources on which elites and subalterns drew in their arguments about the nature of the nation.

Archival incongruity was something Hawhee was, at the time when Olson began encountering it, fairly familiar with without having a name for it, having experienced the incongruity most acutely in the transition from her first to second book. While both books posed questions about bodies in rhetorical history, the radically different time periods and locations (fifth- and fourth-century Greece and twentieth-century US) yielded different materials that demanded radically distinct and flexible methods. The different materials and methods also called for a rethinking of each study's guiding concepts and questions. Two representative images will need to suffice. The first book, *Bodily Arts: Rhetoric and Athletics in Ancient Greece*, begins with an image of a statue found in the shipwreck off the coast of Kythera (2). Hawhee first saw a photograph of this statue in a book and then visited a replica of it at the National Archaeological Museum of Athens. The identity of this statue is contested, but theories that it represents on the one hand an athlete and on the other hand an orator helped her to launch her argument about these intertwined, bodily arts. An equally representative but vastly different image features in chapter 4 of her book *Moving Bodies: Kenneth Burke at the Edges of Language* (81). The image is taken from Walter B. Cannon's 1915 book *Bodily Changes in Pain, Hunger, Fear, and Rage* and is a diagram of the autonomic nervous system, with the brain and spinal cord represented by a long, thin line that looks something like a thermometer, and with pre- and post-ganglionic fibers represented by lines. Tiny sketches of organs connect to the fibrous lines, and the whole thing looks something like a telephone system. The image of a bodily system without a body, when considered next to the muscular, nearly (and once) whole statue that inspired *Bodily Arts*, provides a useful shorthand for the radically different bodies and approaches to bodies available in the respective eras' archives. The available means of research, and the cultural shifts those means bespeak, helped Hawhee tweak her research questions. While both books began with the same general question—"how do bodies and rhetoric come together?"—the available materials refined the questions even as they began to answer them.

The archival incongruity across her first two books helped prepare Hawhee to write the book on animals in rhetoric. As the last section's discussion

of time slicing indicates, animals appear in different milieu, in vastly different forms: at times mute defendants, at other times still artistic renderings.
They also frequently appear in theoretical texts as analogies and counter-
analogies to human animals, and those appearances help frame the other
shapes taken by animals in rhetoric's history. From Aesop's use of animals
as the stand-in for difference to Erasmus's brush with rights-based arguments, and to all the fabulous, visual, and jurisprudential renderings in
between, rhetoric's beasts provide both shifting and remarkably durable
means of thinking about humans and nonhumans alike, as well as about
the art of rhetoric itself.

The realities of archival incongruity aid in the pan-historiographer's efforts to avoid the context-blurring, sweeping conclusions that we discussed
above. Keeping track of the different sorts of artifacts that populate our
slices of time and carefully tracing the sorts of arguments than can be made
using those different artifacts in effect keeps the rhetorical historian both
grounded and humble. To do pan-historiography is to be constantly confronted with the parallels that cannot be drawn and the changing details that
bring texture even to apparent continuities in argument and identification.

Getting Documents and Artifacts to Move

In the thick of researching and writing pan-historiographies, we have both
tried not to lose sight of what is rhetorical: that which moves. And here
we mean "moves" in its fullest (and most multiple) sense, physically and
emotionally. Lester Olson points out that several of the key English-lan-
guage terms of rhetoric derive etymologically from the Latin root *movere*
(*Emblems* xvii). Move, motive, and motif all invoke a sense of action, and
their centrality to the theory and practice of rhetoric urges rhetoricians to
be sure that our historical studies keep an ear open for and an eye on the
live and the lived. For that reason, even as we advocate archival activity,
we urge attention to Diana Taylor's important reminder that archives are
stone silent, their data comparatively immobile, and their contents often
inextricably tied to official narratives. Our studies attempt to keep track of
pan-historical movements, motives, and motifs by considering the bodily
residues that may be found in archives.

Taylor reminds historians that "[e]mbodied performances have always
played a central role in conserving memory and consolidating identities in
literate, semiliterate, and digital societies" (xviii). Therefore, according to
Taylor, "it is vital to signal the performatic, digital, and visual fields as separate from, though always embroiled with, the discursive one so privileged
by Western logocentrism" (6). To this end, she suggests that examining

performances allows a way beyond logocentric biases and encourages attention to scenarios as well as narratives. Scenarios, she explains, need not "reduce gestures and embodied practices to narrative description" (16). Embedded in Taylor's idea of repertoire is Foucault's Nietzschean approach to history as ever-articulated with bodies ("Nietzsche," *Language* 148).

Similarly, Taylor's ventures into Latin American colonial performances demonstrate the interconnectedness of archive and repertoire and the challenge of telling stories about the past without inevitably making them into narratives that serve Western purposes. Historians must often dig through narratives in order to allow scenarios to emerge. Especially when the scenarios sought are those staged or inhabited by marginalized or subaltern populations, however, they are most often found by reading against the grain, finding gestures in omissions, or looking backward from today's scenarios. In this way, we attempt to write histories that strive to become what Foucault calls the "differential knowledge of energies and failings, heights and degenerations, poisons and antidotes" ("Nietzsche," *Language* 156). We contend, that is, that archives can in fact be brought to life, animated by the right mix of scholarly rigor and imagination, the right mix of a long, diachronic view and a more tightly attenuated synchronic perspective. Such an approach allows a broad cultural context even as it offers an opportunity to ask what sense of movement a rhetorical perspective might add to the conversations.

For both of us, finding movement and bodies in the archives has presented both challenges and opportunities. In Olson's study of Ecuadorian national identity, that search has been especially important to the task of seeking out subaltern performances. Faced with archives that privilege the voices of light-skinned, urban elites, she has looked for the scenarios of resistance that lurk beneath those written documents. Reports of administrative failure have been one surprisingly rich venue for encountering the indigenous actors who, over time, challenged, shaped, and appropriated discourses of national identity. For example, indigenous agency pushes to the surface in documents that communicate elite frustration with recalcitrant indigenous labor conscripts. Public works projects in nineteenth-century Ecuador often relied on indigenous laborers who were (often forcibly) recruited from outlying communities, but the residents of those indigenous communities did their best to make conscription difficult. That resistance appears again and again in public records as local authorities report their inability to recruit laborers. Gleaning through reports of failed recruitment, and placing them alongside archival records of indigenous petitions against labor conscription and oral histories of indigenous resistance, yields rich scenarios of contestation. Taking seriously the evidence of indigenous objection that spans texts, performances, and memory emphasizes the conflicts and negotiations endemic in nineteenth-century Ecuador that, in turn, laid the groundwork for later arguments about the nature of the nation.

In researching animals in the history of rhetoric, Hawhee has been surprised to discover just how frequently they come up. They often appear in the service of bolstering the human art, or even, as in Plato's dialogues, to denigrate particular humans in his company, and yet at times they stand as models of training. One challenge of this study is to take care to attend to the lifeworld of its subjects. For example, the political circumstances of conquest that led to Aristotle's having access to elephants (Bigwood; G. E. R. Lloyd) are no doubt worth minding.

The challenges of animating rhetoric's animal life, then, are plain. From animal trials to animal metaphors in rhetorical texts, nonhuman animals are always spoken about and for. And yet the residue of their energy remains in the story of the quail bursting from Alcibiades' cloak when he addressed the assembly (Plutarch 10.1), and in the flame-tongued serpents that twist across early print editions of rhetorical texts. Indeed, it was often the function of animals to enliven and to physicalize ancient rhetorical theory and education, as when Quintilian uses an analogy of birds when discussing the difference between modeling and forcing particular behaviors (2.6.7). One of the functions of the earliest rhetorical exercise—fable—is to breathe life, and words, into the form of animals. Attending to animals, their scurrying and flapping, their barking and cawing, might well fill the archives of rhetoric with more noise and physical life than we could imagine when restricting it to the confines of the human.

Conclusion

In this chapter, we have laid out the case for the relevance of pan-historiography, attended to its challenges and opportunities, and offered strategies for meeting both. Finally, we have raised the degree of difficulty by adding one more aim in the final section: to approach documents and materials, however incongruous, with an eye toward making those materials move, reanimating them in a way that renders visible, audible, and lively a variety of historical figures, voices, and viewpoints. Such an approach requires a combination of patience, imagination, and rigor. We have by necessity discussed our approaches through our current research, since archival, documentary details guide the choices we have made along the way. Our hope is that the vastly different *foci* of our respective studies help to bolster the theoretical dimension of this chapter by uniting the otherwise quite distinct studies under a banner of pan-historiography.

Notes

1. Recent exceptions include Joshua Gunn's *Modern Occult Rhetoric*, which spans most of the twentieth century, with important discussions that hearken back to premodern eras, and John Durham Peters's *Speaking into the Air: A History of the Idea of Communication*.

2. Examples here include Wendy B. Sharer's *Vote and Voice*; Kirt Wilson's *The Reconstruction Desegregation Debate*; Patricia Roberts-Miller's *Fanatical Schemes*; Mark Garrett Longaker's *Rhetoric and the Republic*; Michelle Hall Kells's *Hector P. Garcia*; Cara A. Finnegan's *Picturing Poverty*; Ann George and Jack Selzer's *Kenneth Burke in the 1930s*; Jordynn Jack's *Science on the Home Front*; and Lester C. Olson's *Benjamin Franklin's Vision of American Community*, to name just a few.

3. The best example here is Jessica Enoch's *Refiguring Rhetorical Education*, which draws together analyses of teachers teaching racially and ethnically diverse student populations in the late nineteenth and early twentieth centuries.

4. Charles E. Morris III notes that while "any cursory survey of the field's best scholarship . . . reveals the archive as a long-standing habitat of the rhetorical critic and theorist . . . the archive itself, chief among the inventional sites of rhetorical pasts, has yet to be subjected to sustained critical-rhetorical reflection by scholars in this discipline" ("Archival Turn" 113). Such an observation holds in communication-rhetoric scholarship, but rhetoric and composition scholars have for the past decade or longer been reflecting on their archives. See, most recently, Glenn and Enoch, "Drama"; the special section of *College English* entitled "Archivists with an Attitude"; *Rhetoric Society Quarterly*'s special issue on feminist historiography; and a number of edited collections (Ramsey et al.; Kirsch and Rohan; Enoch and Anderson; and Vitanza, *Writing Histories*).

5. Cf. Foucault, *Archaeology of Knowledge* (186) and Saussure (81–90).

6. Our claim about Foucault calls for qualification. Foucault's notion of genealogy (laid out most plainly in "Nietzsche, Genealogy, History") would be a fruitful place to explore his working between the movements of synchronic and diachronic. There, Foucault notes how genealogy "must record the singularity of events outside of any monotonous finality; it must seek them in the most unpromising places, in what we tend to feel is without history—in sentiments, love, conscience, instincts; it must be sensitive to their recurrence, not in order to trace the gradual curve of their evolution, but to isolate the different scenes where they engaged in different roles" ("Nietzsche, Genealogy, History" 76). Genealogy, that is, favors synchronous movement even as it acknowledges the need for—yet perhaps in its own way resists—a clean diachronous movement. It is rather common to read Foucault as writing histories with a diachronic tendency, such that *Discipline and Punish* is at times taken to be a history of prisons writ large. We should point out that the diachronic *effect* (as with *History of Sexuality*, vol. 1) is achieved through synchronic comparison—the visceral opening scene of a human body being drawn and quartered contrasts with the in-depth commentary on a panoptic structure issuing from a particular inventor at a particular moment (Jeremy Bentham, late eighteenth century). Foucault's engagement with history writing in the College de France lectures transcribed and translated as the volume *"Society Must Be Defended"* is

interesting for the enduring (diachronically so) connections he draws between history and war. A good instance of a diachronic move in Foucault would be his tracing of the evolution of *parrhesia* in *Fearless Speech* (20–24). We are grateful to the anonymous reviewer for requesting clarification on this question and for suggesting possible directions.

7. See especially Ferreira-Buckley's "Rescuing the Archives from Foucault."

8. Ferreira-Buckley does not call attention to this choice, but the fact that she is building a theoretical/methodological argument on the writings and practices of a number of historians seems to necessitate the eschewing of an all-encompassing singular and generic "archive."

7

STITCHING TOGETHER EVENTS: OF JOINTS, FOLDS, AND ASSEMBLAGES

Byron Hawk

The only purpose the discourse of history can legitimately claim
is to designate and transform the field of evidence into *as many
persuasive models as can possibly be fashioned.*
— Hans Kellner, "After the Fall"

Our acts of composition are always collaborative.
— Victor Vitanza, preface to *Writing Histories of Rhetoric*

Victor J. Vitanza opens the collection *Writing Histories of Rhetoric*
with the acknowledgement that the authors and texts gathered there
are a constellation, a molecular agglomerate, a paratactic aggregate (viii).
Despite all of the talk at the time (late 1980s, early 1990s) of categorizing
historiographies (surely a function of the drive to categorize rhetorics that
dominated the time period), Vitanza resists even his own typology. Rather,
he characterizes each essay in the collection as a possible beginning, and
the gathering of beginnings brought together in the collection as setting the
conditions for new future lines of flight for thinking about historiographies.
This attitude toward history seems to have resisted taking hold in rhetoric
and composition. The desire to go back to the archives and read them as
documents, or facts, is still a predominant force in the field (traditional
historiography),[1] and the most recent conference panel on historiography
at CCCC still appears dominated by the desire for recovering excluded
figures from the discipline's view (revisionary historiography).[2] Vitanza's
call for a third category that disperses all categorizations (sub/versive historiography) appears to be the less widely adopted attitude. But I take this
new collection of essays to be a response to this current state. In *Academic
Charisma and the Origins of the Research University*, William Clark quips

in passing, "Often a good sign of decadence, a history appears" (88). He is acknowledging the fundamental rhetorical character of historiography that goes back at least as far as Nietzsche's "On the Uses and Disadvantages of History for Life": new histories are needed when the old ones turn problematic for the promotion of present conditions.[3] Even calls to return to the facts of the past are made in response to current practices and the evaluation of those facts is always grounded in contemporary values. The cyclical calls to theorize history and dispense with theory that we've seen in rhetoric and composition over the past two decades have always been in response to articulations of present conditions and the state of decadence achieved by either extreme.

The call for historiographies is no different than the emergence of histories. A decadence of theory produces a return to the archive; a decadence of resistance to metareflection engenders the production of new methods. But I take Vitanza's characterization of each piece and their collaborative collection as a new beginning to be an acknowledgement that every history demands its own historiography. In *History out of Joint*, Sande Cohen argues that the basis of all historiography is arguing over the method by which events are turned into narratives. From this perspective, history is an assemblage of events grounded in methods of finding, selecting, evaluating, and reassembling events judged from current rhetorical needs. These assemblages are always gathered in collaboration with other methods, other histories, other authors, other texts, other people, and other objects. Methods become situationally specific: they are always for stitching together particular events into assemblages, writing their interminglings and entanglements in rhetorical situatedness, and imagining possible future rhetorical and perhaps historical effects. In this chapter, I imagine a possible historical project and begin to assemble its own historiography. If I wanted to write a history of the collaborative moments in the twentieth century between communication and composition and the circulation of concepts and practices of rhetoric through these emergent events, how would I assemble a historiography that would allow me to stitch them together and trace their convergence and divergence?[4]

Getting the Story Crooked

Following Kenneth Burke, Vitanza notes in his preface that even if we imagine our histories and methods as philanthropic, they will at some point be turned into a "devilish nightmare, because we inevitably 'bureaucratize' our acts of imagination" (*Writing Histories* x). Burke recommends a comic or farcical attitude toward history as a corrective for this inevitability. It is from this perspective that I read Hans Kellner's contribution to *Writing Histories of Rhetoric*, "After the Fall." Kellner provides a comical image of each dominant category of historiography. In his allegory, a mother dies and leaves a chest full of "letters, deeds, accounts, photographs, on top of old clothes, military uniforms, and the like" (24). A first child wants to preserve the documents as an important part of family history; a second child sees the collection as worthless and a burden on the present; a third child wants to give the old stuff to the kids to play dress up or "to see how much better things are today, what with Velcro, diet pop, and all" (24). The children, of course, stand for traditional, revisionary, and sub/versive historiographies. Traditional methods value the past, want to preserve it so it won't be lost, and want the past to speak for itself without any intervention from the historian, his methods, his language, or his culture. But this comes at the cost of shunning rhetoric and language. Revisionary historiography finds the past's power over the present problematic and seeks to judge this power by asserting the present's difference and recovering past excluded rhetorics to counter dominant histories. But for Kellner, "this demystified position actually shows little respect for the power of language," since the past's rhetoric and interests (versus the present's) utilizes language instrumentally to draw general categories or simply correct the existing narrative (27). Sub/versive historiography follows the Gorgian critical or skeptical stance toward reality, leaving the historian to play with language, reperform it again and again. The emphasis on language provides a corrective to the other methods but has nowhere to go persuasively and rests against straw men and on the ethos of the performer.[5]

Kellner, however, provides the possibility for an alternative category that blends a respect for historical reality with an artful attitude toward reading, highlighting the inevitable relationship between language and historical events. In *Language and Historical Representation: Getting the Story Crooked*, Kellner argues that language is the hidden resource of history, engaged in a hidden entanglement with documentary evidence, which coproduces the events of history that are turned into narrative. For Kellner, traditional historians are taught to "not read": "This mode of reading sees a text as a document, a piece of information in a mass of knowledge, a thread in a 'strand of meaning' that must be untangled, straightened out. To do this, the first step, almost inevitably, is to repress the textuality itself, to eliminate the rhetorical joker from the deck" ("After" 31). Revisionary historians question this method; sub/versive historians attack it. But Kellner calls for a different response. He writes,

Learning to write new histories, histories worthy of the remarkable revival of rhetorical consciousness at the present moment, means above all, *to devise new ways of reading*, which will look at the texts as texts not merely as documents, which will look for "other" sources of historical discourse in constant tension with the evidence. What is called for, I think, is "getting the story crooked," looking into the various strands of meaning in a text in such a way as to make the categories, trends, and reliable identities of history a little less inevitable. (32)

Rather than straighten these threads out, Kellner wants to use them to stitch together another story, to show "a deeper respect for reality by reading texts in crooked ways . . . in order to see what is familiar in a different way, in many different ways" (32).

Kellner's primary example is Erich Auerbach's *Mimesis*. In chapter 4, Auerbach reads a passage from *History of the Franks*. Written by Gregory of Tours in the middle 500s, the passage narrates a period of brutal violence and civic collapse. For Kellner, Auerbach reads the passage crookedly. Gregory is writing in the post-Roman world of Gaul, his crude Latin and emerging vernacular depicting the complete fall of society. Auerbach, however, argues that Gregory's tone is positive and optimistic. Kellner reads Auerbach's reading as reflecting his own time and circumstances. *Mimesis* was written after the Nazi takeover of Germany, which left Auerbach exiled in Istanbul. Now cut off from his traditional historical resources—a research library full of treatises—Auerbach was left to write about select passages from a few texts at hand. For Kellner, this is a new method of narrow selection, embeddedness in present conditions, and a crooked, affective reading. Rather than read Auerbach as a traditionalist, which is the typical stance, Kellner sees his radicalism. Auerbach's world was in collapse, just as Gregory's, but rather than despair, Auerbach invents a new model of historiographical reading. The literal and figurative fall of the old world creates the conditions for invention. Kellner writes, "after the fall, [t]he agony was over, the worst had happened, . . . The ruins were to be picked up again, and rebuilt on better terms" ("After" 35). Gregory, and by analogy Auerbach, has his eyes on the future and what might be possible, what might emerge from the ruins. Neither writer despairs; both assemble what is available from the remnants of the past and move forward.

So, I ask, what kind of emergent possibilities for writing histories of rhetoric have been opened up by the historiography debates of twenty years ago, their collection into *Writing Histories of Rhetoric*, Kellner's call for a crooked historiography, and the intervening years of oscillation between traditional and revisionary approaches? If traditional historiography is no longer viable, revisionary historiography has given way to bureaucratic mandates (retrieve the excluded), and sub/versive historiography encompasses another "fall" into anarchy, then "what does a history of rhetoric look like today?" (36). Kellner's response carves out the beginnings of a fourth category. If the purpose of writing history is not to preserve the past, right the wrong of past exclusions, or exercise a performative will to power, then "the only purpose the discourse of history can legitimately claim is to designate and transform the field of evidence into *as many persuasive models as can possibly be fashioned*" (37)—as many historiographies as well as histories. I read Kellner as responding to the rhetorical turn that began in the 1960s and culminated in the 1980s, which is a function of the traditional retreat and return narrative of rhetoric—out of the ruins of the sixteenth through the nineteenth centuries and the fall into positivism that repressed rhetoric and created the twentieth-century split between speech and writing emerges a renewed concern for language and persuasion. But in the twenty years since *Writing Histories of Rhetoric*, a decidedly materialist turn has taken hold of rhetoric and many of the other humanities that engage the works of Gilles Deleuze and Felix Guattari, Bruno Latour, many object-oriented philosophers such as Graham Harman, and a host of complexity theories in a wide variety of versions and disciplines. From this perspective, materiality becomes a part of the other, hidden sources of historical discourse that make it a little less inevitable, a little more emergent. Seen from this new context, Kellner's crooked historiography morphs into a remodeled sub/version, one that is less skeptical of reality, one that is more vitalist in terms of material complexity, one that combines material and discursive conditions for the emergence of histories, and ultimately one that is more performative in terms of discursive enaction rather than linguistic play. If I want a historiography that emerges out of this present moment, one that allows me to stitch together the emergent convergences between communication and composition, what other grounds would I need to assemble?

The Burden of Historiography

For Kellner, potential rhetorics are as limitless as potential historical events ("After" 23), and the constant production of methods is an inevitable outcome of this potential. Kellner is working, in part, out of Hayden White, whose "The Burden of History" makes the case for a more rhetorically inventive approach to historical methods. White argues that nineteenth-century historians saw themselves as mediators of art and science, an image that continues today. When critiqued by social scientists for softness of method, historians claim that history was never meant to be a science but an art. And when critiqued by literary artists for the lack of contemporary approaches to language and style, historians claim history to be a semiscience that is constrained by facts (27). These strategies, however, open up historians to continued methodological critique. Historians, for White, don't have a specific methodology for dealing with these facts, artistic or scientific. He writes:

> What is usually called the "training" of the historian consists for the most part of study in a few languages, journeyman work in the archives, and the performance of a few set exercises to acquaint him with standard reference works and journals in the field. For the rest, a general experience of human affairs, reading in peripheral fields, self-discipline, and *Sitzfleisch* are all that are necessary. (40)

White argues that the arts and the sciences have given up on their modernist predispositions and share a contemporary "constructivist" paradigm,[6] but historians continue methodological training that presumes a mediating role. If scientists have given up on positivist epistemologies and artists have given up on traditional literary narrative, then the only way historians can participate in contemporary conversations is to give up nineteenth-century models of science and art and "[take] seriously the kinds of questions that the art and the science of *his own time* demand that he ask of the materials that he has chosen to study" (41).

White's call to open historiography to its own time aligns with Kellner's call for multiplicity—White is looking for multiple methods that share the same contemporary grounds. When historians today appeal to science, they are thinking more of nineteenth-century positivism than contemporary string theory, systems theory, complexity theory, or ecological models of biology. While White concedes that some contemporary historians are interested in using "econometrics, game theory, theory of conflict resolution, [or] role analysis," few are following suit in the arts. When historians today claim their work is artistic, they are thinking of the nineteenth-century realist or romance novel not "action painters, kinetic sculptors, existentialist novelists, imagist poets, or nouvelle vogue cinematographers" (45). White asks, where are the attempts at "surrealistic, expressionistic, or existentialist historiography" (43)? As of the late 1970s, he sees only two examples: Jacob Burckhardt's *Civilization of the Renaissance* and Norman O. Brown's *Life against Death*. He reads Burckhardt as impressionistic historiography that breaks with a conventional, chronological story: "Like his contemporaries in art, Burckhardt cuts into the historical record at different points and suggests different perspectives on it, omitting, ignoring, or distorting as his artistic purpose requires. His intention was not to tell the whole truth about the Italian Renaissance but one truth about it in precisely the same way Cezanne abandoned any attempt to tell the whole truth about a landscape" ("Burden" 44). Similarly, for White, Brown's psychoanalytic approach uses "a series of brilliant and shocking juxtapositions, involutions, reductions, and distortions" to enable his readers to see the materials through sustained associations in the way John Cage achieves affect through happenings (45). Both examples connect with Kellner's call for more selective and affective ways of reading. Freed from storytelling and its plots, heroes, and villains, these histories employ contemporary methods to stitch together an image of events that no one else had seen before.

Sande Cohen's *History out of Joint* also sees the narrative, story-telling model of history as dead, or at least politically problematic, narrowing the complexity of names and events to support particular political ends. Cohen's antidote is to open names and events to multiple perspectives and potential futures. Following Lyotard's "The Sign of History," Cohen argues that names are signs that collect events, which are analogous to the deal of a deck of cards—based on a limited set of evidence but capable of producing multiple combinations. Signs, such as proper names, are not dependent on the "historical" person as a simple cause but on the operation of complex systems of signs, events, and effects (11–12). Following Deleuze's *Difference and Repetition* and *Nietzsche and Philosophy*, Cohen puts forward a model of these events not as the eternal return of the same, where a proper name would refer to the same "historical" person in each articulation, but as repetition of difference, where repetition is a kind of production that is additive, "something repeatable but not yet over" (*History* 14). So every time Nietzsche's name is invoked it is deployed in a completely different set of multiple events and their collective effects. This form of repetition is never begun or finished because at any given point more differences could be added or a different shuffle of the cards could be enacted. An event as such a process can never be recovered in terms of its complete difference, so a final assessment of its truth-value could never be made.[7] In a contemporary world where naming co-opts events for particular interests and ends via narrative claims on truth, historiography requires not mourning, memory, or nostalgia but continual production, which is the only thing that can outpace dominant claims to truth via names and narratives. All of this is a move toward "readings that resist narrative incorporation of actions, events shifted to issues of *coadaptation* instead of opposition and negation" (222).

STITCHING TOGETHER EVENTS

Cohen's Deleuzian historiography connects well with Kellner's crooked historiography. Coadaptation is less about controlling truth than producing change through affects, or affective readings. And the emphasis on the eternal return as the continual production of difference mirrors Kellner's call to "transform the field of evidence into *as many persuasive models as can possible be fashioned*" ("After the Fall" 37). If narrative history is reactive, narrows possible readings, and establishes a specific historical *telos* (S. Cohen, *History* 226–27), then an active historiography enacts the proliferation of naming events to open possible readings and futures (258). Rather than taking stock of the past, historiography would become a kind of "stocking the future" with new names, events, riffs, openings, connections, and potentialities that coadapt with the present and collectively point toward multiple futures. Generally seen as an effect of history, historical representation would become "a *cause* of what can and cannot have a future" (258). The division between language and reality, discourse and materiality, is flattened into coproductive and coadaptive conditions of possibility. This process is really a form of collective improvisation—an ensemble engaging a text, event, or assemblage, breaking into it, dismantling it, producing new concepts, names, riffs, or sounds through reassembling the past, and putting it back out into the performance to see if someone else can pick up on it, take it up, and remake it again to take it toward new directions in its continual unfolding. From this perspective, a historian does not represent, but *performs repetitions*. This is different, however, than Kellner's reading of performance in sub/versive historiography. Performance in crooked historiography isn't epideictic, about style in present performances, but becomes a continual resetting of conditions for possible futures. History, for Deleuze, "is not about a present overcoming its distance from the past; it is about selections that are made to affect a future" (S. Cohen, *History* 17). It is about working pastness for a passage to the future. It is about performing another shuffle of the cards, taking the field of evidence as a deck of possibilities and reworking it into another possible configuration or assemblage.

For White, "the burden of the historian [is] a moral charge to free men from the burden of history" ("Burden" 48). The fetish for an objective past and the pursuit of attaining it puts an undue burden on life in the present, negating present and future action. White claims that if historians give up on their nineteenth-century presuppositions, then their methodological ambiguity can actually be a positive condition of possibility that no other field really enjoys. The historian would be freer to choose from among many contemporary methods the ones that can best illuminate the past to contemporary audiences and reveal multiple perspectives that can impact both the present and future. In short, the burden of history is lifted when the burden of historiography is opened and freed from the demands of the nineteenth century and its methods. The burden of historiography would become developing methods that emerge from contemporary arts and sciences, that perform events in present rhetorical situations, and that feed back into the present to produce multiple lines of flight to the future. I'm interested in exploring improvisational performance as one model for a crooked, affective, productive, affirmative historiography. But since White's examples mostly come from art, I'm looking for a method more in line with Deleuze's various attempts to pull concepts from both science and art to develop philosophical concepts that are more commensurate with the contemporary moment. If I look at writing histories and developing historiographies as improvisational performances within and through the disciplinary narrative of rhetoric's retreat and return, what combination of arts and sciences might allow me to trace past configurations of communication and composition while at the same time point to future convergences? How might the stitching together of events—combinations of people, texts, practices, ideas, institutions—be modeled?

Complexity Theory and Jazz Improvisation

If the burden of historiography is to invent methods for following and enacting ruptures within narratives that open histories to multiple futures (as in the above discussion of Cohen and Deleuze) and uses common grounds among the arts and sciences to do so (as in the above discussion of White), then I'm proposing David Borgo's connections between jazz improvisation and complexity theory as one possible method for thinking historiographically. In *Sync or Swarm*, Borgo reads jazz improvisation from contemporary complexity theory to provide such a common basis for the arts and sciences. Both ant colonies and jazz ensembles emerge with no central organizer or organization beyond the rules for emergence. Much of complexity theory in biology, for example, deals with the collective behavior of ants. Ants release certain chemical signs when they encounter food or a good location for a nest. These pheromone trails signal other ants to follow the trail. As more ants find the initial trail, more pheromones get released, and the colony moves. With only about five basic chemical signs or rules at this micro level, the ant colony can interact with its environment and exhibit complex emergent behavior or patterns at the macro level with no central organization (Borgo 147).[8] Similarly, for Borgo, improvisation starts with basic rules of music and performance—keys, songs structures, player cues. An individual player recognizes in the musical environment the opportunity for a new musical idea, drops the riff into the mix, leaving a cue for other musicians to follow. As more follow, they drop their own "chemical" cues, and the movement of the whole shifts direction. With basic rules of enaction, the ensemble produces an emergent event (or song) through differences, recombinations, and subversions. This is clearly the kind of repetition that Deleuze is after: the repetition of a riff is never the same but interacts differently with different conditions. These events are the unexpected collisions of the musical, social, cultural, and historical that emerge from specific initial conditions but can't be fully predicted. I'm proposing that Borgo's account of improvisation from the perspective of complexity theory can serve as one possible beginning for a crooked historiography. Following select key terms in Borgo, I'm interested in the predominant patterns of self-organization that operate within historical events: degrees of freedom (assemblages), strange attractors (joints), feedback (folds), and bifurcations (lines of flight). All of these are at play when writers improvise and history unfolds.

Degrees of Freedom (Assemblages)

A phase space is a collective range of possibilities for transformation within a given environmental system. Water, for example, will freeze at 32 degrees and evaporate at 212 degrees. But within these limits are certain *degrees of freedom*—within the range of freezing and evaporating, water has an array of possible avenues for flow within the structures of its environment. Some large-grained structures—mountains, valleys, streams, rocks—can be mapped and some smaller-grained structures—atoms, cells of plants that take in water, sand, organisms that live in or consume water—resist mapping. Borgo gives some basic examples of large-grained mapping: a pendulum can be mapped onto two-dimensional space, and its position and momentum can be charted in that space; a car driving in open space can be mapped onto four-dimensional space, the two directions available and the potential momentum in each direction; a rocket ship, free of gravity and physical limits, can be mapped across six dimensions (69). These phase space diagrams, however, can't exhaust the degrees of freedom within a conditional space; lower dimensional subspaces or small-grained structures also contribute to what is possible within a space. For Borgo, improvisation is a perfect example. Musical notation maps a linear dimension of time, a pitch dimension, and various changes in tempo, dynamics, timbre, and so on (69). Pitches are limited to twelve intervals; time markings have limited numbers of divisions; and markings for dynamics are even more limited in terms of the degrees of freedom made available by various instruments and human enactions. If music performance is expanded to include history of the genre, cultural trends and predispositions, the capacities of listeners, the possible tones and timbres of specific instruments, the volume and tonal capacities of a PA system, the skills and backgrounds of individual performers as part of its phase space, then degrees of freedom become greatly expanded beyond notation.[9] Improvised music expands these finer-grained structures even further into levels of detail that "foreground the dynamic qualities of sound and style that are only hinted at in notated form" (70).[10] All of the large- and small-grained structures assembled for any performance establish its limits and degrees of freedom available to the individual musicians and the ensemble as a whole. The complex interactions of large-grained and small-grained structures produce events through three key types of movement: attractors, feedback, and bifurcation.

Attractors (Joints)

Attractors are regions of phase space that seem to draw the behavior of a system toward it, like the force of gravity pulling water into a valley. Researchers in complexity have outlined three types of attractors that describe the dynamic behavior of many types of systems: a fixed-point or static attractor, a limit cycle or periodic attractor, and a strange attractor. A pendulum settling in to a fixed point or a rock rolling down a hill until it stops are examples of fixed-point attractors. "The final resting point 'attracts' the behavior of the system" (70). For Borgo, "the hills and valleys of a real landscape" can be seen as "hills and valleys of energy" that propel movements of the system (70). A limit cycle attractor is a system that "forever oscillate[s] within a fixed or limited range" (70). A pendulum in a vacuum would continue to swing without the force of gravity pulling it to a null point. But even outside of the ideal state, limit cycle attractors, especially in combination, can model the relative steady states of simple ecologies, predator-prey relationships, and certain weather patterns. More complex systems, however, still elude complete mapping. Even two pendulums linked together in a simulation where the behavior of each affects the other will produce more unpredictable results that can be described by strange attractors. This is the extreme sensitivity to initial conditions of the famed butterfly effect. Borgo gives a simple example:

> Imagine a rotating wheel that allows for a controlled drainage into buckets. When the speed of water supplying the buckets reaches a critical value, the wheel will begin to slow down, reverse direction, and speed up, all with a strange unpredictability. Despite the seemingly controlled nature of this example, even the slightest change in the rate of water flow after the critical point can cause the system to exhibit strikingly different behaviors. (71)

This also describes the tipping point in a system that pulls it toward a divergent steady state based on all of the complex forces, or attractors, at play within its phase space. An attractor in a musical ensemble may be a dominant player, whose continual attempts to inject a new musical riff into the performance begins to draw the other players to it; or a riff that stands out from the white noise so starkly that that it calls for repetition and recombination; or an instrument whose timbre or presence cuts through the collective soundscape and attracts the audience's attention and energy. Borgo notes that people attract and sync with others "when we enter into conversation, timing our phrases and pauses and synchronizing our body postures and movements to facilitate close communication" (136).[11] These are all instances of potential positive feedback.

Feedback (Fold)

The jazz performer's experimentation with degrees of freedom folds back into the phase space to produce both positive and negative feedback. Negative feedback operates in simple systems such as thermostats to maintain a particular steady state. Similarly, steering a boat with constant adjustments to the negative feedback from conditions keeps the boat on course. Even judicial systems function through negative feedback to keep actions within standard parameters. But in complex systems, feedback is often positive. Rather than keeping actions within narrow parameters to sustain a steady state, positive feedback is in excess of steady parameters and sends the system in new directions. As Borgo puts it, "if negative feedback regulates, positive feedback amplifies" (72). For example, two pinballs released into a machine with only slightly different trajectories or speed will follow significantly divergent paths when they encounter the positive feedback of the bumpers—the bumpers send the pinballs in more unexpected trajectories. For Borgo, this kind of positive feedback has gotten a bad rap. The screeching sound of a microphone feeding back through a PA or the bandwagon effect of ideas circulating through mass audiences is seen as a problem. But these forms of positive feedback can lay the conditions for Jimi Hendrix or the writing of the Declaration of Independence. "In nonlinear dynamical systems, positive feedback can become a generative or organizing force" (72). In musical settings, negative feedback is crucial: playing within established musical structures or practicing specific songs within ensembles sets the initial negative conditions or rules for emergence or performance. But in a more improvised setting, positive feedback plays a bigger role. Each gesture, decision, or enaction can produce sudden or drastic movements in the overall performance. Borgo writes,

Positive feedback undoubtedly plays a role in musical creativity of all types; on both the macro level, as artistic ideas can spread rapidly within a community, and on the micro level, as a minute performance gesture or compositional germ may blossom into an important creative moment or full-blown work. . . . Even a small change in the first performance gesture—a shift in dynamic level, attack, or articulation, etc.—can lead to a sudden divergence from the evolution of a system started with nearly identical initial conditions. (73)

Noise, unpredictable combinations, and intended interventions can all positively feedback into a performance to add complexity to the degrees of freedom available within a system. Here, *system and performance become almost synonymous* through the production of multiple lines of future development.

Bifurcation (Lines of Flight)

The effects of positive feedback lead to bifurcation points by incorporating difference into a system. More stable attractors such as valleys or common chord progressions maintain relatively steady paths or trajectories. But strange attractors both draw in surrounding trajectories and generate feedback loops, which enhances the complexity of the system and creates new initial conditions or degrees of freedom that bifurcate into new directions. Borgo's example is ping-pong balls on the surface of the water. Drop one in and release another deep in the water. Both will be attracted to the surface of the water. But once there, they bob and weave in response to the waves and run into each other, only to bounce off, bifurcate, and follow new paths established by the renewed degrees of freedom. Ants function in a similar way. When an ant finds food, it drops a chemical signal for other ants to follow. If another comes across the signal, it drops more of the chemical. At first this functions like an attractor, but as more ants respond to the growing chemical signals, a tipping point is reached, and the swarm shoots off in the direction of the food. For Borgo, improvisation works through such (strange) attractors, feedback loops, and tipping points. In his analysis of "Hues of Melanin" by the Sam Rivers Trio, Borgo notes that bifurcations occur at shifts in beat and tempo, whose catalysts tend to be trills, repeated tones, or gradual descents in tones or notes that signal a slowing or changing of tempo. Five and a half minutes into the performance, Rivers lands on a trill that prompts the drummer to shift tempo and groove. The ensemble drops that musical cue rather quickly, but upon another saxophone trill at thirteen minutes, the group picks up the same beat and explores it further (79). The trill becomes an attractor that functions as positive feedback and initiates a bifurcation. The first trill and beat change drops the idea (or chemical signal), but it isn't taken up by enough of the other players to create a bifurcation. The next time around, once more players pick up on it, the trill generates more feedback and reaches a tipping point that creates a bifurcation and the group moves in the new musical direction. The trill or beat is an attractor that eventually garners enough feedback to change the direction of the musical performance. All of these bifurcations, however, are deeply influenced by the entire history of the system—Western musical tradition, the social and cultural context of the performance, the skill and experience of the players and their particular responses to the emergent musical patterns, the physical affordances of the instruments, the energy of the room and crowd. Borgo's model is interested in the transitions among phases and movements of stability around musical strange attractors that feed back into performances and the lines of bifurcation that follow from their interactions. His model doesn't seek to explain the movements causally but instead provides a language for *reading* performative events beyond the language of notation. What if I examine the convergence of communication and composition in particular moments of the twentieth century as these kinds of performances? What lines of flight could be opened up for rhetoric through the production of such a history?

Conclusion: Insect History

In a section titled "Insect Music," Borgo outlines the connections between complex adaptive systems such as ant colonies and jazz ensembles based on a kind of swarm intelligence or self-organization (141–47). Steven Johnson connects this kind of collective, swarm-like production to the historical emergence of ideas in his book *Emergence*. Johnson argues that both the "great man" approach to history and the "paradigm-shift" model are insufficient for conceptualizing and mapping the historical emergence of ideas. The great man theory, where a single thinker has a eureka moment that transforms a discipline or culture, neglects the more distributed, communal effort that lies behind intellectual advances. The paradigm-shift model, where theories hold sway for long periods of time and then a key problem arises that disproves the theory and leads to the development of a new theory that solves the problem, has difficulty explaining the more microevents that lead up to the shifts and the actual developments of the new paradigm. Johnson argues that a basic slime mold simulation is a better metaphor for the way ideas evolve. He writes:

Think of all of those slime mold cells as investigators in a field. Think of those [pheromone] trails as a kind of institutional memory. With only a few minds exploring a given problem, the cells remain disconnected, meandering across the screen as isolated units, each pursuing its own desultory course. With pheromone trails that evaporate quickly, the trails leave no trace of their progress—like an essay published in a journal that sits unread on a library shelf for years. But plug more minds into the system and give their work a longer more durable trail—by publishing their ideas in best selling books, or founding research centers to explore those ideas—and before long the system arrives at a phase transition: isolated hunches and private obsessions coalesce into a new way of looking at the world, shared by thousands of individuals. (64)

This bottom-up model of historical change as emergent behavior clearly connects with Borgo's model of improvisation. It is a collective behavior that interacts with its environment (finds food), establishes attractors (drops pheromones), feeds back into the environment (adding new chemical properties to the system), and points toward new lines of movement (the trails that attract future movements of the colony).

If the phase space of such a performance is seen from a larger historical scale, Borgo's model for reading performative events establishes a model for participating in stitching together events. Borgo recognizes that the role of theory or modeling systems is not simply a form of negative feedback. Models of systems create intuitive responses at the level of embodiment and enaction that positively produce new lines of development. The theories, models, and emergent intuitions of a performer inject difference and new possibilities into a system. Borgo quotes John Briggs and David Peat from *The Turbulent Mirror*:

Nonlinear models differ from linear ones in a number of ways. Rather than trying to figure out all of the chains of causality, the modeler looks for nodes where feedback loops join and tries to capture as many of the important loops as possible in the system's "picture." Rather than shaping the model to make a forecast about future events or to exercise some central control, the nonlineaer modeler is content to perturb the model, trying out different variables in order to learn about the system's critical points and its homeostasis (resistance to change). The modeler is not seeking to control the complex system by quantifying it and mastering it causally; (s)he wants to increase her "intuitions" about how the system works so (s)he can interact with it more harmoniously. (qtd. 73)

There may not be a better description of what historiography might look like from the perspective of history as complex systems. Rather than control through negative feedback or the limiting narratives Cohen responds to, the historian's attempts to model history through writing could positively feed back into the system to contribute to the grounds for other histories, other models, and other future lines of flight. A history might: find key nodes or joints, moments or events, within a historical phase space; model their networks, feedback, and bifurcations; and fold that model back into the current disciplinary system or set of histories.[12] Such a history might, when placed in a particular contemporary configuration or phase space, coproduce new bifurcations, new intuitions about possible disciplinary configurations or new approaches to possible histories, nonlinearly.

Aligning Johnson's model of history with Borgo's method of the modeler provides a potential image of historiography, one possible way to think about tracing the convergences of communication and composition in certain moments of the twentieth century. If we take the model of complexity and improvisation above seriously, then we could never know what such a history would look like until it has been written. But we might take Borgo's key principles as rules for emergence. A historical modeler might take each principle as a chapter, select particular moments of convergence (such as conferences, organizational meetings, particular department or program configurations, or collective editorial projects), and map, diagram, or trace each stage of conditions and enactions to produce a networked history that emphasizes movement rather than stasis:

- *Degrees of freedom*: A chapter or section on phase spaces might produce networked maps of the conditions of possibility for moments of convergence between communication and composition. These could function at larger macro scales to include institutional configurations (universities, conferences, organizations, all of the participants, their writings, all of their associations, genealogies, and interactions). They could also delve into smaller scales that these larger diagrams might not illuminate (the affective nature of disciplinary or departmental politics; the mood or qualities of particular meetings, departments, associations, people; the skills of the individual players, the technologies they have access to, the role of drinking for social cohesion or division; all of the things that might affect any performer/performance). In short, the modeler produces a networked map generated from a database full of information from this phase space. The written portion of such a history might not fully reflect the new digital methods that such diagrams might require. Just as Borgo uses fractal programs to try to model the degrees of freedom exhibited in particular instruments that traditional notation can't account for (94), new technologies and methods will be needed to generate new views of these phase spaces. Traditional nineteenth-century narrative structures would no longer be sufficient models.

• *Attractors*: A networked history would identify the key attractors (collective, individual, microbial—places and institutions, people and texts, ideas and affects) and chart their relative force of attraction, intensity, or "weight," tracing how they pull, push, and coproduce movements within the diagrammed phase space. Who dropped what chemical or improvisational signs? Which ones were picked up or left behind? Why? Which ones are fixed-point attractors, limit cycle attractors, strange attractors? What repetitions built up stronger attractive forces? How do their combinations generate stronger attractions? What emergences were simply unpredictable? If examining rhetoric and practices in these moments of convergence, what models of rhetoric held sway and why? If new digital methods are required to diagram phase spaces, perhaps traditional archival and interview methods might provide insight into the affective attraction of particular people or places. New digital citation and networking models would then trace and reveal particular textual or ideational points of attraction connected to the affective moments identified through more traditional methods.

• *Feedback*: Such a history could trace the directionality of relationships among attractors by marking the moments of feedback in each event. What are the key institutional, economic, political, or disciplinary elements of the phase space that function as negative feedback? What combinations of attractors function as negative feedback to keep rhetorical concerns within established parameters? What were all of the forces, people, texts, exigencies that converged on the particular moments to bring communication and composition together across rhetorical concerns? How were the concepts of rhetoric, institutional practices, or pedagogical practices transformed through their circulation and moments of positive feedback? What key players dropped cues that took hold through positive feedback? Through what networked paths did the people, ideas, or practices circulate and feed back? How did unpredictable combinations add complexity to the degrees of freedom and allow the system to become performance? In order to articulate such relationships, a network history might import methods from complexity theory, systems theory, or ecology. Ant models of complex adaptive systems, models from performance studies, and approaches to discourse analysis could all be digitized and amplified to show how ideas don't simply replicate but mutate as they circulate and feed back. The functionality of any of these possibilities would depend on the historical material assembled and the particular attractors being modeled.

• *Bifurcation*: The above conditions of possibility set the stage for tracing various emergences from the events, showing, for example, how communication and composition diverged yet again, retreating to their respective departments, disciplines, or configurations. A networked historiography asks, in each event, how difference is incorporated into the discursive, disciplinary, or institutional system. Once attractors and moments of feedback have been gathered or mapped, the modeler can trace the entelechial drives they touched off. What attractors gathered up enough intensity to turn the movements of the event toward new directions? What reinventions of the concept of rhetoric circulated among and emerged from these networks of people and places? Toward what problems were they deployed? How did they set new conditions for the emergence of divergence? Why did communication and composition take new and different lines of flight from these moments of convergence? In terms of method, these movements can be modeled in the ways software programs model the swarms of ant colonies and beehives.[13] What combinations of methods would be needed to show these movements? If historical ideas are nothing more than ant pheromones circulating through colonies or trills dropped in a larger musical improvisation, can the circulation of concepts of rhetoric, or pedagogical practices, or the divergences of disciplinary groups be modeled on these bifurcations? What other elements or attractors did these ideas or practices need to attract in order to bifurcate? What historical assemblages of material objects, forces, and movements made these turns possible? How do their combinations generate stronger attractions that drive the particular event toward particular futures? How would such perspectives allow us to read performative events materially? What might we learn about disciplinary movements from such models?

• *Conclusion*: If such a history were to follow a chapter breakdown, the conclusion might examine questions such as: What future lines of emergence from the present does the above historical articulation suggest or make possible? In what ways may this historical account function as a strange attractor or produce positive feedback? Into what current conditions might this articulation circulate and feed back? What other elements may need to be gathered around it to produce a strong enough attractive force to create a bifurcation or tipping point? In short, this approach gives the historiographer a new model of rhetorical situations that would potentially reveal as much about the current moment as the historical events.

A networked historiography based on complexity and improvisation involves a break with the simple or causal chains of narration and story. It operates on diagrams or models of various partial views at various levels of scale for specific historical events and traces movement and change. Writing history would become tracing pheromone trails, seeing where they drop off, aren't picked up; seeing where they coalesce and the trails builds; mapping where that collective action goes and what follows from it.[14] They may simply be maps, drawings, diagrams or tracings, databases or moving visual graphs. Or these models might be the beginning points for chapters, some telling micronarratives, some projecting future effects, some tracing the circulation and transformation of ideas through the networks articulated by the models. One can't know for sure what such a history built on its own historiography would look like until the methods are developed, the models built, and the written improvisation performed.

The role of the writer and historian becomes synonymous with the role of the jazz improvisationist: engage the system through performance to enact positive feedback loops within the parameters of the system—in short, follow emergence to become a strange attractor. Historians both describe these movements and contribute to them, folding their work back into the historical conditions that other historians will be responding to,[15] either by way of static attraction, a steady ecological state of historical thought, or the new developments enacted by multiple strange attractors. This chapter, for example, is a function of improvised reading. Starting with initial conditions, a response to the original volume *Writing Histories of Rhetoric*, I started reading. Certain authors and texts began coalescing as strange attractors. I started writing through them. More micropoints of attraction emerged. As I continued to write, new lines of thinking and new connections opened up. I followed them, but their trajectory took shape because of the way I read crookedly and because of the paths I chose to follow at certain moments along the writing performance. This is the collective, improvised, material performance of history itself and of writing history.

I see the perspective I'm putting forward as folding back into the collective discussion on categorizing historiographies in *Writing Histories of Rhetoric*. John Schilb's contribution identifies the zeal for classification in the field as an anxiety for control that ultimately closes off difference and simplifies the complexity of history, noting the particular preference for "the mystical number three": traditional, revisionary, sub/versive (Vitanza); cognitive, expressionistic, social-epistemic (Berlin); expressivist, transactive, poetic (Britton); scholars, researchers, practitioners (North); or play, game, purpose (Lanham) (Schilb 129). What Kellner and, by extension, White suggest is an extension beyond this trend into a fourth category. White, following Nietzsche, wants to extend Nietzsche's base categories of monumental, antiquarian, and critical historiographies to Nietzsche's own suprahistorical model ("Interpretation" 52–53). The way Kellner sketches out Vitanza's categories suggests a similar extension into fours with his crooked historiography. Whether one reads crooked historiography as a step beyond sub/versive historiography depends on how strongly Kellner's parody is taken. If we read his characterization as completely accounting for sub/versive historiography, Kellner's model is distinct. But if we read Vitanza's performance crookedly as improvisation rather than play, both begin to look like methods of complexity. Even though Kellner seems to set up his approach as a fourth alternative, there is a close affinity between sub/versive and crooked historiographies, with perhaps a key difference being the critical connotation of sub/versive and the more inventive, paratactic connotation of crookedness and its proliferation. But this is also characteristic of Vitanza's call for parataxis.[16] This perspective sees sub/version not as critique but as *sub*sequent *version*ing, repetition of difference.[17] Clearly, this is Kellner's call as well: "The only purpose the discourse of history can legitimately claim is to designate and transform the field of evidence into *as many persuasive models as can possibly be fashioned*" ("After the Fall" 37). And this is precisely what complexity as improvisation does. Borgo's method ultimately sets up a version(ing) of rhetoric for historiography: writing history is the ability to see (and feel) the available degrees of freedom in a given assemblage and fold/feed back into this phase space to attract new lines of flight, producing collective, collaborative possibilities for more histories and historical enactments.

Notes

1. A number of recent works in rhetoric and composition have espoused archival work from traditional and revisionary perspectives. See Connors; Carr et al.; Gold; Kirsch and Rohan.

2. The most recent Octalog continued the emphasis on revisionary history with the implication of developing a more inclusive (i.e., factual) history.

3. See J. Poulakos for Nietzsche's basic argument and categories ("Nietzsche and Histories").

4. Pat Gehrke and I are in the beginning stages of such a possible collaborative project. What follows is just a beginning point for a historiography that will also be emergent and collaborative. We won't know what the history will look like until it is written. This is a function of the principle that every history demands its own historiography. Thanks to Pat for some comments on this rebeginning.

5. For an alternative view of rhetoric and historiography, see Graff and Leff.

6. White doesn't identify social construction by name, but he is invoking such shared assumptions. See Crowley for the distinction between essentialist and constructivist historiographies ("Let Me").

7. Cohen's Deleuzian approach problematizes revisionary history. Cohen writes, "Hence, the current fretting about the loss of memory, collective brooding about repression of the past, or demands for liberation from various inherited blindnesses are mostly rationalizations that support recoding, not conceptual disorientation, let alone configuration of new arrangements" (S. Cohen, *History* 223).

8. See S. Johnson for discussions of ant behavior. See M. Taylor for discussions of fractal programs that produce emergent behavior from a few simple initial rules.

9. White noise has infinite degrees of freedom, but as soon as a particular instrument is used to produce sound, its physical qualities impose limits on noise that close its degrees of freedom and allow it to be mapped (Borgo 94). Borgo discusses new fractal programs that map the degrees of freedom of different instruments, getting into the physical details of the phase space that notation can't account for.

10. Freer forms of jazz improvisation without strong ties to notation are more flexible with regard to tempo, tone, and timbre, and explore a wider range of degrees of freedom. Borgo notes, "Jazz history . . . is littered with . . . performers from Pee Wee Russell to John Coltrane who, when given a detailed transcription of their improvisations, could not perform them" (70).

11. Borgo discusses this in terms of sync and entrainment. Sync is the intuitive or tacit synchronization within the body and its relations with the outside world: cells' chemical and electrical synchronization in the body that allows it to perform key functions; the body's synchronization among its organs that range from regulation of the heart to regulation of brain functions that produce consciousness; the synchronizations between bodies and their environments, whether sleep cycles, attunements to weather or seasons, or female attunement to menstrual cycles via pheromones. Entrainment is the way multiple bodies and systems tend to synchronize in order to produce ecologies (136, 139).

12. There are many emerging digital methods that produce models or visualizations. For one example see Jennifer Howard's recent *Chronicle* article "Citation by Citation, New Maps Chart Hot Research and Scholarship's Hidden Terrain."

13. For more on ants and the "insect logic" in our current discourse on networks, swarms, and digital agents, see Jussi Parikka's *Insect Media*.

14. Johnson's description of slime mold pheromone trails outlines the strengthening of these trails and how they coalesce or attract more movement (S. Johnson, *Emergence* 63). A related phenomenon happens in the brain and the relative "weights" of neural connections. Borgo similarly discusses the notion of weight or intensity of connections in improvisation (79).

15. Whether in historians or jazz musicians, the ability to elicit response is critical to positive feedback. See Davis's discussions of responsibility, "responsible responsiveness," and response-ability (*Inessential*).

16. See "An After/word": "some more" (220); "Taking A-Count": "dissoi paralogoi" (184) and "paratactic" (187).

17. See Casey Boyle's upcoming article, "Versioning Compositions: On Engaging Abundant Digital Memory," for an extended discussion of versioning.

8

RHETORIC'S NOSE: WHAT CAN RHETORICAL
HISTORIOGRAPHY MAKE OF IT?

Jane S. Sutton

The title of this essay is unusual. I open this essay, therefore, by keying
in the title to a contemporary scene of rhetorical historiography. This
scene serves as the deep background for understanding my motive for writing about a nose. One large facet of the historiographical scene in rhetoric
is the 1980s. In "Octalog: The Politics of Historiography," James J. Murphy
argued that what is at stake in rhetoric is not differences in methodology
alone, "but varying perceptions of what ought to be discovered for the good
of the community" (5). Varying perceptions may lead to new ideas of rhetoric, daring ideas presumably. Another facet of the scene is the 1990s. In a
multiperson discussion format, Roxanne Mountford wrote emphatically, "At
a time when the [community] is increasingly in need of rhetorical exploration, we must *risk* looking for rhetoric," looking "for rhetoric where it has
not been found" ("Octalog II" 34; emphasis added). While the scene changes
with differences of opinion, of subject, and of mood, there is a similarity
among them as voiced by Murphy and Mountford that is striking in its vision. Both address a need to discover, to find, to create—to invent. Specifically, they refer to this need in terms of a dare and a risk. This is where the
title of my essay enters the scene; it signals my taking a dare.

This essay is a venture into a radical metaphor. What it leads to is a description of how rhetoric advanced theoretically through a nebulous metaphor and how this prefigured rhetoric's containment, as well as how it creates
chances for new ideas in writing the history of rhetoric today.

While reading the *Rhetoric*, I was caught unawares when I came across
a passage in which Aristotle makes a comparison between democracy and
a type of nose. Here is the passage:

> Thus democracy loses its vigor, and finally passes into oligarchy, not
> only when it is not pushed far enough, but also when it is pushed too

far; just as the aquiline and the snub nose not only turn into normal noses by not being aquiline or snub enough, but also by being too violently aquiline or snub arrive at a condition in which they no longer look like noses at all. (1360a 25–30; cf. *Politics*, 1309b)

The names of these noses are not often used. I pause to describe the two types of noses. The best description can be found in Fanny Fern's lesson in Greek and rhinoscopy at a mock commencement exercise around the turn of the twentieth century. She says, "Nose + Nose = proboscis [concave nose]. Nose—nose—nose = snub [flat nose]" (qtd. in Richards et al. 48). An aquiline nose is also called a concave nose. It protrudes like a beak. A synonym for the snub nose is the flat nose.

I mentioned earlier that I was caught unawares by the nose in *Rhetoric*. Even if readers notice it, they often dismiss it as incidental and thus not worth exploring. In fact, after querying a colleague (one too many times I admit) about this passage, he told me I could just take a black magic marker and cross out the passage to render it invisible, and I would have not affected the idea of rhetoric. Presumably the same could be said for the history of rhetoric. (That history elides the nose became an important clue as I ventured into a metaphor.)

I had my black marker ready when I noticed that the nose was smack dab in the middle of the chapters (1359a–1366a) cataloguing the topics of deliberation. George A. Kennedy characterized these particular chapters as the "early core" of rhetoric (*On Rhetoric* 56). When I considered the location of the passage on the nose in *Rhetoric*, I thought it not incidental: to use a body part (a nose, for gawd's sake, not an ear, not an eye), rather than to incorporate some property of rationality to stabilize or fix the center of rhetoric in relation to the civic realm, is not the standard view of how rational speech is invented, much less how it functions in the context of democratic deliberation (for example, see Fisher). Yet Aristotle turns to the nose to stage the form and function of rhetoric. (The exceptionality of the nose is the clue that enabled me to find a way to pursue new ideas.)

What is the connection between rhetoric and democracy, and how does the nose resemble it? At first glance, shape seems to constitute their point of likeness. So, in the context of rhetoric and democracy, the nose, metaphorically speaking, illustrates perfect straightness and thus balance, just as a poet might use (the shape of) a particular fruit to illustrate the perfect chin and thus a balanced visage. However, the more I thought about the metaphor of the nose, the more the idea of shape began to lose its luminosity, until finally the connection completed faded from view.

Here is how the idea of shape and its attendant features of straightness and balance lost its power. I wondered, if it were the feature of straightness that the nose was meant to designate, why didn't Aristotle just continue his comparison with the metaphor of the carpenter's rule that he introduced earlier in the *Rhetoric* (1354a 25)? Elsewhere, I have described how Aristotle employs the metaphor (of the carpenter's rule) to envisage *logos* as the rule(r) that enables intelligent and reasonable action (Sutton, "Death" 217–18). A warped carpenter's rule is divergence from the straight; this divergence refers to the possibility of decisions going wrong and of the hearer succumbing to poor judgment. Extending the carpenter's rule to the scene of democracy would be a valid next step, so I thought. Would it not measure effectively the straight and right line of democracy? The carpenter's rule is not used to measure the logical aspect of deliberation vis-à-vis the ends of government. There must more to the metaphor of the nose than simply shape, I reasoned.

I, therefore, changed my approach. I viewed the nose in terms of what it does. It smells. What is this *sense* of rhetoric? How might a sense of smell be metaphorically equivalent to the performance of rhetoric in democracy? As I reflected on this idea, I wondered about the other senses—sound (ear), sight (eye), touch (hand), and taste (tongue). I thought the sense of smell— the nose—a very odd selection. The more I considered the nose, the more exceptional it seemed. Wouldn't it be more appropriate to stage the activity of rhetoric through any one of the other senses?

Eventually, it was Gertrude Buck's writings on metaphor that turned my attention from the nose qua nose to its exceptionality—the accidental quality—of the nose inscribed within the topic of deliberation. To venture into a metaphor, I follow Buck's insights to explain what the metaphor of the nose does. In particular, I make three turns from the idea that a new metaphor constitutes "a nebulous and undeveloped perception of a situation" (274). This situation refers to rhetoric's problematic relation with contingency and the solution to it develops generationally.

Briefly, here is Buck on metaphor: In the development of her idea, metaphors eventually reach a point beyond which they cannot go. When this happens, a new metaphor arises, but unlike the old one, the new metaphor is undifferentiated; it perceives a sense of something. It is a feeling more or less. The verve of a metaphor is evident in *Rhetoric*: I surmised that the metaphor of the carpenter's rule had reached its final point in its ability to measure the three means of persuasion (*ethos, pathos, logos*) which effectively straightened out Aristotle's predecessors, the Sophists (Sutton, "Death"). According to Buck, there is a sign when a metaphor reaches its end of development: it articulates a judgment, and this is especially true of the metaphor of the carpenter's rule. It renders *logos* the "straightest" of them all in order to specify the means by which moral judgment accrues in rhetoric. And this is how I came to the conclusion that Aristotle needed a new metaphor. This is how I came to view the nose as vital to understanding rhetoric and deliberation in the context of democracy.

I begin by turning to Buck's notion of the new metaphor. That is, a "nebulous and undeveloped perception of a situation" (274) could not be a more accurate depiction of E. M. Cope's take on the nose. The nose is unexpected. Apparently, Cope figures that Aristotle would use one of Plato's favorite metaphors—that of the lyre (1: 69). In addition to the carpenter's rule, there seems to be yet another standard or usual image circulating in the culture upon which Aristotle could have drawn to specify the situation of rhetoric in relation to the ends of government, but he didn't. The metaphor of the nose is vague and unformulated. Cope reasons that the metaphor of the nose must be a substitute for the lyre and thus shares the same meaning. To screw up or relax the strings in order to produce a different pitch or tone denotes ideas of harmony and balance (1: 69). The nose, like the lyre, identifies the health of the body politic.

There are political undertones in the notion of sound because the lyre can implicate a balanced or harmonious state of affairs. But who can play the noses? I am barely able to suppose (with Cope) that there could be noses, so to speak, playing deliberation; in his line of thinking, the snub nose, being flat and thus depressed, would substitute for the act of lowering the strings of the lyre, and its concave form would raise them. By implication, all voiced noses would be interconnected and engaged in deliberation. This could be playing the noses. However, to envisage the nose as a lyre is to presuppose it as an instrument of sound, not smell. Moreover, it assumes that the health of the body politic is the situation about which the metaphor of the nose is concerned. This leads me to the next turn. What is the situation that the nose, albeit nebulous and undeveloped, is picking out? That is, what is the nose being used to develop for rhetoric? This is rhetoric's problematic relation with contingency, to which I now turn.

Deliberation concerns the future tense, which means rhetoric is immersed in events and happenings. When it comes to making claims about the future, the task for rhetoric is to figure out how to respond to situations. Toward that end, rhetoric seeks to observe [*theorein*] and to succeed "by habit" rather than "accidentally" (Kennedy, *On Rhetoric* 29). The metaphor of the nose offers access to what rhetoric needs, as well as how it manages to get this need met and thus succeed by habit.

In rhetoric, the notion of "happening" is ubiquitous. A happening evokes rhetoric. It defines rhetoric, actually setting it apart from all other arts. It is common for rhetoricians to talk about a happening as contingency. A contingency is something that may happen. A happening sits in the semantic domain of the unexpected, the exception, and the accidental. As an abstract principle, a happening in rhetoric is ruled by a line of argument called the probable and improbable. Connected to the topic of probability, a happening becomes attached not only to the means of making arguments but also to the form of contingency. When this happens—when rhetoric is connected topically and formally to the notion of making arguments—rhetoric is implicated by deliberation. The function of deliberative discourse is to tell what is happening and going to happen in the form of argument. This is not prophecy but rather a way of employing the means of persuasion vis-à-vis the topic of the probable and improbable and based on that to deliberate or to reason about the future. For this and more, rhetoric needs to smell. That is, it needs to think.

What is the relation between smell and deliberation? What Lyall Watson says about smell, in his *Jacobson's Organ and the Remarkable Nature of Smell*, indicates to me that a strong relation exists. Before sight and sound hijacked our attention, humans shared with all life a sort of common sense, a chemical sense that depended on direct contact with matter in the water or the air. This chemical sense was smell. According to Watson, "it is even possible that being able to smell was the stimulus that . . . turned a small lump of olfactory tissue on its nerve cord into a brain" (12). Thus, he concludes, "we think *because* we smelled" (12). In effect, the nose qua metaphor "notices" the differences between a kind of rhetorical deliberation developed by habit and one developed accidentally. The sense of smell, a kind of thinking, enables rhetoric to widen its deliberative capacity, which limits the range of the accidental. I now turn to explain how the metaphor of the nose enacts the separation from the accidental and leads to the development of democratic deliberation.

As an undeveloped metaphor, the nose is perceptible only in certain moments such as strange images or in dreams (Buck). If these images are pursued, it is possible to cultivate the metaphor. Such a strange image exists in Aristotle's discussion of the teleological process when the process is comparable to the action of human development. Entering something of a dream state, I have created a script to frame and describe how the metaphor unfolds to resolve the problem of contingency. To plot the action, I cast two characters: child and adult. In terms of this script, I follow Aristotle's lead and use children to specify them as the snub type of nose. As they morph into the nose, children enter the story to signify the accidental. According to Aristotle, "Children are inferior to adults owing to the great amount of restlessness and motion [change] in their souls" and thus must be made accountable (*Physics* 248a 1; 405a 5–406a 1). Insofar as children are prone to the accidental, they represent raw materiality—something like random contingency—which Aristotle renders as snub. Again, he turns to children to characterize it: "All children are snub-nosed (*simoi*) (*Problems* 963b 15). Unlike Aristotle, I let the adult represent the aquiline nose, which allows me to identify the peculiar way rhetoric means to show itself on the incline, rising in the world, nose bent in an uphill pattern. In sum, the adult performs contingency as change that is well behaved. And so the adult schematizes rhetoric's deliberative side, rendering as "that which holds for the most part" (*Rhetoric* 1357a 34–b1), which is the sign of "probability."

As a human art, an art embodied by the people (*demos*), rhetoric has a nose. Noses are "*human* organs as distinct from snouts" (Grene 61). But there are two shapes of noses: one is snub (or a flat nose) and the other is concave (or an aquiline nose). Insofar as these two shapes are human, the problem of how to deal with a happening—the topic of change and the accidental—is appropriate in terms of "*man*, not of an old animal" (Grene 61). The two (shapes of) noses (like men, say Socrates and Coriscus) do not differ in terms of humanity. Two shapes, two noses: what accounts for their differences, politics aside?

Of essences or of things defined, Aristotle writes in his *Metaphysics*, "some are like snub [flat], and some like concave [aquiline]" (1325b 30). The nose as abstract principle helps us to understand what constitutes a definition. He goes on to say that the noses

> differ because snub is bound up with matter, while concavity is independent of perceptible matter. If then all natural things are analogous to the snub in their nature—e.g. nose, eye, face, flesh, bone, and, in general, animal; leaf, root, bark, and, in general, plant (for none of these can be defined without reference to movement—they always have matter), it is clear how we must seek and define the essence in the case of natural objects, and also why it belongs to the student of nature to study soul to some extent. (1025b 30–1026a 6)

So the nose is not just a nose, but yet it is concrete (Bambrough). The snub is the sign of matter, movement, the stuff of a happening (*Physics* 194a 3–7; *Metaphysics* 1030b 16–23; 1064a 19–23). The snub is not divided from the aquiline, just as the child is not divided from the adult. It is a relation of dependence. In effect, the snub is *in* the aquiline (C. Chen); the two kinds of noses are not oppositional. Born out of Aristotle's systematization of thought, the child is snub matter—movement or change. In effect, the snub/matter/child in Aristotle embodies motion as *emotion*—the "hexis or pathos of substance" (Grene 59)—and is expected to grow up, submit to a form, and move to its end, all of which by smell and time denote substance and teleology. This is the adult. So, rhetoric's relation with contingency, once homogenous and undifferentiated as signified by its human matter of the snub nose, evolves through the desire for normalcy but with a slight elongation, as an aquiline nose, toward substance.

Insofar as rhetoric may be viewed as incorporating a specific set of actions, namely seeking *to break away* from the accidental and, specifically, from the Sophists due to their connections with the accidental (Classen; Cherniss), the script that best translates the metaphor is an escape narrative. According to Tzvetan Todorov, the narrative takes "escape" as its theme, which doubles as a logic (36–37). To parse this logic is to unpack rhetoric's desire characterized by "wanting what it does not have and fleeing from what it has" (36). Configuring the metaphor as an escape narrative, I have followed the logic by dividing it. There is the aquiline nose line plotting rhetoric as wanting what it does not have (characterized by habits), and there is the snub nose line plotting rhetoric as fleeing from what it is (characterized by the accidental).

Through the nebulous metaphor of the nose, rhetoric changes theoretically in at least two ways: Physically speaking, the nose is a sign of rhetoric's relation to raw materiality coming to rest. What is at rest is stable and regular and creates the condition of succeeding by habit. The lyre could have told this story. But the nose offers the sense of smell. Smell is a distinct sense from the sense of sound. Sound whose sign is the lyre has aspects of movement, a movement that does not follow a straight line but rather a circular one. The heavens move in a circle, and the lyre resembles the heaven, as its namesake the constellation Lyra implies.

In effect, the metaphor of the nose enacts an escape narrative. This is the story of rhetoric fleeing from sound because it wants to think, and this means it must smell the opportunity, grasp what is afar, and lead the listener straightaway to an understanding of it. So the phrase "lead them by the nose" carries the idea of straight-line thinking implied by the carpenter's rule but adds something. It signifies the progression of rhetoric into the realm of deliberation, getting what it wants while fleeing from what it is—accidental change. The sound of the lyre is the reminder of a form of rhetoric without a deliberative capacity capable of smell. This is a rhetoric that functions accidentally. As rhetoric develops and matures, it moves out of its snub matter and lengthens, like an aquiline nose. It is, I think, no accident that Aristotle uses the nose—not the lyre, not the carpenter's rule—to specify the relation between deliberation and democracy. Besides, the nose is the body part that is most easily observed by others and counted during the process of deliberation.

In the first part of this essay, I developed the perception of the nose by differentiating its elements. It is one thing to imagine the nose as communicating something about rhetoric and quite another to take it seriously to consider further and pose an answer to the question: What can rhetorical historiography make of the nose? I offer two suggestions.

Professor, historiographer, and recipient of the Pulitzer, Bancroft, and Parkman Prizes, Daniel J. Boorstin points to the accidental as the key to understanding our present circumstances. The perfect embodiment of the accidental is Cleopatra's nose; Boorstin turns to the *Pensées* of Blaise Pascal, who wrote, "Cleopatra's nose, had it been shorter, the whole face of the world would have been changed" (qtd. in Boorstin ix). Is there an image like Cleopatra's nose in (the event of) rhetoric around which its script can be conceived? Strangely, accidentally, it is the nose, namely that passage in *Rhetoric* mentioned earlier.

Now when it comes to connecting the nose to the writing of history, the statement on Cleopatra's nose arguably is not the best way to introduce an accidental historiography to rhetoricians who are familiar with the nose as it relates to themes of exclusion, especially of women, in the history of rhetoric. In *Borderlands/La Frontera*, Gloria Anzaldúa writes, "I am visible—see this face—yet I am invisible. I both blind them with my . . . *nose* and I am their blind spot. But I exist, we exist" (1601; emphasis added). Anzaldúa embodies her nose, and this is her rhetorical experience of being in the social practice; her nose reveals her as a "foreigner" who has entered the realm of rhetoric, while at the same time it puts her behind a barricade that constructs a communicative praxis (1602) without her kind of nose. The authors of "Octalog: The Politics of Historiography" raised the question of women's exclusion (10) and observed rhetoric's "material conditions" (11). Perhaps they are related somehow to snub matter. At any rate, Anzaldúa is one who brilliantly recounts not only rhetoric's material conditions but also the suffering associated with them, namely of being excluded from history, theory, and practice of rhetoric.

But there is another way to think about exclusion, and this way does not involve rhetoric's nose in relation to an individual's nose, like Anzaldúa's nose. This way does not regard the metaphor of the nose as a point of departure for writing a people's story, of women's noses, of Cleopatra's nose, of Chicanos' or Chicanas' noses. A category of exclusion that goes beyond considering people in rhetoric's traditional framework concerns how metaphors, although magically marked out, establish the ground to substantiate the realm of rhetoric vis-à-vis democratic deliberation. In this view of exclusion, the elided metaphor forgets to say how rhetoric "grew up" and gained its formal identity as a "people art" in relation to democratic deliberation.

Although I have said an accidental historiography is not interested in the shape of either Cleopatra's nose or Anzaldúa's nose and how this shape manifests their exclusion—from within history or Texas and ostensibly within rhetoric, I do imagine the possibility that the nose in rhetoric could implicate the authority of women. But this possibility goes beyond my question. At the very least, the answer to the question (what can rhetorical historiography make of the nose?) means developing the metaphor to understand how it envisages rhetoric. Do enactments of rationality belong to the complex image of the nose? Could the social practice of deliberation be represented by noses? Could an analysis of noses reveal prejudices constructed theoretically within the model of deliberation? To inquire is sure entry into the fray, a political arena where more than the history of rhetoric is at stake.

Returning to Boorstin—he is not luring us towards the nose and then asking us to play "what if" (what if asparagus were blue or what if Cleopatra's nose were shorter). The nose is the instantaneous moment that catches us unawares. *The nose is the breakthrough of the accidental.* Catching sight of a nebulous metaphor like the one of the nose is a form of discovery. To focus on this breakthrough requires framing the metaphor in a script in order to engage it. In this way, I presented the nose in an escape narrative in which rhetoric is seen fleeing from what it is (contingency through and through) and wanting what it does not have (a means of managing what it is). As such, the goal of my writing is to explore how rhetoric was or can be transformed by the accidental. This transformation is not about defining rhetoric's trajectory as neither moving from ignorance to knowledge nor as moving from a negative to a positive version. An accidental history permits us to explore from the perspective of an accidental image the process by which rhetoric can reconfigure itself as an agent of change.

If effect, I can now say that Aristotle implicates rhetoric in the accidental: It is what brings rhetoric into existence, and it is what he wants to control and thus extend rhetoric politically. In Aristotle's terms, rhetoric is the art of pure movement, and he goes to battle with his predecessors over rhetoric with an exceptional metaphor (Classen.) I would paraphrase Pascal and say this: Had rhetoric's sense of itself been an eye, the whole face of theory would have been changed.

Lastly, I want to return to the image of the nose from the standpoint of the child. As raw materiality, this figure could reverse the direction of rhetoric toward rest—the adult form of contingency configured as likelihood—and explore the accidental in contemporary terms of change, including various views from Newton to chaos theory (Buckley; Zimmerman). This would be a radical step of exploration because in rhetoric it would mean writing/speaking like a child.

I remember being at a child's birthday party. There were ten adults and five children. The children were outnumbered, even at the party for a child. In the middle of my conversation with Chista, her daughter ran into the room holding a present and screaming,

"Mommy! Mommy! Look what I got."

Then the mother interrupted her daughter and said, "Don't tell me in English. Tell me in Farsi."

"But, Mom," she said, directly, "it happened to me in English."

To return to rhetoric as the art of managing a happening—a contingency—that is coming or has come upon us for good or ill: the mother wants the child to specify this "happening" as an external event and to use suitable language cast in the form of deliberation. This language traffics in probability, and although probability meant something different for the ancient Greeks than it does for us, the notion of probability was able to impose a rational way of dealing with eventualities as they arise (see Kraus; Hoffman). A form of rationality is how "it"—for example, the Challenger exploding in space—is translated, its accident a means of deliberating the future of the space program. Staying in character with the birthday party, I would say that when the adult tells about such an event, he or she employs a standard language. The child, however, experiences what happened from within snub matter, but she versions the presence of "it" differently, at least not in terms of probability. If we (dare) bear a childlike attitude toward the happening and let this child allow "it" to break through, we discover the presence of a happening in rhetoric's theoretical beginning. In a received history, this child's version of what happened in rhetoric is—well—trivial and unexpected. After all, it does feature the nose.

Why listen to a child: actually, why listen to a nose? What could a child possibly observe of rhetoric *as such*? If the adult would admit this possibility, what might the tropical child/nose reveal about the art?

The foreword in Jean-François Lyotard's *The Postmodern Explained* coaxes us in the contemporary world to ask such questions. Arguably, Lyotard sides with child as he raises the question about the human condition: "What would happen if thought no longer had a childhood?" (ix). In this manner,

I wonder what would happen if rhetoric no longer considered its childhood? The postmodern condition is less about relations of power as only can be imagined between adult and child than it is about another kind of *imbalance* having to do with the child's ability to translate when the adult deems the child's language—well—childlike. Working from the angle of the child, I cast Lyotard's question ("what would happen if thought no longer had a childhood?") to refract a politics of translation, but it is not based on a language, like English or Greek, but on a language involving "the possibility of thought 'happening'" (ix). To let the (snub) nose speak, if you will, is to discover the child/raw materiality/possibility of thought happening in rhetoric. How can the child speak of "it"—the presence of a nose in *Rhetoric*—when the adult—or whatever form of power—always already interrupts, closing off doing and thinking about experiences?

It was "being caught unawares" that prompted me to take a risk that Murphy and Mountford called for, and I looked at the metaphor of the nose. Being caught unawares is a phrase from Samuel Taylor Coleridge's "Rime of the Ancient Mariner," on which Gregory Bateson and Mary Catherine Bateson warrant a perception as productive (73). The poem's protagonist was stuck, ironically, upon the flow (of water), a predicament that came to an end when out of the corner of the mariner's eye he saw fish, their silver bellies shimmering. The flash (of perception/fish) was not direct, but sideways—out of the blue, like the nose in *Rhetoric*. The answer to the question—what can historiography make of the nose?—is twofold: The presence of nose provides a model of Aristotle using an accidental image accidentally—a child speaking. It can lead to writing an accidental history of rhetoric. As was the case with the mariner, being caught unawares creates change, and it denotes a variety of perception that initiates a "contingency of value" (Smith) to look for rhetoric where it has not been found.

9

HISTORIOGRAPHY AS HAUNTOLOGY: PARANORMAL INVESTIGATIONS INTO THE HISTORY OF RHETORIC

Michelle Ballif

[I]n order to watch over the future, everything would have to be begun again[,]
namely with haunting, before life *as such*, before death *as such*.
                                        —Jacques Derrida, *Specters of Marx*

Given that a *revenant* is always called upon to come and to come back, the [writing] of the specter, contrary to what good sense leads us to believe, signals toward the future. It is a [writing] of the past, a legacy that can come only from that which has not yet arrived—from the *arrivant* itself.
                                        —Jacques Derrida, *Specters of Marx*

We begin and end this corpus/corpse of the (un)canny (un)dead by reckoning with Jacques Derrida's claim: "There has never been a scholar who really, and as scholar, deals with ghosts. A traditional scholar does not believe in ghosts—nor in all that could be called the virtual space of spectrality" (*Specters of Marx* 12). He continues to assert: "There has never been a scholar who, as such, does not believe in the sharp distinction between the real and the unreal, the actual and the inactual, the living and the non-living, being and non-being . . . in the opposition between what is present and what is not" (*Specters of Marx* 12). This essay, then, undertakes to accept this challenge: to become a haunted scholar of rhetoric by investigating the paranormal possibilities for the historiography of rhetoric reconceived as "hauntology" (Derrida, *Specters* 10), as an ongoing conversation with ghosts, real or imagined, dead or very much alive. By so doing, by becoming, all of us, "ghost whisperers," we would be "calling, calling, calling to the Other" (Vitanza, *Negation* 50), and by communing with them, we could invent our future and "learn to live finally," ethically (Derrida, *Specters* xvi).

Why this ghastly ghosting? Why this uncanny conjuration? I begin with the presumption that historiography *is* always already the writing of the "history of death" (Derrida, *Aporias* 43). As such, our key *responsibility* would not be to write the history of death as a "grand" nor even "petit" narrative of our past. Rather, it would be to lend an ear to the ghostly whisperings of that which (continues to) haunt rhetoric, to investigate all those burials of our history—all those textual crypts[1] that have served to ontologize the remains of "our" history of rhetoric. The *ethical* obligation to listen to these unfamiliars is not motivated by a desire to render them (finally) familiar, which—again—is an attempt to bury the remains (finally), but rather to render *ourselves* unfamiliar (as scholars, and as a discipline).

But, already, we are too many steps out in front of ourselves, which is where we will want to have been: awaiting (the return of) the *arrivant*. As is often cited, Derrida in his exordium to *Specters of Marx* claims that "to learn to live" "finally" is a lesson that cannot be learned from life, but only from "the other and by death. In any case from the other at the edge of life. At the internal border or the external border, it is a heterodidactics between life and death" (xvii). Further, "nothing is more necessary than this wisdom [to learn to live finally]. It is ethics itself" (xvii). Our relation to death, to our own, to the other's—whether as the possibility of impossibility (Heidegger) or, particularly, as the impossibility of possibility (Levinas)—structures our being and our ethical relation to the other (see R. Cohen). Thus, ethical—and just—being (in-the-world) necessitates stepping to and beyond the (impossible) border between life and death, demands listening to, learning from, conversing with those inhabitants of this border: the dead as undead, the *revenant* as the *arrivant*. This, I propose, is our ethical injunction for a *just* practice of historiography to re/member the ghost, and it requires a certain uncertain step toward the border.

---

1. Hauntological historiographies might begin by investigating the foundations of already written histories of rhetoric—or, more to the point, by investigating what has been repressed, textually, by already written histories of rhetoric. What has been buried, for example, in a footnote? How does this burial haunt—irrepressibly—the text? It is precisely this haunting that hailed Byron Hawk, that conjured his "counter-history" of the field of composition studies. Two footnotes from one source and one from another, as so many verbal apparitions, appeared as ghosts to Hawk, and his conversation with them defamiliarized our field's defining, foundational conception of itself as opposed to any sort of so-called "vitalism." That is, the "living" field of composition studies necessitated the burial, the sacrifice, of an/other: "vitalism." The history of the field of composition studies—as a living entity, made present to itself, as a discipline—demanded a corpse. Hawk's ensuing "counter-history" lent an ear to this corpse, which had been buried "alive." As another example, Jane S. Sutton's

But towards a border that is impossible to cross—and to know: Where does the border begin and end between the living and the dead? Does it exist? Even if it did, could one know it? Even if one could know it, could one communicate it? The ghost haunts our borders of life and death, of knowing and not knowing, and of communicating or not communicating. For a hauntological practice is not an ontological one—it makes no claims of *being,* nor is a hauntological practice an epistemological one—it makes no claims of *knowledge.* For the ghost "is" insofar as "one does not know if precisely it *is,* if it exists, if it responds to a name and corresponds to an essence" (Derrida, *Specters* 5). Derrida continues: "One does not know: not out of ignorance, but because this non-object, this non-present present, this being-there of an absent or departed one no longer belongs to knowledge. At least no longer to that which one thinks one knows by the name of knowledge" (5). It, the ghost, defies our categorical ways and means of knowing. Yet, this "thing," this unknowable, undead "thing," which *is* not *as such,* calls to us, "the living," and demands a (responsible) response.

A hauntological historiography would acknowledge this responsibility, but it would also necessitate, as we will have investigated, a certain uncertainty regarding temporality and address. That is: a hauntological historiography writes with/in a haunted, uncanny sense of the past, present, and the future—indeed, with a sense that linear, historical time is "out of joint," and that the borders between the past and the future remain—not only permeable, but—impossible. Likewise, a hauntological historiography performs a certain uncertain writing habit in that the historiographer can never know who is addressing whom—nor know the difference between addressor and addressee. There is no certainty, and there is no rest from the restless dead; no historiographer will have ever laid to rest the wandering specter nor rendered familiar the unfamiliar. The responsibility never wanes, and the hauntological

---

"counter-history," *The House of My Sojourn,* follows the ghostly whisperings of the women interred in the basement of the "house of rhetoric." That is, as she de/monstrates: "living" rhetoric—since classical times—has necessitated the erection of a structure that was/is founded on the repression/the burial of female rhetorical agency.

As are Hawk and Sutton, I am interested in how histories are written upon the graves of repressed histories. But the (non)point of investigating these crypts is not to offer a "better" or "more accurate" history—as if either were possible, for *any* history would necessitate its own series of burials, precisely because history is for the living, and hence requires its dead, its logic of mourning, its cultural rites of burials—real or imagined. A hauntological historiography, although interested in crypts, is not interested in *decryption*—it has no desire to render meaningful the secrets buried (for its "meaning" *is* its function of having been buried). There is no "truth" in the casket, awaiting its resurrection. A hauntological historiography has

historiographer will never enjoy the false satisfaction of good conscience because there is no possibility of certainty, and indeed—s/he will "run from" any "assured form of . . . subjective certainty" (Derrida, *Aporias* 19).

A hauntological historiography responds to a call, which comes from a radical singularity that defies/exceeds any categorization. Derrida dedicates his *Specters of Marx* to the "memory of Chris Hani," who was assassinated—sacrificed as a substitution for a "communist." Derrida enjoins: "one should never speak of the assassination of a man as a figure, not even an exemplary figure in the logic of an emblem, a rhetoric of the flag or of martyrdom. A man's life, as unique as his death, will always be more than a paradigm and something other than a symbol" (xiv). Likewise, a hauntological historiography would dedicate itself to radical singularity—by refusing to put rhetoric under the "logic of an emblem," or to erase its singularity to a "paradigm." The infinite responsibility is to live (with) this radical singularity—that which is murdered/repressed/excluded under the banner of a "grand" narrative—or even in a "petit" narrative.

We will have re/turned to all: the *arrivant* as the *revenant*.

Hauntological Historiography

To begin our ghastly conversations as historiographical dialogues, we must distinguish our "hauntological" (non)methods from what has been heretofore produced as "histories" or accounts of the dead (rhetoric).

In Michel de Certeau's estimation, the writing of history is to construct sepulchers for the dead, or—more to the (non)point—to construct the dead,

---

no hermeneutical desire, to lay open the grave, to lay bare the corpse. More akin to hermetics, the crypt displaces understanding, listening toward the *threshold* of understanding (Derrida, "Fors" xii–iii). (For more [on] "secrets," see Joshua Gunn's *Modern Occult Rhetoric*.)

Might a hauntological historiography have been written according to the (non) logic of cryptography—as "sub/versive hysteriography" (Vitanza, *Negation*)? Might it be a conversation with the ghosts haunting, paratextually, the footnotes of a history? Lending an ear to the "supplement," that which cannot be incorporated into the text without resulting in some "loss or impairment" to the text (Genette 328)? ("The obvious impairment," Genette writes, "is that incorporating a digression into the text might well mean creating a lumpish or confusion-generating hernia" [328], that is, creating a discursive monster—perhaps a zombie, a confusion of the boundaries of understanding, a figure of the living dead.) What might such a paratextual "history" be? A dancing on the *threshold* of the grave. A paratext, writes Gerard Genette, is "more than a boundary or a sealed border, the paratext is, rather a *threshold*" (2). (This chapter is a prologue to a greater project—in process—investigating the threshold: the paratextual, paranormal history of rhetoric.)

as dead, for the purpose of constructing the living. De Certeau writes: "writing plays the role of a burial rite . . . ; it exorcises death by inserting it into discourse" (100) and "[wr]iting speaks of the past only in order to inter it. Writing is a tomb" (101). The writing of history, then, as traditionally, or even revisionarily composed, is a rhetorical maneuver with the aim to *bury the dead:* to make sure the remains remain put. As such, historiography is a mourning of the dead that "consists always," Derrida writes, "in attempting to ontologize remains, to make them present, in the first place by *identifying* the bodily remains and by *localizing* the dead" to "make certain" that the remains *"remain there"* (*"Fors"* 9). This process of ontologizing remains is symptomatic of a panicked rhetorical process, compulsarily repeated, to make the dead materialize as dead.

The remains must be buried in order to construct the living—*as such.* Burial rites, funeral orations, and other such cultural rituals surrounding the mourning and handling of corpses serve a rhetorical function of articulating the conceptual border between the dead and the living: to hail the "not-dead," the survivors, *as the living,* and thereby to re/circumscribe the relations between the living (see, for example, Ochs; Loraux). As Derrida has it: "to pronounce dead" is "a performative that seeks to reassure but first of all to reassure itself by assuring itself, for nothing is less sure, that what one would like to see dead is indeed dead. It speaks in the name of life, it claims to know what that is" (*Specters* 59).[2]

Judith Butler, in her *Bodies That Matter: On the Discursive Limits of "Sex,"* articulates how "sexual difference" is engendered by a panicked, rhetorical reiteration. Coopting her explanation, I have substituted "the dead" for all

---

2. We begin, again, with a haunting, with a spectral footnote. In *The Invention of Athens: The Funeral Oration in the Classical City,* Nicole Loraux writes, in a footnote (which, regrettably, does not materialize in her 2006 abridged edition):

> After I had finished this book, P. Vidal-Naquet suggested to me that the dramatic date of the *Menexenus* (386) makes the dialogue between Aspasia and Socrates, both of whom had long been dead, a dialogue between ghosts. A dialogue of ghosts on the speech to the dead, denounced as an illusion because it carries the Athenians to the Islands of the Blessed: the parodic intention becomes multiplied to infinity! This certainly throws some light on the celebrated "anachronism" that has so puzzled critics. (466n303, qtd. in Rosenstock 331)

This cryptic suggestion evokes for us the possibility of rereading the *Menexenus* as hauntological historiography. In addition to dialoguing (with) ghosts, we have a haunted temporality, and we have a haunted address. Let us proceed with this paranormal investigation, then, to see where we might arrive.

If, as Loraux, has demonstrated, the funeral oration in ancient Greece served a

instances of "sexual difference" or "sex" that appeared in her original prose to demonstrate how "the dead" is, likewise, materialized by a panicked, rhetorical reiteration:

> Consider first that ["the dead"] is often invoked as an issue of material differences. ["The dead,"] however, is never simply a function of material differences which are not in some way both marked and formed by discursive practices. Further, to claim that ["the dead"] are indissociable from discursive demarcations is not the same as claiming that discourse causes [death; although clearly it can]. The category of ["the dead"] is, from the start, normative; it is what Foucault has called a "regulatory ideal." In this sense, then, ["the dead"] not only functions as a norm, but is part of a regulatory practice that produces the [living] bodies it governs, that is, whose regulatory force is made clear as a kind of productive power, the power to produce—demarcate, circulate, differentiate—the bodies it controls. Thus, ["the dead"] is a regulatory ideal whose materialization is compelled, and this materialization takes place (or fails to take place) through certain highly regulated practices. In other words, ["the dead"] is an ideal construct which is forcibly materialized through time. It is not a simple fact or static condition of a body, but a process whereby regulatory norms materialize ["the dead"] and achieve this materialization through a forcible reiteration of those norms. That this reiteration is necessary is a sign that materialization is never quite complete, that bodies never quite comply with the norms by which their materialization is impelled. (1–2)

To repeat: "That this reiteration [of what is "the dead"] is necessary is a sign that materialization of ["the living"] is never quite complete." "The living"

---

historiographical purpose: to invent Athens by historicizing it, then—indeed—Plato's rendition of Aspasia's funeral oration demonstrates a further historiographical purpose: to invent a future Athens by historicizing it anachronistically. This spectral temporality (a writing of the future from the past/a writing of the past from the future) is accomplished through spectral address—Socrates appears in the future (as the *arrivant*) by returning from the past (as the *revenant*). Bruce Rosenstock's "Socrates as Revenant" addresses this address, the *Menexenus*, by noting the variety of ways in which the "dialogue" complicates any understanding of who is speaking and to whom one is speaking. Of course, to begin, we have the address of Socrates haunted by Plato, who channels a dialogue between the dead, to the dead, and for the dead. In the oration, as Rosenstock points out, Socrates "adopts the rhetorical trope of prosopopeia, speaking in the voice of the dead, first to their sons, then to their parents. . . . No other extant Funeral Oration employs prosopopeia this way" (336). He continues to argue that this rhetorical gesture seeks "to persuade the audience

is never quite materialized *as such,* despite all of our burial rites—cultural and discursive (which amount to the same thing), because of the uncanny fear and disavowed knowledge that "the dead" can and will rematerialize: that there is no crypt that can properly contain/refrain the dead, and they walk amongst us—indeed, *in us,* as the living (un)dead.

What I will have suggested is that when a scholar risks the challenge of the dead's rematerialization, and thereby risks the instability of the conceptual border—the "sharp distinction" between the living and the dead—and when a scholar resists a historiographical practice that aims to bury the dead, eulogize the dead, memorialize the dead *in order to* "lay to rest" the dead, then we effected, haunted historians would thereby conjure the "restless" dead to "address" them, to remember them only insofar as we (re)member them. Let the dead bury the dead, which is—of course—as impossible as the possibility of the living burying the dead.

Risking this challenge of the dead's rematerialization is, of course, an uncomfortable enterprise. The rematerialized undead do not want us to feel comfortable in our living skins. That is why the hair goes up at the back of our neck when we encounter them. A haunted historiography is *uncomfortable* precisely in its uncanniness. We will not feel at home in a hauntological history, and, unlike Odysseus, we will not hail the inhabitants of the underworld, ply them with sacrificial blood, for the purpose of *finding our way home.* On the contrary, our encounters with the (un)dead will leave us, too, restless: uneasy, uncertain, unhomely. And in that restless moment, we experience the event, the ethical moment of radical otherness, which—we will have experienced—is with/in us.

This provocation/invocation to the ghost is a historiographical overture that does not protect itself from the uncanny, from that which is unknowable

---

that the dead are somehow present among them, guiding them toward the future" (338), and "in this rhetorical context all 'natural' perceptions of what is past or present or future are challenged" (339), as are the same of what is alive and what is dead. Indeed, Rosenstock claims, "the ghostly Socrates is revealed to be more alive than the living, who, in truth, inhabit a realm of shades" (339).

This is, to be sure, a case of a historiography that invents the "not-yet" of Athens; however, despite the haunted address and haunted temporality of the "dialogue," is this a case of a hauntological historiography? I say not, not-yet—as the ghostly apparition, apparently channeled by Plato, is a case of using the dead, once again, for the purposes of the living. Plato resurrects Socrates, animating a corpse, in another use of prosopopeia, but not to hear what the dead might say, but rather to use Socrates, once again, to condemn the Athenian people, who fall prey to the orators' abilities to bewitch (γοητεύουσιν), who can—in the funeral orations—"hypnotize men's souls . . . by confusing life and death, past and present" (235a 2; Loraux 268, qtd. in Rosenstock).

as such. "When historical scholarship," Peggy Kamuf writes, limits itself "to what it is possible to know," it forecloses the "possibility of other histories, in all their plurality, and even the possibility of other pluralities" (229). "The fundamentally apotropaic gesture of scholarship," she continues, "is put in place as a protection against the *trope* of plurality, against the *more than one* but also the *other than one*" (229). And yet I would press this further, to suggest that this "apotropaic gesture," which turns from the ghost, protects us not only from the "*trope* of plurality" but also from the plurality of *tropes.* That is, our impossible hauntological scholarship aims not (only) to conjure a plurality of histories (or petit narratives) but also to forestall any satisfaction that thinking the "*impossibility as also possibility*" of plurality (229), which relieves us of our ethical obligation to think the *possibility* (of plural histories) *as also impossibility.* That is, that there always remains an excess in any historiographical account, and hence any "knowledge" of any historical moment, any narrativization of such, denies the event its uncanniness.

"Knowledge" is precisely what renders the impossible possible. When the radical singularity of an event is encountered, the desire to endow that event with "meaning" elides its radical singularity precisely by subjecting it to categorical norms that cannot—by definition—include the radical singularity of the event. As Nietzsche long ago explained: there is no singular "leaf." To speak of "the leaf" is to speak of the *concept* of "the leaf," which means—by necessity—that the infinite variety and innumerable apparitions of "leaves" are reduced to the conceptual understanding of "the leaf," *as such.* To make "the leaf," *as such,* iterable is to forget the radical, distinguishing differences in order to make it an object of knowledge ("On Truth and Lying" 249). What a hauntological practice of historiography must wrestle with is the epistemological certainty presented by "the leaf," or more to our (non)point, "the dead."

Derrida criticizes the so-called historian of death, who "knows, thinks he knows, or grants to himself the unquestioned knowledge of what death is, of what being-dead means" (*Aporias* 25). Of course—as with all knowledge/ power systems, this knowledge passes itself off as common knowledge, as self-explanatory: "everybody knows what one is talking about when one names death" (25). This "knowledge" allows the historian of death to claim for "himself all the criteriology that will allow him to identify, recognize, select, or delimit the objects of his inquiry" (25). We're reminded of Nietzsche, once again: "If I define the mammal and then after examining a camel declare, 'See, a mammal,' a truth is brought to light, but it is of limited value. I mean, it is anthropomorphic through and through and contains not a single point that would be 'true in itself,' real, and universally valid, apart from man" ("On Truth and Lying" 251).

The same epistemological motor motivates traditional (or even revisionary) historiography. The historian knows, thinks he knows, or grants to himself the unquestioned knowledge of what has "happened." This is the "comfort" of a historian, a "certainty" of knowledge, produced by the very categorical criteria that allows one to recognize the "past," *as such*, as an object of knowledge. The radical singularity of the event must be elided in order to compose a historical account of the event—and so a truth is brought forth, but—again—it is of "limited value," in that it tells us what we already know, what we can already know, what is possible to know.

A hauntological historiography, on the contrary, "would entail a certain affirmation of intellectual or psychical uncertainty, a certain 'lack of orientation' (to recall a term used by Jentsch)" (Royle 56–57). Freud's essay "The Uncanny" uncannily enacts this "lack of orientation"; his "history" of (the term) "the uncanny" continuously undoes itself. It sets up a dichotomy of "heimlich" and "unheimlich," only to have the pair con/fused, only to illustrate a certain disorientation. Nicholas Royle characterizes Freud's essayistic foray into the uncanny as bordering on the comedic, as Freud attempts to

> draw up an inventory, an exhaustive list of what is uncanny. It is as if he thinks, or is willing to pretend that we might think, that the uncanny can be collaged, classified, taxonomized. But one uncanny thing keeps leading on to another. Every attempt to isolate and analyse a specific case of the uncanny seems to generate an at least minor epidemic. (13)

"Freud's essay demonstrates," Royle continues, "that the uncanny is destined"

> to elude mastery, it is what cannot be pinned down or controlled. The uncanny is never simply a question of a statement, description or definition, but always engages a performative dimension, a maddening supplement, something unpredictable and *additionally strange* happening in and to what is being stated, described or defined. (15–16)

"The maddening supplement" can never be contained, never be accounted for; hence, even an infinite plurality of histories will never be "enough." The remains will never have been remaindered.

Hauntological Temporality

Burying the dead, as an ontological move to reify the dead as the dead (and the living as the living), effects not only humanity and culture, but also (linear) historicity: through "closure," we constitute a past; through "perpetuation," we constitute a future; and through both, we constitute a more present (to ourselves) present (see Runia 325). History as burying the dead, as ontologizing remains, sees to it—finally—that what is *past* is *past.* However, a "hauntological" reading of history notes the uncanny *ambivalence* of "closure" and "perpetuation"—the irresolution of paradox, just as paranormal hauntings remind us that all bodies do not stay buried, that the repressed will return, and that the past is made manifest by virtue of the present and the future (for example, the compulsion to repeat).

"Haunting is historical, to be sure," Derrida writes, "but it is not *dated,* it is never docilely given a date in the chain of presents, day after day, according to the instituted order of a calendar" (*Specters* 3). He continues:

> What is the time and what is the history of a specter? Is there a present of the specter? Are its comings and goings ordered according to the linear succession of a before and an after, between a present-past, a present-present, and present-future, between a "real time" and a "deferred time"? If there is something like spectrality, there are reasons to doubt this reassuring order of presents and, especially, the border between the present, the actual or present reality of the present, and everything that can be opposed to it: absence, non-presence. . . . There is first of all the doubtful contemporaneity of the present to itself. Before knowing whether one can differentiate between the specter of the past and the specter of the future, of the past present and the future present, one must perhaps ask oneself whether the spectrality effect does not consist in undoing this opposition, or even this dialectic, between actual, effective presence and its other. (*Specters* 48)

Hauntology's implication for history: it reveals the concept of linear time as an ontological category of historical understanding. In its (non)place we experience haunted temporality: "A spectral moment, a moment that no longer belongs to time, if one understands by this word the linking of modalized presents (past present, actual present: 'now,' future present)" (*Specters* xix; see also Bevernage). A haunted historiography, then, works with/in spectral temporality and without presenting a linear linking of so many "modalized presents" to "historicize" "the past." Indeed, haunted temporality renders the borders between the "present" and the "past" aporetic, and—instead—calls to a time of the "not yet," as a "future to come or as death . . . it is not yet" (*Aporias* 14).

The "past" is already a phantasm, conjured from the future. As an "effect" of the "present," which is an "effect of an effect," the "past" is, therefore, only ever known insofar as it has been historicized after the fact, aprés coup, and hence comes from the future. So, in this sense, a haunted historiographical practice is writing the future—not the "past," as such, yet not simply "the future," as a temporal tense in linear succession of the past and the present. This is a future—like the *revenant*, which is "summoned," but is "the very thing that will never present itself in the form of full presence," the very thing that will *never arrive* as such, and yet—this "not yet" future is to be summoned, just as the *arrivant* is to be summoned, as "an alterity that cannot be anticipated," as the "event that cannot be awaited as such, or recognized in advance therefore, to the event as the foreigner itself, to her or to him for whom one must leave an empty place, always, in memory of the hope—and this is the very place of spectrality" (Derrida, *Specters* 81, 82). Indeed, Derrida suggests, this "not yet," but a hospitably (without reserve) awaited future is the "condition of the event and thus of history" (82). It is "the impossible itself, and that this *condition of possibility* of the event is also its *condition of impossibility*" (82).

Haunted temporality, then, summons a historiographical practice that lives on border lines—not only the border of the living and the dead as the "undead," but also the border of the past and the present as the "not-yet future." The ghost, as *arrivant*, according to Derrida, is "whatever, whoever, in arriving does not cross a threshold separating two identifiable places, the proper and the foreign" but "affects the very experience of the threshold" (*Aporias* 33). Writing *at the threshold* with these uncrossable thresholds— possible yet impossible, impossible yet possible—is to write histories as a hauntological practice. At this threshold, this uncanny temporal space, we experience the event (the arrival of the ghost) as *both* a first time—a wholly other, radically singular event—*and* as iterable, as the ghost *will return,* "again and again" (*Specters* 10). The *arrivant* is always already a *revenant*, and one can portend neither its arrival nor its return as anything other than the im/possible event at the threshold with/in spectral temporality—where the future, but also the past, is "not yet."

A hauntological historiography, haunted by a spectral temporality, attends to the radical singularity of the event, which linear history elides by subjecting it to a narrative—with beginning, middle, and end—or to a paradigm, or to a case study, or to a representative anecdote, saddling all events with signification and meaning, subjecting them to the tidy explanatory world of causes and effects, which presume and necessitate a buried past and a predictable future.

Embracing the uncertainty of haunted temporality is to accept the "absolute risk" that a just historiography would necessitate. This uncertainty amounts to foregoing any "subjective certainty" or "good conscience" about one's historiographical work. To not accept this risk is to write histories that are "protect[ed]" by the "assurances" of "knowledge," or "by the certainty of being right, or of being on the side of science, of consciousness or of reason," and it is—therefore—"to transform" the spectral event, the uncanny encounter, into narratives that elide the remains, that ask the remains to remain, where they are—buried, so that the eulogic narrative may serve to reconstitute the "living," and to justify the existence of the discipline of rhetoric—*as such* (Derrida, *Aporias* 19).

Hauntological Address

As we noted above, the hauntologist experiences a "radical uncertainty" in regards to historical temporality but also in regards to "who is speaking and to whom is one speaking when one" writes histories of rhetoric (Royle 56–57). This radical uncertainty caused by an encounter with the uncanny engenders a disorientation where one might be said to have dissolved, as such, and indeed the threshold of self and other seems sur/passed.[3]

In his essay "The Uncanny," Freud notes that his study of the uncanny "might indeed have begun" with "*es spukt*"—a German phrase resistant to easy translation, uncomfortably rendered, variably, as "it haunts" or "it spooks." And, this is where we—in his stead—will have begun our address on the address: A hauntological address addresses an indeterminable ghost. The subject position of the haunting is unidentifiable: "it" spooks, "it" haunts. To speak to ghosts, then, is to speak to the "it spooks." And therefore, without a proper address, one may never be certain that

---

3. We begin, yet, again, with another haunting, another footnote. In *Negation, Subjectivity, and the History of Rhetoric,* Victor J. Vitanza writes that his work, including the aforementioned text—perhaps "especially," is a conversation with the/a dead, specifically the ghost of Jim Berlin. As such, Vitanza ponders his rhetorical conundrum: "How does someone argue with an other who was so much alive but who is now (the) dead?" (343n3). This is what has been haunting, heavily, this entire essay: the *mourning* of the dead other. As Alessia Ricciardi notes in *The Ends of Mourning,* as Jean Laplanche wrote: "there is certainly no mourning without the question, what would he say, what would he have said, without the regret or remorse of not being able to hold a sufficient dialogue" (208). Although a full discussion of mourning is beyond the scope of this brief essay, we will nod—briefly—to Derrida's dissatisfaction with psychoanalytic treatments of mourning (and/or melancholia) as potentially pathological. Without rehearsing the distinction between incorporation and introjection, we will—alongside Derrida—prefer modes of mourning the dead and addressing the dead that provide a space for the (dead) other to remain other—in his/her radical singularity, irreducible to our self (with the caveat that the dead "is no more"—"in himself, by himself, of himself," but with the further caveat that "*we* are never *ourselves*," in ourselves, by ourselves, of ourselves [Derrida, *Memoires for Paul de Man* 28]). Derrida—via de Man—writes:

it has reached its destination—or an/other. For both the so-called addressor and the so-called addressee: "it" spooks, "it" haunts empties out
both positions.

This reformulation—or rather deformulation—of the "rhetorical situation" or "communication triangle" challenges the foundational presumption
of our discipline that a "rhetorical stance" begins with a rhetor (be he virtuous or not) speaking (be it well or not). In his "Three Countertheses: Or, A
Critical In(ter)vention into Composition Theories and Pedagogies," Victor
J. Vitanza explores Jean-François Lyotard's analyses of a variety of language
games; and, although "for us, a language is first and foremost someone
talking," Lyotard writes, "there are language games in which the important
thing is to listen" (qtd. in Vitanza, "Three" 153; cf. Ratcliffe). A hauntological
historiographical practice would be one such language game, insofar as "one
speaks [writes] only inasmuch as one listens; that is, one speaks [writes] as
a listener, and not as an author" (qtd. in Vitanza, "Three" 153). That is, as
Vitanza explains, this "language game," which Lyotard calls the "pagan
game," is a "counterrhetoric" to "homological-totalitarian, philosophical-
political thinking [. . . that] favors a rhetoric of the speaking subject," that
relies on the "exclusive categories of either addressor or addressee" (Vitanza,
"Three" 152–53; 152). This "counterrhetoric," this pagan listening, therefore,
is *not* reducible to a addressor/addressee relationship in which the positions of either are clearly delineated. The "it spooks" of the ghost renders
indistinct *as such* either an addressor or an addressee. The previously posed

> The possibility of the impossible commands here the whole rhetoric of
> mourning. . . . Upon the death of the other we are given to memory, and
> thus to interiorization, since the other, outside us, is now nothing. And with
> the dark light of this nothing, we learn that the other resists the closure of
> our interiorizing memory. With the nothing of this irrevocable absence,
> the other appears *as* other, and as other for us, upon his death or at least
> in the anticipated possibility of death, since death constitutes and makes
> manifest the limits of a *me* or an *us* who are obliged to harbor something
> that is greater and other than them. . . . And the figure of this bereaved
> memory becomes a sort of (possible and impossible) metonymy, where the
> part stands for the whole and for *more than* the whole that it exceeds. . . . It
> speaks the other and makes the other speak, but it does so in order to let
> the other speak, for the other will have spoken first. It has no choice but to
> let the other speak, since it cannot make the other speak without the other
> having *already* spoken, without this *trace* of speech which comes from the
> other and which directs us to writing as much as to rhetoric. (34; 37–38)

In this way, mourning *is always already a rhetorical—and haunted*—relation
between the living, the dead, the living dead, and, therefore, the very "structure of
mourning is that of an ongoing conversation with the dead" (Kirby 467).

questions—who is speaking and to whom is one speaking when conversing with the ghost—are mis-stated. I'll, therefore, repose as: Who is listening and to whom is one listening when conversing with the ghost? And the "answer" is: "it spooks." There is *no one at home* in *either* the addressor or the addressee position. The "it spooks" "occupies places belonging finally neither to us nor to it" (Derrida, *Specters* 216–17). There is, finally, just "it spooks" and *just* listening.

How to address the "it spooks"? There are no codifiable set of *technai*—despite a long history claiming the contrary. The ancient Greeks, much to Plato's dismay, "were adopting new techniques for communicating with" the dead, "particularly for compelling them to serve the living" (Johnston 102). Sarah Iles Johnston, in *Restless Dead: Encounters between the Living and the Dead in Ancient Greece*, informs us that goêtes were professional ghost communicators, and Plato, in his dialogue *The Sophist*, characterizes the Sophists as goêtes, having the power to "bring to light 'verbal ghosts' . . . with their words" (103). We shouldn't be surprised, I suppose, to have returned to the Sophists—or, that is, we should be surprised eternally by the return of the (repressed) Sophists. As Jane Sutton has argued, a traditional historiography of rhetoric assumes the so-called "death of the sophists," but it is a "hyperbolic" death, just as the claims to their "exTermination" are, likewise, greatly exaggerated, as Vitanza notes. Just as the Sophists never remain buried, "a ghost never dies, it remains always to come [*l'arrivant*] and to come-back [*le revenant*]" (Derrida, *Specters* 123).

Hauntological historiography, which addresses the ghost as an addressee, is not reducible to "automatic writing" or psychography where the historiographer is (merely) a medium, as in a séance, (merely) channeling the words of the ghost, and vomiting up so much ectoplasm in the process. Such a language game would be akin to Lyotard's description of the "Moses game," transcribing so many commandments on tablets of stone, obligated to listen to authority, situating the ghost in the author function (Vitanza, "Three" 152). What remains excluded in such a transaction is the so-called "third man," as characterized by Michel Serres, as the "prosopopoeia of noise," as "the *demon*" (qtd. in Vitanza, "Three" 155), which is the demon of "it spooks" that expropriates the subject position. Hauntological historiography, which addresses the ghost as an addressee, is not reducible to "ghost writing," as it is said of speech writers who lend their words to the author/ity of another, as Aspasia was accused of doing in Plato's *Menexenus*.

To write as if a listener is to listen precisely to that which is excluded, to that which our modes of understanding have excluded, to that which—therefore—lies at the threshold of our understanding. And there, at that (non)place, at that border or threshold, the uncanny manifests itself in a continuous "unsettling (of itself)" (Royle 5).

A haunted historiography would, likewise, unsettle itself, continuously. That is, not only would it unsettle "history," or "the rhetorical tradition," but it would also unsettle its own uncanniness. Of Freud's 1919 essay, translated as "The Uncanny," Royle writes:

> There is, in short, something strange about the qualities of Freud's text: sometimes a passage or a single sentence can appear to open up entirely new worlds of thought. At other times it can seem strangely incoherent, curiously repetitive and inconclusive. We may feel, on occasion, that we are "familiar" with Freud's text, but then something new and unexpected will shift into focus. . . . The uncanny [including the text of the same name] thus consists in what Shoshana Felman has referred to as a "reading effect," continually open to being re-read but re-read always strangely differently. (7–8)

As well as a "writing effect," continually open to being rewritten but rewritten always strangely differently.

Avital Ronell conjures this "writing effect" as "haunted writing" in *Dictations* and presents it as an "ethics of haunting." Reminding us of the etymological link between "ethos" and "haunt," Ronell extrapolates: "The relation to a past that, never behind us, is hounding and calling up to us, on good days friendly and populated, implicates nothing less than an ethics" (Preface 154; see also Jarratt and Reynolds). For Ronell, this haunting amounts to a "visit, which is to say: a relation has been opened to another text which manifests itself without presence yet with infinite nearness. Henceforth, one [is] . . . taking dictation from a text of the Other" (Preface 154). Diane Davis reads Ronell, here, as arguing that "any true conversation involves a kind of haunting; and writing, which amounts to a conversation with the departed (dead or alive), is necessarily an experience of hauntedness" (*UberReader* xxvii), and it behooves one to respond ethically, "with boundless generosity," by refusing to make the other familiar to the I (xxvii).

Hence, historiography as hauntology accepts the ghost's conversational overtures as an ethical gesture, as opening a space for an address as a "passive movement of an apprehension, of an apprehensive movement ready to welcome" (Derrida, *Specters* 216), a simultaneous moment of welcome, but also of apprehension, for one can never foretell, predict the arrival of the *revenant*.

10

WRITING FUTURE RHETORIC

G. L. Ercolini and Pat J. Gehrke

In the preface to *Elements of the Philosophy of Right*, G. W. F. Hegel wrote that "when philosophy paints its grey in grey, a shape of life has grown old, and it cannot be rejuvenated, but only recognized, by the grey in grey of philosophy; the Owl of Minerva begins its flight only with the onset of dusk" (23). Minerva, for whom the owl was both symbol and companion, was the Roman goddess of wisdom, contemplation, technical arts, and defensive warfare. She sprang into the world from the head of Jupiter fully grown and fully armored, without need of a past of her own. This was Hegel's archetype for history and a fitting figure for the desire to know the future: at the twilight of history's articulation, privileged by being at the cusp or the dawning of a radically new moment or an apocalyptic shift, coming into the present fully formed and armored by the articulation of history's reason. For Hegel, only at twilight is wisdom possible—the twilight of one's life or the twilight of a particular moment in history, when all is grey on grey. A pattern or reason in history is only sensible to those witnessing the end of its articulation. Yet what a strange figure for history is Minerva's owl; imbued with powers to discern what others cannot in the twilight, the owl's task to survey remains one of diligence and repetition, always to be done (or to have been done), folding wisdom upon wisdom in a future that is figured as a present-progressive.

It was Michel Foucault, perhaps more than any other thinker, who struggled with Minerva's owl and the potency of Hegelian history. Foucault's critique of history made optimism for deeper wisdom in the twilight difficult, but he also amplified the necessity of attending to both our pasts and futures. For Foucault, patterns of history are formed, articulated, re-formed, and re-articulated ad infinitum in a process that calls into question the unity of history and, hence, the unity of self and metaphysics implicit in theories of history grounded in either nature or reason. Foucault's revolutionizing of history, as Paul Veyne called it, recasts Minerva's owl into a new role: one that surveys not the past but the present in its own twilight. Foucault, in meditating upon the work of Gilles Deleuze, transforms the owl of Minerva into a recursive flight of infinite vigilance, writing the interstice:

> What ceaselessly reactivates it, what causes the endless rebirth of the aporia of being and nonbeing, is the humble classroom interrogation, the student's fictive dialogue: "This is red; that is not red. At this moment, it is light outside. No, now it is dark." In the twilight of an October sky, Minerva's bird flies close to the ground: "Write it down, write it down," it croaks, "tomorrow morning, it will no longer be dark." ("Theatricum" 185)

Between Hegelian and Foucauldian history lie not only how we remember and inscribe the past, or solely how we understand our moment in the present, but more importantly, what we can imagine in our tomorrows yet-to-come. Orienting oneself towards the future is the political question at stake in attitudes toward history. When we speak of the future, we often relate it to a present and past, or perhaps more properly a continuum of simple past into present-progressive: a has-been that is-coming. We talk of a future as an articulation of a movement of the present that has reached a culmination of our past. We utter a prediction in the echo of Hegel's voice.

Today, as we stand in the dawning of a new millennium, we are surrounded by predictions of every sort: technological, social, political, and even academic. Authors conjure futures that depict the political, ecological, and technological present-progressives as futures in articulation. Scholars in the humanities, and particularly in rhetoric, have not often engaged in such substantive predictions, but every now and again a moment arises—the anniversary of an association, the fiftieth issue of a journal, or the onset of a marked calendar change—that brings even the wisest to summon the future. These predictive moments sometimes forecast what is to come and other times prescribe a "better" future. In either case, such predictions often obviate and forestall the potentialities of the future while at the same time occlude the possibility of writing the future as a transgressive act of self-experimentation. In rare cases, however, writing the future can also offer a mutagenic space that alters our consciousness of the present and past, a fictive future (as if there could there be any other type) that fissures our present-progressive: a *ficture*.

Predictions: Or into the Future, Darkly

When reflecting on past predictions (whether forecasts of scientists or premonitions of psychics), we often chuckle at their apparent naïveté. Predictions made by mid-twentieth-century academics may strike today's reader as similarly humorous. In all fairness, we should remember that such predictions were usually made in the midst of some jubilee or centennial and at the request of an association officer or journal editor. Acceptance of such a task demonstrates at least a gracious willingness to participate in the epideictic moment. A symposium on the twenty-fifth anniversary of the Pennsylvania Communication Association, published in the November 1965 issue of *Today's Speech* (now *Communication Quarterly*), offers a particularly imaginative and quite singular example. This silver anniversary symposium took the form of a hypothetical future epideictic occasion: the fiftieth anniversary of the Pennsylvania Speech Association to be held in the then-future of 1989. The document's singularity rests in how the predictions were framed. Under the title "The Year is 1989," the writers adopted a position twenty-five years into the future and wrote as if describing the then-present and the changes they had seen over those coming twenty-five years. The three short essays and editor's commentary, although written in the present tense, take the future anterior orientation of a hypothetical 1989.

In the symposium, William S. Tacey describes how we each drive a hovercraft with electronic controls, wear a "Dick Tracy combination TV transmitter-receiver" on the wrist, and have an instant translating device (24). In this fictive 1989, while English departments have entirely disintegrated, rhetoric is restored to its rightful place in the world due to expansion of business and democracy, making several years of rhetorical education mandatory. Theodore Clevenger Jr. cheered the future-present discovery of rhetorical universals, "properties of discourse which appear to be common to all languages and cultures," enabled by advanced language instruction and the attendant disappearance of language barriers, where anyone can "learn practically any language in a few weeks" (12). Of course, regardless of the smartphone, video-conferencing, the anxieties of humanities professors, or the claims of universalists in philosophical anthropology, our wrists lack video, English departments live on, rhetorical education struggles, we treat universals as dubious, and learning Chinese remains difficult.

Despite whether these predictions were playful imaginings or earnest forecasts, their specific form reveals a presumed progression of the present into the future. A common forecast made in Tacey and Clevenger's time, oft-repeated today, foresees the extinction of the print book. In 1965, Clevenger speculated that by 1989 all research would be published only on magnetic tape (13). The digitization of texts and the continuation of magnetic tape as preferred media led Harry L. Weinberg to speculate that by 1989 we would "no longer have books in our libraries" (28). Tacey thought that media would make the very act of writing largely obsolete, replaced by computer-mediated face-to-face communication (25). Of course, the proliferation of electronic mail, forums, blogs, and chat rooms have made the written text even more common (regardless of the rise of YouTube and video blogging), while optical and solid-state devices are increasingly phasing out magnetic storage. Likewise, shifts in production of knowledge and proliferation of media exponentially expanded the amount of information produced. Clevenger's assumption that huge amounts of information would be stored by central computers and then broadcast to users sounds suspiciously like internet research databases, until one understands that by "huge amounts of data" Clevenger meant one million bits, and today we store dozens of billions of bytes of information in the space of a fingernail.

Weinberg in the same symposium was somewhat correct to predict that computers would solve "the problem of acquiring, with minimal effort, adequate content" for rhetorical critics (27). He could not know that with the proliferation of information systems and full-text databases, the expectations for what constitutes "adequate content" would also increase. Likewise, his prediction, like almost all the predictions surrounding the rise of electronic organization and storage of information, did not take into account the disparity between the types of information that would be instantly accessible. A host of unpredictable social, economic, and political events had to come together in a particular way in order to privilege access to daily newspapers, popular magazines, social networks, and "lolcats" over books and academic journals. Unexpected changes in society and technology have radically altered the future from what these communication scholars predicted but at the same time have been folded into a narrative of progress that today gives rise to new predictions.

In addition to this symposium in *Today's Speech*, one can find other scholars of rhetoric in the twentieth century who were tempted to more conventional forms of prediction. For example, Rupert L. Cortright asserted in 1949 that "quality will always be more important than quantity" (151), which is still a part of our discussions about contemporary hiring and promotion. Jerry Hendrix claimed in 1970 that the rhetorician of the future "won't feel a necessity to relate his [or her] criticism to rhetorical theory at all," a point for heated argument between rhetoric scholars even today (104). Whether or not we still rely upon materials published before 1950, as Clevenger predicted (11), or the bounds of our field continue to disappear, as Hendrix expected (102), the accuracy and value of these predictions are inextricable from ongoing political and normative debates about what counts as good scholarship in the field of rhetoric.

Attitudes towards the Future

Up to this point, we have focused predominantly upon the inaccuracy of prediction. However, we should acknowledge that our interest in these claims does not primarily concern their accuracy. Rather, their accuracy only tangentially relates to the fundamental operation of forecasting and prediction: a reliance upon certain historical assumptions and their disciplining forces. Some "predictions," such as William Work's claim that the trend toward narrow specialization will continue "unless the pendulum swings back away from specialization," are so noncommittal as to be little more than assertions of noncontradiction (21). More definite forecasts and predictions, however, commonly ground themselves in the same fundamental principles that support traditional historical studies.

The predictive move places the present in a series of moments that map out an articulation. In Hegelian terms, prediction looks back not to see what is possible but to find the articulation of reason in the movement of history. As Réal Robert Fillion put it, "the point Hegel makes . . . is that we cannot *bring* sense to history, we can only *discern* it" (81). This "cunning reason" of history is precisely what Foucault worked most of his life to complicate. Foucault contended that to take oneself as the "object of a complex and difficult elaboration" of history, rather than seeing oneself as a point "in the flux of passing moments," limited the possibilities for freedom and self-transformation ("What Is Enlightenment?" 311). The search for such a reason or articulation, he wrote, constitutes part of why traditional historians focus on long periods of time, hoping to find "the stable, almost indestructible systems of checks and balances, the irreversible processes, . . . the great silent, motionless bases" that lie "beneath the shifts and changes in political events" (*Archaeology* 3). Prediction is predicated upon such knowledge of these currents or trajectories, which traditional histories articulate. Prediction follows the Hegelian model of seeking in the past an unfolding reason that extends toward the future.

Predictive studies largely rely either upon historical-transcendental or empirical-psychological interpretations. Philosophical predictions such as Hegel's coming World-Spirit or literal readings of Immanuel Kant's prediction of the end of war and rise of global governance are grounded in what Foucault calls the historical transcendental: "the opening of an inexhaustible horizon, a plan which would move backward in time in relation to every event, and which would maintain throughout history the constantly unwinding plan of unending unity" ("History" 34). As Fillion's explication of Hegel has well argued, these may come in many forms and, in the case of Kant and Hegel, depend to varying degrees on an underlying principle of nature or reason.

Scientific predictions that dominate contemporary politics are grounded in empirical-psychological interpretations. Yet these predictions rely upon the same foundations as their historical counterparts: "detecting the hidden meanings which were lying silent and dormant, . . . following the thread or destiny of these meanings, describing the traditions and the influences, fixing the moment of awakening" (Foucault, "History" 34). Countless hours and dollars are spent in the business of discerning this code to history within contexts of politics and economics, even though time and again we find that what is predictable and what is important are rarely the same. Indeed, predictive models of economics based on rational agents and normal distributions have recently become embattled due not only to global economic crises, but also to challenges to their core assumptions (cf. Bogle; Gehrke, "Crisis"; Taleb).

Cortright's explanation of his predictions in communication studies testifies to the naturalized Hegelian attitude toward history: "in today already walks tomorrow" (150). Similarly, John Deethardt's call for more predictive studies by communication scholars exemplifies the forms of study challenged by Foucault. Deethardt said that with futurized communication studies "we gain a knowledge of trajectory and ends, which . . . helps us set policy or make ready for disaster" (280). Both Cortright and Deethardt typify how prediction relies upon a projection of current themes into the future. By its very form, prediction takes what is known and experienced and carries it forward, such as the assumption in the 1960s that magnetic tape would continue to be the preferred method of data storage. In prediction, the future is an extension of the present-progressive.

A belief in unchanging elements of reason or humanity may also support this extension of the present. Foucault noted that the historian's history "finds support outside of time and pretends to base its judgments on an apocalyptic objectivity" only because of a belief in "eternal truth, the immortality of the soul, and the nature of consciousness as always identical to itself" ("Nietzsche," *Language* 152). Similarly, the possibility of prediction depends upon stable or constant elements that serve as the guiding principles by which the predictor organizes the other variables. This may be a logic that governs history, a view of humans as rational decision-makers, or a belief in a substratum that brings the universe into coherence. In any case, the contingent elements that predictors presume as stable are functions of events that have come together at a particular moment in history and can just as easily slip from the scene, crumbling the predictor's present foundation.

This dependence upon firmament belies the predictor's "heroizing" of the present. Prediction reflects upon the past to lay out trends, trajectories, and logics that lead the *now* present to the threshold of the *new* future: a future that might finally yield to us what we have toiled for so long to achieve, a future that might promise the culmination of our collective efforts as a species (as humans or as scholars). The religious prophet must emphasize the importance of this particular moment in the divine plan. The humanist prophet must likewise emphasize the importance of this particular moment in human development. As Foucault points out, the modern subject cannot be satisfied with a vision of the present as fleeting or a perpetual movement without overarching purpose or logic ("What Is Enlightenment?" 310). To be part of the world at this moment is not enough, but instead every subject is made a hero of history, a grand contributor to the forward movement and progression of humanity (even if only by her or his own folly).

Cortright's fantasy of speech becoming the "overwhelmingly transcendent" discipline before the end of the millennium (155) and Clevenger's belief that by now we would have discovered "true rhetorical universals" (12) both manifest the need to envision oneself as standing at a critical moment in history, a unique point in the articulation of the future. Rhetoric sometimes gives itself an especially heroic purpose, picturing the work it does as training citizens of the world to lead us into a better future, usually one in alignment with certain liberal democratic ideals (cf. Gehrke, *Ethics*). Cortright compared training in oral rhetoric to "the life guard who plunges in to save a drowning person. And in a world where freedom is drowning, men and women who command speech are needed" (155). Such a statement not only betrays our hubris but also testifies to the vision of rhetorical pedagogy and scholarship as a critical element in the realization of our "ideal" future.

Foucault characterized these forms of historical and predictive analyses as "intangible, sacred, and all-encompassing" (*Remarks* 129). In contrast, the practice of genealogy, the close and diligent reading of historical texts, when done without imposing a faith in metaphysics, reveals that behind things lies "not a timeless and essential secret, but the secret that they have no essence or that their essence was fabricated in a piecemeal fashion from alien forms" (Foucault, "Nietzsche," *Language* 142). By eschewing both transcendental-historical assumptions and the strategy of empirical-psychological interpretation, Foucault sought to engage in a critical or "effective" history—a genealogy. Heeding Friedrich Nietzsche's admonition, Foucault analyzed the object of study as an event or occurrence without the assumption of its relationship to an origin, a trend, or a trajectory ("On the Ways" 283). From these methods, rather than describing the unity of history or a predictive trajectory, he described "for each discursive practice, its rules of accumulation, exclusion, reactivation, its own forms of derivation, and its specific modes of connexion over various successions" (*Archaeology* 220). An event thus multiplies and disperses through historical study rather than remaining unified or collected. History makes myriad and tangled paths to a present that has infinite possible futures, just as convoluted and accidental.

This genealogical method neither traces an ancestry that might resemble the evolution of a species nor maps out the destiny of a people. Rather, it identifies "the accidents, the minute deviations—or, conversely, the complete reversals—the errors, the false appraisals, and the faulty connections that gave birth to those things that continue to exist and have value for us; it is to discover that truth or being do not lie at the root of what we know and what we are, but the exteriority of accidents" (Foucault, "Nietzsche," *Language* 146). If Foucault identifies connections between events, practices, discursive formations, or an episteme, such a succession of heterogeneities, as Veyne put it, "does not trace a vector we can call progress" (167). Rather, heterogeneities and their successions testify to the fact that reason, desire, and consciousness fail to operate as "the driving force behind the kaleidoscope" (Veyne 167). There is, quite simply, no hidden engine to history.

However, this does not mean that the genealogist can simply write history any which way and cavalierly toss about predictions. Quite to the contrary, what differentiates genealogy from traditional historical studies is its refusal to presume a *telos*, an *esse*, or an *arche* that would hypostatize historical events. Foucault made clear that genealogy "cannot be the product of large and well-meaning errors" ("Nietzsche," *Language* 140). Rather, it is "gray, meticulous, and patiently documentary. It operates on a field of entangled and confused parchments, on documents that have been scratched over and recopied many times" (139). It properly requires "patience and a knowledge of details and it depends on a vast accumulation of source material" (140). Such a study of history can be neither arbitrary nor trivial. Quite to the contrary, if it is to be effective in rising like Bellerophon to combat the chimera of Hegelianism, historical study must take up the reins offered by Minerva and treat the past with a perpetual vigilance, mobilizing history as a demonstration of the anarchic.

Genealogy mobilizes history to intervene into our present and possible futures by putting at risk our assumptions about the naturalness or necessity of what we are, do, think, and know. In this way, the study of history is the study of the self and a process of self-transformation—a mutation. In seeking out the dispersed and heterogeneous events of history, one opens the possibility of reactualizing them, not as repetition, but as application and transformation (Foucault, "Critical" 45). Genealogy thus deploys history as a tool in the Nietzschean dictum to experiment with one's self, to make of oneself a work of art, and to live dangerously.

Prediction and forecasting obviate such transformation and mutation in the extension of the present-progressive. Prediction and forecasting operate as domestications of a great unknown—forcing the infinite otherness of the future to conform to current parameters. In this way, predicting and forecasting can be understood as technologies of discipline that deploy history as authority and evidence. The forecaster or predictor inscribes a norm from the past and the present-progressive onto an as-yet unformed future. Such normalization is the central technique of discipline: "creating or specifying a general norm in terms of which individual uniqueness can be recognized, characterized, and then standardized" (P. O'Malley 189). To weave all of human life and action into an articulation of reason or nature not only thus disciplines the past and present but also domesticates the future as a yet-unrealized but already written articulation.

In her study of the ideology of the future in political rhetoric, Patricia L. Dunmire notes two kinds of representations of the future: deontic, "the modality of 'ought' and 'should'" that expresses "obligation, conviction, and permission," and epistemic, "the modality of 'will'" that expresses "knowledge, belief, and truth about the future" (484). The interplay between the deontic and the epistemic constructs a space where historical knowledges are mobilized as evidence for futures that give virtual presence to the stakes of competing ideologies and relations of power. By producing histories that are solid, that give meaning and substance to the present as an articulation of reason or nature, the future is domesticated to produce an epistemic dictate for a deontic controversy. We *should* take one action because if we do not, then this *will* happen. The deontic argument depends upon an epistemic claim of the future grounded upon a past, extended into a present-progressive, taken as at least coherent if not governed by an articulation of reason or nature.

Epistemic arguments over the past mobilized as grounds for deontic arguments function to colonize and domesticate the future. Sohail Inayatullah articulated the movement of such futures in the modern state:

> Planning and futures research then become innovative social inventions which, as with the behavioural sciences, can aid in the triumph of liberal democracy and capitalism, of individuality and rationality. Planning and futures as used in the West are destined to take their places among the social sciences, but at a higher level, for they have a value component (preferred future) and a praxis component (policy analysis), albeit a problem of no data and little theory. (121)

Prediction makes the future a property of present knowledge untangling the tangled mix of events and discourses, refusing the future its status as unknown. While historians, like Minerva at her loom competing with Arachne, weave the past into texts and interpretations that argue their point, futurists bring the future to the present as an object of knowledge by extending that past through the present-progressive. The job of predictors and forecasters remains, first and foremost, to "manage and domesticate time" (Inayatullah 121). In speaking of the events to come, the forecaster forestalls them, comforts against their surprise, and removes the uncertainty of what-is-not-yet with the security and stability of the what-is-coming. Thus as we predict the future, we write it as a past that is yet-to-come, treating history as an articulation that will and must follow a logic that we have "discerned."

Rhetoric scholars are often concerned with the future of the field, even if we are more often prescriptive than predictive. Roy D. Murphy wrote in 1964 that "the immediate future of speech education should be a matter of deep concern to us" (5). The September 2010 special issue of *College Composition and Communication, The Future of Rhetoric and Composition*, likewise repeats this common refrain. Yet, our predictions will always foretell a future that shares a great deal with the present because the elements of life left stable in our analyses overwhelm what we expect to change. As Inayatullah puts it, you cannot expect to do a study of the future of the nation-state using the nation-state as a prime category of analysis and not at the same time inscribe the continuation of nation-states as organizing principles into the future (135). Rhetoric scholars likewise inscribe vast aspects of their perceptions of the present into a future that is, as yet, undeterminable. How could we expect to do a study of the future of rhetoric using the author, the orator, the text, the university, or even rhetoric as a stable category of analysis and not commit the same error?

What is at stake in making such predictive claims—especially predictions grounded on scientific arguments or on progressive histories—is the possibility for thinking about the future as a site of mutation or upheaval. At the point that one engages in predictive future studies, the elements of analysis left constant become knowledges that constrain imagination and will. This inversion of the relationship between will and knowledge—where will becomes subordinate to particular knowledges—is the articulation of prediction and forecasting as a system of restraint. Such a system is intolerable if it "becomes intangible as a result of its being considered a moral or religious imperative, or a necessary consequence of medical science" (Foucault, "Sexual Choice" 149). We might likewise say that the scientific and historical justifications for prediction and forecasting have brought such activities to a status of naturalness and necessity. Further, forecasting and future studies generally have "left naturalized" the "theoretical assumptions about what is foreseeable, data assumptions about what is observable, and value assumptions about what is preferred, and, most importantly, the categories of theory, data, values, and their ordering" (Inayatullah 116). All of these uninterrogated assumptions led Inayatullah to conclude that future studies "simply reinscribes the present even while it 'predicts' the future" (115). One can witness precisely this extension in rhetoricians' obsession with whatever marks our current age or controversy when they make predictions or prescriptions.

Forecasting has the same effect upon the forecaster as traditional views of history have upon historians: "The objectivity of historians inverts the relationships between will and knowledge and it is, in the same stroke, a necessary belief in Providence, in final causes and teleology" (Foucault, "Nietzsche," *Language* 158). Thus, the historian finds no choice but to see a particular future as dictated by the past; an understanding of the purposes and capacities of reason is deigned to guide the future. For example, Deethardt writes that "we must develop practitioners of futuristic rhetoric to guide the movement of the whole colony. To such persons purpose is clear" (280). While one might cringe at the idea of a chosen few guiding the colony, what Foucault points out is that the guides themselves are already guided by what they take to be true. When will falls under the sway of particular knowledges, it becomes a machine of obedience that replicates itself and forestalls mutation. As James Darsey has argued, "The prophet cannot be held personally culpable for his message. . . . So long as the prophet serves as God's trumpet, his activity is not only justified but mandated" (17). Note that Deethardt does not say that practitioners of futuristic rhetoric can mold new purposes or risk the transformation of the future. Rather, he says that the "purpose is clear." It is present and visible, instantiated and extant outside of the knowing subject, already written if only we knew how to read it. Such scholars of the future have already surrendered their possibility for paradigmatic shift or the transformation of systems of knowledge. Rather, they engage in reproduction of the present under the sign of discovery.

The problem here lies not in accuracy or adequacy of data. Forecasting relies upon the fundamental principle that "more information about the future will lead to administrators making better decisions" (Inayatullah 117). Supplementing the hermeneutic problems with this position, Foucauldian genealogy aptly demonstrates quite the opposite: more information most often disturbs the unity and coherence of history. The past, the present, and the future can only be constructed as unified and coherent if one overwrites details and excises anomalies. Moves toward "better" prediction, more accurate forecasting, and more information "forget the structures, the regimes of truth that create our selves and order, that create our notions of what we call the future" (Inayatullah 134). In short, more information in forecasting is only the search for similitude within the bounds of the present-progressive.

The task of the historian or scholar as intellectual is neither prediction nor prescription: "the role of the intellectual today is not that of establishing laws or proposing solutions or prophesying, since by doing that one can only contribute to the functioning of a determinate situation of power that to my mind must be criticized" (Foucault, *Remarks* 157). If one desires to find what spaces might be available for action—what ways we might risk mutating our subjectivity rather than replicating the same instantiations of domination—then the task with which to concern ourselves is "determining problems, unleashing them, revealing them within the framework of such complexity as to shut the mouths of prophets and legislators: all those who speak *for* others and *above* others" (159). This is precisely why Foucault was not a strict historical determinist. His genealogical studies do not say "this is how things are, look how trapped you are. I say certain things only to the extent to which I see them as capable of permitting the transformation of reality" (174). The future, as much as the past, is a site of such possible transformation, once unmoored from Hegel's reason and Kant's nature.

Writing Future Otherwise

Other than prediction and forecasting, what ways might emerge for writing the future? Inayatullah proposes an alternative futures perspective, seeking a better and more complete view of multiple diverse possible futures (134). However, a multiple-scenario view of the future cannot engage the task of placing subjectivity at risk of mutation, if it merely branches traditional historical methods into lines of probabilities in the search for a future that is still written and knowable, even if probabilistic. As Inayatullah argued of traditional futures studies, multiple-scenario predictions hold a core concept or central element of the present as constant, given, or unexamined. As Lawrence Grossberg argues, the dominant alternative modernities "assume that all possible modernities are simply variations on the universal model of euro-modernity. Such theories of 'alternative modernities' constrain the ways we can imagine other realities, and hence, the ways we can analyze the present" (259). Multiplying futures while leaving a fundamental element unquestioned, be it the nation-state or euro-modernity, only proliferates scenarios constrained within a presumed necessity or naturalness, not only leaving that element intact but insulating it from being imagined otherwise.

It may be impossible to write the future from a position adapted from Foucault, given that the future's dusty tomes and archival materials (essential to genealogy) are yet to be written. Inspired by Victor J. Vitanza's work on the future-anterior in *Writing Histories of Rhetoric*, we offer a rumination on another way to write transgressive futures, mobilizing the possibility of the as-yet-unimagined to call into question the normal and necessary. We might also consider the dystopian present-progressive as an articulation of a not-to-be that puts the "now" into sharper relief. At heart, such writings of the future cannot inscribe a new order or trajectory but instead destabilize our thoughts of the future and lead us to what R. J. Goldstein identified as one of the central themes of Foucault's work: "our constant task must be to keep changing our minds" (14). Neither prediction nor prescription, it writes of a not-now as neither the yet-to-come nor the desired outcome.

In the process of writing the future, we can cut across limits that govern contemporary thought in order to demarcate those limits. Transgression crosses a limit, "an action which involves the limit, that narrow zone of a line where it displays the flash of its passage, but perhaps also its entire trajectory, even its origin; it is likely that transgression has its entire space in the line it crosses" (Foucault, Preface 33–34). Transgression neither breaks nor destroys a boundary. It neither removes the limit nor does its penetration leave a hole for others to follow. Rather, "the limit and transgression depend on each other for whatever density of being they possess: a limit could not exist if it were absolutely uncrossable and, reciprocally, transgression would be pointless if it merely crossed a limit composed of illusions and shadows" (34). The value of transgression lies in the flash at its crossing where it demarcates the limit and shows the limitedness of the limit. For example, discussions of the civil rights of not-yet-real computer-based artificial intelligences, androids, manufactured lives, or human consciousnesses separated from the body play with the bounds and operations of subjectivity and with conceptions of rights submerged in discourses that took them as given, necessary, and natural. From the classic science fiction of Isaac Asimov (*I, Robot*), Ray Bradbury ("There Will Come Soft Rains"), and Philip Dick (almost his entire corpus) to the Japanese manga of Masamune Shirow (*Ghost in the Shell*) and anime of Ryūtarō Nakamura ("Serial Experiments Lain"), we are frequently given examples of the imagination of futures that interrupt the present-progressive.

Likewise, writing the future may be put to the purposes of the dissociation of identity: the unsettling of stable bases for subjectivity. In writing the future we might be able to discover some of what Foucault sought in genealogy: "distinct and multiple elements, unable to be mastered by the power of synthesis" ("Nietzsche," *Language* 161). In this way we can emulate some of the purposes of genealogy, such as the "introduction of discontinuity into our very being, dividing our emotions, and dramatizing our instincts" (154). Consider how discussions of genetic engineering lead to imaginations of genetic modification mid-life. The mastery of the genome provides for imagining the manipulation of the genetic structure of people at any point in their lives. Imagine a world in which after a week in the hospital one's entire genetic makeup could be reworked and the body adjusted. Alternatively, the science fiction commonplace of human teleportation can have profound implications for the uniqueness of each individual subject. One common explanation for how teleportation works (*The Fly, Star Trek*) is that the teleporter converts the matter of the person in the device into energy, beams the energy to a location, and then uses that energy to build a duplicate of the matter of the being or thing being teleported at the destination site, often relying upon some kind of quantum entanglement or unexplained technology to get any ephemera from the person's source version to the destination version. In fact, many *Star Trek* episodes have presented scenarios in which multiple copies are generated ("The Enemy Within") or left behind ("Second Chances") by aberrant teleporters (transporters), as well as teleporters restoring persons to a previous saved version ("Lonely among Us"). In the episode "Daedalus," the inventor of the transporter device even discusses the protests and debates over the metaphysical implications of teleportation for our understanding of human nature and consciousness.

These science fiction imaginations provide futures that are at once fictive and yet offer the possibility of a fissure with our present, with our relationships to time and to ourselves. They pose the possibility of becoming *fictures*: picturing fictional futures that fissure. Such rupturing is given greater functionality when it can be made not only in the imaginative, but in the deployment of the simple past and present-progressive given wild aberration. Larry Niven's *Ringworld* trilogy posits an artificial world constructed as a ring around a star, wholly manufactured and populated by human and nonhuman species. What made *Ringworld* especially fascinating was its completeness and accuracy. Such worlds are theoretically possible by our current understandings of science and one can today find a Ringworld simulation on NASA's Ames Research Center space settlement website. When stabilizing the simulated ring posed problems, physicist Freeman Dyson proposed an alternative spherical structure, which the simulators found more reliable. What has often made science fiction especially powerful as social commentary and philosophical vehicle is that it speaks with and through what we believe to know about science, about ourselves, about our past and our present-progressive, while at the same time inserting (or pointing out) the fissures in those knowledges. In short, much of future-oriented science fiction is *ficture*, and a few fans of the genre already have taken to calling works of fictional futures by that term. Ficture interrupts the present-progressive via an imagination of a future anterior, reflecting where we have been and where we are. Is this not an apt description of George Orwell's *1984*? Its original *New York Times* reviewer called it "crushingly immediate" and expressed worry that its salience to its own time was so strong that it might become lost to literary history in the decades ahead (Schorer). It was a book of a future not predicted or prescribed, but offered as an interruption of the narratives and prophecies of Orwell's own age.

Ficture aims to write the future with an eye toward self-experimentation. Such writing cannot be oriented toward the what-will-be but seeks to risk the subject of knowledge and engage in experimentation upon the self—two of the goals of genealogy. Writing ficture no longer inverts the relationship between will and knowledge but is an act of will-to-knowledge. Ficture practices self-constitution through what Foucault called self-writing (Foucault, "Self-Writing" 214). In some ways, like the journals and notebooks (*hupomnēmata*) that one might keep and consult, the writing of fictures is not focused on the future, but instead is a writing of the present moment. They both, though in different ways, "capture the already-said, to collect what one has managed to hear or read, and for a purpose that is nothing less than the shaping of the self" (211). However, ficture is far more a kind of correspondence that moves out from the self to a future anterior, and then returns to the self, potentially as advice, admonishment, or exhortation, or perhaps also as an opening or invitation to further imagination. That one writes such ficture for or to others, as Seneca did in his letters, involves one in a kind of training that is also a self-training at the same time. As a revealing of oneself to others in the act of writing, the ficture as correspondence, even more than as *hupomnēmata*, is an act of constituting oneself "through the appropriation, the unification, and the subjectivation of a fragmentary and selected already-said" (221). As such, ficture can be part of the means to outfit oneself with truths, to work on oneself, and thus to take up what Foucault articulated as a foundation for ethics, politics, and freedom: a care of the self (Foucault, "Ethics" 285, 299).

Among those rhetoric scholars in that 1965 symposium on the future of 1989, Weinberg stands out as thinking and writing in the direction of ficture. In his essay, rising concerns over methods of behavior modification and the moralism frequently found in 1960s rhetorical scholarship are combined to produce a somewhat comical dystopia. He describes the invention of the "Daser" technique or "De-ethication Amplification by Stimulated Emission of Resistance" (28). The Daser removes any question of ethics from rhetoric so that we need only be concerned with the effectiveness or functionality. Of course, like much science fiction, something goes wrong. In this case, a student stumbles upon a line from Plato's *Apology*, "The unexamined life is not worth living," which interrupts the Daser and spurs ethical inquiry, and then all hell breaks loose. Weinberg, while neither an Orwell nor a Bradbury, nonetheless tries his hand at ficture and makes an attempt to constitute an imaginative future injected into the simple past and present-progressive as a mutagenic agent, effecting the disruption and transformation of the what-might-be.

His example, if unpolished, demonstrates like so many fictures that eschewing prediction and forecasting is not to slink away from activism. Rather, it is an articulation of Foucault's warning that everything is danger-ous—which is not exactly the same thing as bad: "If everything is danger-ous, then we always have something to do" ("On the Genealogy" 256). The dystopias, utopias, and fantasies found in ficture do not leave us stultified. Quite to the contrary, "there are a thousand things to do, to invent, to forge, on the part of those who, recognizing the relations of power in which they're implicated, have decided to resist or escape them" (Foucault, *Remarks* 174). This resistance does not promise a better future that we might prescribe or prophesy, and this escape does not yield a prior state or a natural freedom. Quite to the contrary, it resists by problematizing and risking mutation while escaping only by moving from subjection to subjection with an in-determinacy that refuses to permit any one subjection the density required to reach a state of domination. If we can write the future in this way, as we submit ficture might, we engage in the task of the intellectual, which Fou-cault articulates profoundly:

> The job of an intellectual does not consist in molding the political will of others. It is a matter of performing analyses in his or her own fields, of interrogating anew the evidence and the postulates, of shaking up habits, ways of acting and thinking, of dispelling commonplace beliefs, of taking a new measure of rules and institutions. . . . It is a matter of participating in the formation of a political will, where [the intellectual] is called to perform a role as citizen. (*Remarks* 11–12)

Rather than molding the political will of others through prediction or pre-scription, ficture offers a different mode of intervention into the present. Thinking ficture has broader implications and applications than being a new genre of writing in rhetorical studies—it offers a critical attitude, a mode, an orientation of encountering the figure of "future." Even if one does not write a ficture, adopting a fictural relationship to the future performs the task of the intellectual by preserving the future's capacity to open questions, problems, and concerns of the present.

Ficture, as that subgenre borrowed from science fiction, has appeared on occasion in communication and rhetorical studies as a form animating the imaginative space of the future anterior (for example, the Daser technique). However, one does not need to recite various battles about what counts as scholarship and the associated anxieties about professional advancement to highlight the practical and ethical limitations of cavalierly proposing and exhorting ficture as a genre of academic writing (although we encourage such experimental rhetorics). Nonetheless, we believe writing fictures could have a place in published forums, academic blogs, occasional pieces in professional publications, or on the occasion of an anniversary or perceived turning point. However, more importantly, ficture offers rhetoric a critical disposition or a modality of engaging the future. Ficture's possibility as a critical frame already resides in the work of rhetoric scholars who retreat from colonizing the future so as to open its potential as a site of experimentation.

In 2010, in "Research in Rhetoric: A Glance at our Recent Past, Present, and Potential Future," Raymie McKerrow made ten predictions about rhetorical scholarship that curiously neither predict nor prescribe (nor proscribe). Perhaps more accurately, they occupy the predictive form while evacuating it by positing the admitted groundlessness of the predictions, instead offering them as "indicators of rhetorical health." While neither explicitly ficture nor future-anterior, the predictions suggest the directions the field of rhetoric might have gone if it was to have thrived and remained healthy (continuing to challenge various problematics). In a different manner, in *Cultural Studies in the Future Tense*, Lawrence Grossberg continues his commitment to reworking conjuncturalism (complexification of context) as a critical approach for cultural studies. Examining how modernity has taken a very specific form (euro-modernity) that could have been otherwise, he takes one step towards opening up other ways of theorizing the problem and, hence, imagining other possibilities for the future. Cultural studies in the future tense largely involves intervening in the present (through the past) to open up the future. While neither McKerrow's nor Grossberg's writings are ficture, they do (in differing ways, to differing degrees) exhibit critical attitudes sympathetic and compatible with ficture.

A fictural orientation relates to the future as a site of experimentation and open possibility, rather than colonizing the future by making it an object of present knowledge. Such a disposition can not only be practiced in writing but can also shift our more general reading and thinking. By subordinating

criteria of accuracy and veracity, a fictural reading offers a comic corrective to the predictive mode's tragically static future. A fictural reading of
a literal prediction inverts its position from colonization of the future to a
dislocation of the present. History is one of the vital tools of such a disposition, be it in the writing of fictures or fictural reading. Historical study, as
the dispersion of genealogy and the accumulation of pasts, equips one to
make the future, as well as the past, a space in which we can shake up old
habits, dispel commonplace beliefs, and interrogate evidence and postulates.

After all, Minerva did not command Bellerophon to battle the chimera,
and she did not direct Perseus to kill Medusa, but to the first she lent a har-
ness and to the latter a shield. She did not weave the destiny of mortals like
the Parcae but did make tapestries of the past that told tales as warnings and
as inspiration. Such is what history can do; it can equip us with tools and
tales with which we can set out upon our challenges and expeditions and
make new paths and new futures that might defy the predictions and pre-
dilections of mortals and gods alike. History provides the raw materials for
deploying fictures that open the possibility of making new spaces for living.

11

A PHILOLOGY FOR A FUTURE ANTERIOR:
AN ESSAY-AS-SEMINAR

Victor J. Vitanza

For John Poulakos

I cannot imagine what would be the meaning of classical philology in our own age, if it is not to be unmodern—that is, to act
against the age and, by so doing, to have an effect on the age, and
let us hope, to the benefit of a future age.

—Friedrich Nietzsche, *Unmodern Observations*

We . . . say of some people that they are transparent to us. It is,
however, important as regards this observation that one human
being can be a complete enigma to another. We learn this when
we come into a strange country with entirely strange traditions;
and what is more, even given a mastery of the country's language. We do not *understand* the people. (And not because of not
knowing what they are saying to themselves.) We cannot find
our feet with them.

—Ludwig Wittgenstein, *Philosophical Investigations*

[T]he Greek word *opiso*, which means literally, "behind" or
"back," refers not to the past but to the future. The early Greek
imagination envisaged the past and the present as in front of
us—we can see them. The future, invisible, is behind us. Only
a few very wise men, can see what is behind them; some of
these men, like the blind prophet Tiresias, have been given this
privilege by the gods. The rest of us, though we have our eyes, are
walking blind, backward into the future.

—Bernard Knox, *Backing into the Future*

Introduction as Predispositions

When I was in secondary school with the good nuns, I collected words.
One was the word *philology*. But it was a roundabout way that I arrived at this word *philology*. It was an accidental detour, an inclination, from

all other words, that began with my collecting the word *Logos*. This *word of words*, as I have come to understand it, was introduced to me in a catechism class. Drawn in all caps on the blackboard! No one dared to erase the word.

As for *philo-logy*, I learned the connection between *philos* and *logos* as *the love of the word, the love of Logos*, or *the love of the word of God as The Word*.

Years later, however, I discovered the word *misology*. [1]

And *from* and *with* that strange word, I learned about the dis/connection between *misos* and *logos*. I learned that the word of words misfires. Henceforth, I eventually, and yet hesitantly, placed ~~LOGOS~~ under erasure.

My predisposition, ever since, has been to become-pagan, to become-Heraclitus, to stir and to listen to the coals, their firings and misfirings. I dis/engage in drifting here, d.rifting t.here. Oscillating. Se.arching. For the dis-ease in *logos* itself. I have attempted *to make* some things, intermittently and perpetually, with these misfirings. These specters that haunt *the history of rhetoric*. And the maternity of modernity. Hung up in utero.

My approach, in this attempt, is to write *an essay-as-seminar* on philology. [2] I would write such for *We historiographers* who would be *We philologists. Classicists*. In the facelessness of Modernity. As for myself, when it comes to philology, I am ignorant. I must become an autodidact, knowing, all along, that I will never know what I would *dream of knowing*. To *be* a philologist, after all, is impossible for me. I do not suffer from delusional fantasies of omniscience. One can only *become* a philologist. Perhaps at best an *amateur* philologist.

And yet, primarily, I am called to become *responsible*, not as some colleagues would have me be "responsible," but as I am called to increase *my ability to respond* to the other, as well as others. In *logos*. And I can best accomplish that end through *collaborations with logos* in its various (mannerist, baroque) ramifications, by following *traces* (or remainders) left by *logos*. Simply put, I find myself obliged to read-think-write countless traces.

My hybrid *essay-as-seminar* will have been, perpetually in notes taken. Assignments given. Test Drives that contest. [3] But in every way, aphoristically and contradictorily. And yet, coherently. As in a (lucid) dream logic of desires providing for "coherent contradictions." [4] And in all ways, misunderstood by way of an *ex-stasis* of misologies. *Ecstacies*. While these notes are addressed, reflexively to myself *in the future anterior* and to *logos*, these notes are also addressed to a *Society of the Friends of the Text*, transversally across *depart*ments.

My predisposition, therefore, is that the love of language, or *logos*, studied by philologists, so-called expert or amateur, is not a love that can be trusted.

Logos is not trustworthy enough to be our guide (*hegemoon*).[5] Any attempt at a fixed, disciplined relationship with (the) *logos* is always already ill-fated.[6] Hence, the hermeneutics of suspicion (Ricoeur)! And then abandonment (Vitanza)! And yet, again, the *assignments* given will call for *assignations* with *logos*. Or with what would prove to be a perverted love, a marriage of heaven and hell, a metamorphosis of philology into the *Science of Antiquity*. In the grand, Germanic name of *Altertumswissenschaft*. Alas Babylon. The eventual divorce and, then, dissipation were inevitable. Yes, my inclination is sub/versively to exploit this perversion. Beyond good and evil. For a general transvaluation (cf. Kofman).

My further approach is to query the *mise en abyme* (or the *Abgrund* **in** the *Grund*) of philology for *hetero*graphies of rhetorics by way of suggesting reexaminations of a varied series of philologies within the old philology and their rebirths as new philologies, and yet, at a third level, rebeginningly, by way of *a philology of the future anterior* as thought in notes, assignments, and test drives by Friedrich Nietzsche (1844–1900) and others.[7] (I will always attempt, stubbornly, to become *untimely*, or better put, *unmodern*!) But *Thoroughly Modern Millie* persists to play, even if off Broadway.

My primary considerations of philology, or in a different sense "classical studies," are as a *backdrop* for rethinking, rereading, and rewriting histories of rhetorics. My sense is that, after all of our efforts, "we" have yet to begin thinking, reading, and writing such histories. Nor have we yet returned to philology to think history-writing of classical rhetorics through modern rhetorics. We, for example, think in terms of time chronologically so as to correct the transgression of being anachronous, as if human thinking will ever avoid being-anachronous! Machine thinking, yes! But human thinking? Why bother! The irony here that I allude to is that colleagues would insist on using a scientific, modernist set of philological principles and lawful tools *to know* the past, the Greek past. But the issue is not about knowing what constitutes being-Greek, centuries ago or today, but about knowing what constitutes *human, all too human*-beings. Perpetually *posthumous* human-beings. And yet, I take great dis/comfort in Sophocles' *Antigone*:

πολλὰ τὰ δεινὰ κοὐδὲν ἀνθρώπου δεινότερον πέλει.
τοῦτο καὶ πολιοῦ πέραν πόντου χειμερίῳ νότῳ
χωρεῖ, περιβρυχίοισιν
περῶν ὑπ' οἴδμασιν.
θεῶν τε τὰν ὑπερτάταν, Γᾶν
ἄφθιτον, ἀκαμάταν, ἀποτρύεται
ἰλλομένων ἀρότρων ἔτος εἰς ἔτος
ἱππείῳ γένει πολεύων.   (332–75)

Sophocles reminds me that "we" *cannot find feet* with *others*. "Ours" are *swollen* (with excess) feet. There are more than enough translations[8] of this passage (above) to suit numerous desires and contexts, even the desire of detextualization. I associate this passage from Sophocles on the nature of human beings paradigmatically, here, with the birth and death of tragedy! Specifically, to Nietzsche's concerns.

The *task of history writing*—its ex-status—is always already *anachronous*. *We*, as a field of study, have not even begun to think philologically in *untimely* (that is, *unmodern*) ways.[9] In the future anterior. So let us *will* to have begun histories for the advancement of *living*.

Approach *the Seminar*, at y/our own pace. And detour from my suggestions—the clusters of readings—as you will, with a source here generating other sources on other paths to elsewhere. What I give you has been my own path of study. Inevitably, you will return here. Again, these suggested readings are offered not as *assignments* but as *assignations*. Give what I have modestly proposed here a chance. Give an impossible love of *logos* a chance.

§ Philology 1

Questions concerning the History of Philology, or Classical Scholarship:

Assignments: To *read* and yet to *study*. By secondary habit, I turn to the *Encyclopedia Britannica,* eleventh edition. Specifically, Peter Giles and William Dwight Whitney's article on "Philology" for a scholarly context. Mostly their approach is a placement of philology as a division of anthropology, while the rest is a discussion of philology as the science of linguistics and as a classification of language families. Their optimistic claim: "linguistic philology has been actually created . . . out of the crude observations and wild deductions of earlier times, as truly as chemistry out of alchemy, or geology out of diluvianism" (415). The central player is "the German scholar [Franz] Bopp, that founded the science of linguistic philology" (415). Try reading the ninth edition.

Additional primary-secondary works to restart with: Ulrich von Wilamowitz-Moellendorff's *History of Classical Scholarship*, as well as the Hugh Lloyd-Jones introduction.

Notes: As Lloyd-Jones points out, Wilamowitz-Moellendorff never mentions Nietzsche, but Lloyd-Jones introduces Nietzsche's contributions, preparing the way for a later discussion. One such is Lloyd-Jones's own "Nietzsche and the Study of the Ancient World."

The *crucial issue* for me, as I would make the issue for the field, is the clash of Wilamowitz-Moellendorff against Nietzsche. The timing in modernity

—which has never taken place—distinguishes, simply put, between *Wissenschaft* and *Weisheit*. Translated, *science* and *wisdom*. (See Geuss and Speirs, Introduction, *The Birth of Tragedy* xxviii; cf. Nietzsche, *Gay Science* x–xi. Also read Nietzsche's "The Struggle between Science and Wisdom" in *Philosophy and Truth*).

Lloyd-Jones, early in his introduction to Wilamowitz-Moellendorff's book, recommends both Sir John Edwin Sandys (1844–1922), *A History of Classical Scholarship*, and Rudolf Pfeiffer (1889–1979), *History of Classical Scholarship*. Sandys refers once and then, in a footnote, on page 333, to Nietzsche and Wilamowitz-Moellendorff, and his smear campaign. And Pfeiffer was no friend of Nietzsche.

There are, earlier and later, exceptional philologists in the West (antiquarians, compilers, classicists, and so on, such as Erich Auerbach, Walter Benjamin. Ernst Robert Curtius, E. R. Dodds, M. I. Finley, Eric Havelock, Wilhelm von Humboldt, Werner Jaeger, Arnaldo Momigliano, Walter Ong, Jacqueline de Romilly, Norman O. Brown, Leo Spitzer, Lorenzo Valla, Marcus Terentius Varro, Pierre Vidal-Nanquet, Jean-Pierre Vernant).

Most interesting, for me, however, is Joseph Justus Scaliger (1540–1609). His *Opus de emendatione temporum* (*On the correction of dates*) would be worthwhile to read. Anthony Grafton's two-volume work, *Joseph Scaliger: A Study in the History of Classical Scholarship*, especially the second volume, focuses on Scaliger's attempt to establish chronologies based on astronomical calendars. Be sure to study Grafton's earlier account on chronologies: "Joseph Scaliger and Historical Chronology." Here is evidenced Scaliger's mix of both Biblical and pagan sources as being required to cross-check chronologies in order to establish events with Hebrew and Greek sources. Grafton, thereafter, gives an account of *the decline of time frames* and yet some rather interesting twists and turns in multiple chrono-logics, namely, Scaliger's struggle to justify *before the creation* (that is, "proleptic time") and *after creation* ("historic time"). This struggle by Scaliger, as contradictory as both times are, will later manifest itself analogically in high modernity, through psychoanalysis, as Freud's "*Nachträglichkeit.*" Scaliger found it difficult to be a pagan-Christian. But Francis Bacon (1561–1626), as Timothy J. Reiss says (*Discourse* 198–225), found it difficult to be an adolescent, and, therefore, Bacon wrote *Temporis partus masculus* (*masculine birth of time*) (Bacon, "Masculine"). Chronos, not to be confused with Cronos, is a father to deal with.

We will discuss time and calculations, below. Philology, in attempting primarily to come to peace with father *time*, ignores the *event* (the disaster).

Test Drives: Read Moses Hadas (1900–1966), who in 1954 writes, in *Ancilla to Classical Reading*, that "[c]lassical philology in its broader sense . . . is not a subject but a complete curriculum" (120–21). What subjects (or disciplines) does Hadas include in that curriculum? What would you add to the list for today, 2012+? What have others added? Keep in mind, however, the more added, the more impossible the task of philology becomes.

If philology is not a *subject* but a *complete curriculum*, then, is philology a *discipline* or what? Read François Hartog's "The Double Fate of the Classics" and Sheldon Pollock's "Future Philology?" For a broader scope, spend some time with various other discussions in the special issue of *Critical Inquiry* on the status of disciplines (*The Fate of the Disciplines*). And yet, you must spend some quality time with Salvatore Settis's *The Future of the "Classical."*

§ Philology 2

The *crucial issue*: I insist that the histories of philology, mentioned above, should be studied along with the Nietzsche *and* Wilamowitz-Moellendorff event (*Ereignis*), as *propriative* or rather as appropriation, and yet, expropriation (*exstasis*).[10] This rift is *a moment of finitude*, the limit, that makes for modernity, which, given the *event*, never takes place. In chronological time.

Assignments: Study Nietzsche's "Philology of the Future" (or rather, *The Birth of Tragedy*, both the 1872 and 1886 editions with their prefaces) and Wilamowitz-Moellendorff's response, "Future Philology!"

On Nietzsche's *The Birth of Tragedy*, read Porter's *The Invention of Dionysus*. And James Whitman's "Nietzsche in the Magisterial Tradition of German Classical Philology." And Jason Winfree's "Before the Subject: Rereading *The Birth of Tragedy*." And Peter Sloterdijk's *Thinker on Stage* (15–32).

On Wilamowitz-Moellendorff's response, read Robert Norton's "Wilamowitz at War." And William Calder's "How Did Ulrich Von Wilamowitz-Moellendorff Read a Text?" Additionally, read Calder's "The Wilamowitz-Nietzsche Struggle," which continues answering the question of why Wilamowitz so "hated" Nietzsche and "attacked" him perpetually through life and unto death with remorse. (Is Wilamowitz's problem a case of *misology*, leading, as Plato would say, to *misanthropy*? See *Phaedo* 89d–90). And be sure to read Wilamowitz-Moellendorff's *My Recollections, 1848–1914*, especially 78, 150–52.

Study, then, Nietzsche's "Homer and Classical Philology," which is Nietzsche's inaugural address delivered at the University of Basel, May 28, 1869. This is the presentation that landed Nietzsche the position *Ordinarius* Professor of Classical Philology. And then read James I. Porter on Nietzsche's Homer in "Nietzsche, Homer, and the Classical Tradition."

Others on Homer: Continue by reading Giambattista Vico's (1668–1744) discussion of the search for Homer, in *The New Science* (301–28). For balance, read Samuel Butler's (1835–1902) *The Humour of Homer, and Other Essays*. And of course Butler's *The Authoress of the Odyssey*. And Christa Wolf's *Cassandra*. And then a book that contributes to some cohaggling: Victor Davis Hanson and John Heath's *Who Killed Homer?* Be sure to read the preface to the paperback edition. Then, a forum in the journal *Arion*: see individual exchanges, listed in the suggested readings below, by Willett, Martindale, Green, and then Hanson and Heath's rejoinder ("The Good, the Bad, and the Ugly").

Notes: Historically, philologists-classicists, drag each other around the walls of Troy more than once. For a generic set of examples, see C. Robert Philips's "Classical Scholarship against Its History." There is little dispute among most philologists about whether Wilamowitz-Moellendorff was correct in his assessment of Nietzsche's *Birth*. Yes, he was! And yet, Nietzsche obviously did not follow the dominant protocol. But why? There are a series of complicated answers to this question. There is the issue of Nietzsche dis/engaging in *cultural critique*, which allows for necessary self-reflexivity contributing to numerous recoils. From such a begged perspective, Wilamowitz-Moellendorff, however, was incorrect in other rather serious ways: His response to Nietzsche can be read as pathological and as creating a *differend* (Lyotard). The question begged is that *philology* (the science), as the youthful Wilamowitz-Moellendorff and others would practice it, should *be* the norm and, therefore, the basis for assessing an/other's work.

In a scholarly work, we today would still expect Nietzsche to establish a claim, with a literature review, and state why he is against the status of philology. While Nietzsche accomplishes this method in his work on Homer, he, in *The Birth of Tragedy*, radically shifts his tone, in a dramatic cultural shift in tone, by opening his discussion with two *images*, and then ironically turning the very "object" of study itself into a post-critical object. The two images (pictures) are *Apollonian* (as Johan Joachim Winckelmann dreamed of) and *Dionysian* (as Nietzsche had invented, or what he would take as the excluded remainders created by the Germanic fantasy and institutionalization of the Apollonian). (Cf. Porter, *Invention* 16–47, 131–42; Nietzsche, "The Dionysian Worldview.") For now, we need to understand that Nietzsche, much like a future anthropologist, is dis/engaging in a *cultural drift* away from the positivist field of philology, as well as the nationalistic aspirations of Germany.[11] Nietzsche attempts to make the field of philology *strange* so that it could be experienced as such, but it was not received as such. And yet, he wrote for the future, knowing all along that his contemporaries would not appreciate him in their own time.

The difference between Wilamowitz-Moellendorff and Nietzsche is the difference between the *will to Truth* (as Wilamowitz-Moellendorff would define it) and the *will to power, a revaluation of all values* (as Nietzsche developed the notion). From my perspective, Wilamowitz-Moellendorff and Nietzsche were speaking at cross-purposes. There is no point of *stasis* for them to agree to disagree. Nietzsche achieves *exstasis*, from which *eventually* to think and write. Given that Nietzsche is excommunicated from the academy, he writes ex-statically against academia, Germany, and Europe. And yes, Nietzsche critiques himself and engages in a turn (*Kehre*)—in the second edition of *The Birth of Tragedy*, moving from a subtitle of *"Out of the Spirit of Music"* (1872) to *"On Hellenism and Pessimism"* (1886)—thereby, further reestablishing his views of a future philology. But then again, it is Nietzsche's way to dis/engage, perpetually turning and re-beginning. The aphoristic style makes demands of the reader, which often "modern man" does not measure up to (see Nietzsche, *On the Genealogy*, preface, 8). We are still trying to learn how to read Nietzsche.

Lest we forget, Nietzsche's prior discussion of and presentation on Homer is his *opening* thought. In public. Originally, as Porter points out, the title was "On Homer's Personality" ("Nietzsche, Homer" 19; Porter, *Nietzsche* 4). In a primary way, the name "Homer" is a *McGuffin*. And yes, I've just committed the fallacy of anachronism! As Porter writes:

> Homer is the product of a particular kind of fascination. . . . Classical scholarship has itself mystified Homer and killed him in the process. . . . Homer was never, in fact, a stable entity from which a sure base of culture and learning could flow, and this was part of his attraction. . . . (In Greek, *homerizein*, "to Homerize," after all can mean "to lie.") (*Nietzsche* 9)

In an extra-moral sense! The signature "Homer" is a *mise en abyme*. Nietzsche, in his job presentation, asks: "The figure of Homer? *Was the person created out of a conception, or the conception out of a person?* This is the real 'Homeric question,' the central problem of the personality" (qtd. in Porter, *Nietzsche* 6; Nietzsche's emphasis). Hence, perhaps, Vico and Butler's responses! Of course, we cannot forget Friedrich A. Wolf and his *Prolegomena to Homer* (1795), which was exceptionally controversial in its day. (See Grafton, "Prolegomena" and Porter, *Nietzsche* 69–81.)

Again, the issue is not merely one person's text or an accumulation of texts under the name holder of "Homer"! Rather the issue is the fascination with *subjectivity* or an *entity* for any one or more stakeholders. In later works, Nietzsche writes: "But there is no such substratum; there is no 'being' behind the deed, its effect and what becomes of it; 'the doer' is invented as an after-thought,—the doing is everything" (*On the Genealogy* 1: 13; cf. Hamacher, "Degregation"). The doers? Homer? Socrates? Plato? Nietzsche? What this faith in grammar, or the subject-object paradigm, or *the thing in the world*, leads to is a general notion of a *false causality* (see *Beyond* #16–17, 21, 34; *Twilight* vols. 3 and 4; *Human* 1: 11). Nietzsche had no expectations that a modern reader would understand such a non-relationship. What he says remains both too early and too late.

The *event* (again, *Ereignis*) issues a distinction between *Wissenschaft* and *Weisheit*. Science and wisdom. But even then, these two words, in various usages, become interchangeable through equivocations with other substitutions. After all, Nietzsche and others were caught up in an Enlightenment *crisis of representations*, with the German words—*Vorstellung* (*vorstellen*), *Darstellung* (*darstellen*), *Anstellung*, and so on, becoming the most equivocal, depending on various thinkers with as many interests (see Reiss, *Discourse* 21–54; cf. Seyhan, *Representation* 136–62). Often the word *wisdom* becomes *image* or *art*. But Nietzsche begins with *science* and *art* early, in discussing philology at Basel ("Homer" 3). And yet, in this *presentation* on Homer, Nietzsche also makes fun of philologists and philology. Thereafter, he becomes increasingly direct in a *wisdom* or *art* (aesthetics, or making presence, pictures, images) that even today many *scholars* simply deflect.[12] Nietzsche spelled out in great detail precisely *what he would do* if offered the position at Basel.

(But again, really: Part of the crisis of representation, of course, is discovering ourselves in the position of having *to present the un-presentable*! *We cannot find our feet*, much less the grounding!)

What always makes Nietzsche difficult to read is not only his use of aphorisms but also his very aesthetic-ironic practice of writing. Porter best explains this style in terms of "philology as critique." Simply put, Porter reads Nietzsche as quasi-"subject" (as masked entity, author, skeptical philologist) taking on the very sensibility of the particular "object" itself under study. So as Porter argues, Nietzsche, in writing about Democritus of Abdera, "begins to emulate Democritean physiology itself" (*Nietzsche* 55). Thereby Nietzsche, the skeptical philologist, dis/engages in a critique of philology, by setting aside modernity's "subject-object" relations, in what Gregory Ulmer would call an instance of "post-critical object" thinking and writing. As a re-beginning, we can say, therefore, that Nietzsche takes a post-hermeneutical and post-critical ex-stance against Wilamowitz-Moellendorff's presumption. Nietzsche, posthumous man, lives (on) in the future anterior (cf. Waite).

Test Drives: Take "Truth and Lying in an Extra-Moral Sense" for a test *drive* (*Trieb*). The translator, David Parent, gives a "complete" translation of the first two sections, whereas earlier, Walter Kaufmann, in *The Portable Nietzsche*, translated only the first section. For yet another rendering, see Daniel Breazeale's translations of "On Truth and Lies in a Nonmoral Sense" (in Nietzsche, *Philosophy and Truth*). Breazeale includes Nietzsche's thoughts beyond the second selection with three additional numbered, very brief, sections, and several more extensive notes by Nietzsche. While the content is Nietzsche's, the numbering is not. As a developing philologist, how would you approach these three variants? (See Cerquiglini, *In Praise of the Variant*.)

§ Returns to Philology

In recent time, there have been a number of calls for *the return to philology*. Each call is quite different from the others. I select here only a few of many such calls.

Assignments: Study Paul de Man's "The Return to Philology." Republished in *The Resistance to Theory*. Read Albert Friedman's "Ontology Recapitulates Philology."

Study the forum "On Philology" in *Comparative Literature Studies*. Republished the same year in the book *On Philology*, edited by Jan Ziolkowski (a reprinted forum, "On Philology," originally published in *Comparative Literature Studies*).

Likewise, study the forum "The New Philology" in the special issue of *Speculum* (edited by Nichols). The focus is on medieval, manuscript culture.

And, then, study Edward Said's "The Return to Philology" (originally presented in 2000). The work along with other presentations is in *Humanism and Democratic Criticism*. For Said, read Andrew Rubin's "Techniques of Trouble" and Said's translation of Erich Auerbach's "Philology and *Weltliteratur*." Also, Ned Curthoys's "Edward Said's Unhoused Philological Humanism." Said was deeply influenced by both Auerbach and Leo Spitzer.

Notes as questions: What motivates these various calls for the return of philology? What is "new" in these calls? How does each call appropriate philology and for what interests?

Test Drives: Try yet another return to philology in Hans Ulrich Gumbrecht's *The Powers of Philology*. We will return to Gumbrecht's thinking in terms of *time* and *space* as well as future meditations on philology. And Hamacher's "From '95 Theses.'"

§ Being in Time

Initially I had Being *and* Time separate. But for Nietzsche, being and time are inextricably one. Also, Place/Space are one and the same in *Being* in *Time*. So I bundle the three or four together. Given that Nietzsche affirms different ways to think about being in time and place/space, I will suggest these ways in subcategories, though all are an assemblage or can be experienced as collages.

Assignments: *Rhythm and Meter*: Study Nietzsche's lecture notes: "Nietzsche: On the Theory of Quantitative Rhythm" and "Time-Atom Theory." Then, "On Rhythm." For commentary, read Porter, "Being on Time" in *Nietzsche* and in "Nietzsche's Atoms." Additionally Elaine Miller's "Harnessing Dionysos." And Manuel Dries's collection *Nietzsche on Time and History*. And especially see Henri Lefebvre's *Rhythmanalysis*, which is an extension of Nietzsche's work.

Space/Place/Time (physiology): Study Keimpe Algra's *Concepts of Space in Greek Thought*. Therein is the simple, yet forever complicating, triad of *topos, kenon, chôra*. *Kenon*, as the middle term, is the void. But for Nietzsche, physiology creates the conditions for the possibilities of the (experienced) time of the body in space/place. Nietzsche writes: "the right place is the body, demeanour, diet, physiology" (*Twilight*, #47). Most importantly read Eric Blondel's *Nietzsche: The Body and Culture*. Therein *philology* becomes *physiology* (136). For references to physiology, study Nietzsche on Heraclitus in *The Pre-Platonic Philosophers* (53–74). And Nietzsche's *Beyond Good and Evil* (#28) and "Why Am I So Clever" in *Ecce Homo* (#1–2). Read Page duBois, *Sowing the Body*. This topic of *pulse and metabolism* is dear to me, a project of my own, as I rework it through cinematic time.

Eternal Return (Redemption and Revenge): Read Nietzsche's "Of Redemption" in *Thus Spoke Zarathustra*, which focuses entirely on time, revenge, and then eventual voluntarism, leading to time as *eternal return*. And then turn to Richardson's "Nietzsche on Time and Becoming." The best two books on the Nietzsche's thinking on *the eternal return* and then on *the ancients* and the *anachrony of the time-fetishes* are, respectively, Pierre Klossowski's *Nietzsche and the Vicious Circle* and Ned Lukacher's *Time-Fetishes*. Therein lies *chronos, kairos, aion*, and *khôra/khôragus* as an "anachrony within being" (20–28). And study Lukacher's *Primal Scenes*.

Real (chronological) Time!: Go figure. Go calculate. Do what you have to do to calm your modernist anxiety. Start with Dershowitz and Reingold's *Calendrical Calculations*. But, in recalling the dictum not to confuse the *map* for the *territory* (place/space), I would add, we should not confuse the *mashed-up calendars* for *temporality*.

Psychoanalytic Time (conscious-unconscious, time-memory): Study Rainer Nägele's *Reading After Freud*. Study the entire book, especially the third section on Freud and Habermas and the last section on "*Nachträglichkeit* and *Berspätung* (belatedness)" (67–90, 169–201). Here is a presentation of the reverse of tic-toc, as toc [ ] tic, or as ~*too early* [event] *too late*~. Perhaps the closest that we get to a *writing of the event* is as exemplified in Gumbrecht's *In 1926: Living at the Edge of Time*. Gumbrecht's is no mere representation of technological-linear time (rational, scientific), but of simultaneous time. And read Luce Irigaray, *Marine Lover of Friedrich Nietzsche*.

Cinematic Time: Study Mary Ann Doane's *The Emergence of Cinematic Time*. (Doane's is indoubtedly the most important book any writer of history can read on the *shock* [Freud and Walter Benjamin] of the *mechanical representation of time*. See Doane 1–32.) Also, Zielinski's *Deep Time of the Media*. And so many others, including Henri Bergson (*Matter and Memory*; *Creative Evolution*) and Gilles Deleuze (*Cinema 2*).

Notes: While history writing for the most part is locked into chronological-linear time with a teleology directing it, *time* itself, as a concept and practice, has a motley history, and a problematic one, given that time, as we have come to live and experience it, from the early Greeks to the present, *can be out of joint*! Read Daniel Wilcox's *The Measure of Times Past*.

As a reading of Nietzsche's tragic grounding of history, Nägele, in *Echoes of Translation*, gives a close reading of the opening (cesarean) sections of *Birth*. There are echoes of Schiller's as well as others' thinking on the tragic grounding that is a unity [*Ur-Eine*] of *Grund* and *Abgrund*. Nägele writes: "In Nietzsche, the Dionysian and Apollonian become the figures of *Darstellung* or, more precisely, the figures of a specific thinking of *Darstellung* as the duplicity of a lost unity. . . . Nietzsche see[s] tragedy as the presentation of an original fissure [breach or event]" (82)—which points to *being out of joint*, being hopelessly *anachronistic*. And yet, joyfully *ecstatic*. (Cf. Nietzsche, "On the Uses and Disadvantages of History for Life" (1874) in *Untimely* [*Unmodern*] *Meditations*.) And John Poulakos, "Nietzsche and Histories of Rhetoric."

Being anachronistic: . . . . is being *thoroughly modern*. (See my *Negation* 140–43; cf. Ballif, *Seduction, Sophistry, and the Woman with the Rhetorical Figure* 33). And yet, being *thoroughly postmodern* is an attempt, given Jean-François Lyotard's reading, of dealing with the drama of event's trauma. Of dealing with the question concerning a dramaturgy of traumaturgy or vice versa. On its way to bearing witness to new idiomatic-hysteriographies/schizographies. Perhaps the best way productively to mis/understand this kind of un/thinking is to jump into *trauma* (and violence) *studies*. We "moderns"—all suffer from (massive) *shock*. From. A Primal Scene. Uncovering ourselves. In. Writing the Disaster. RE-Writing—historiography itself—has become the very scene of *Nachträglichkeit* and *Berspätung*.

View Chaplin's *Modern Times*. Make a film of Maurice Blanchot's *The Writing of the Disaster*. (Read Robert Toplin's "The Filmmaker as Historian"

and Hayden White's "Historiography and Historiophoty" in preparation
for making the film.)

Let's finally come to an understanding that *anachronisms are an error
in chronology*. Not *in time*. We must ask the ignored question of *What is
chronology an error in?* We must avoid begging the question, or creating
a *differend*, constructed by privileging chronology as *the time* that should
adjudicate all other times as false, in error. While chronology is the time
informing modernist historiography, "we" have never been modern![13] And
besides, time travel by philologists or anyone is perpetually subject to what
is called the *grandfather paradox*!

Test Drives: By ways of *perspectives by incongruities/anachronies* (Nietzsche, Kenneth Burke, Lyotard) take three works on *Empedocles* and read
them a/historically across each other: From *chronological* through *poetic*
to *deep time*. *Make* something of them together. But without criteria. With
What will have been done. I recommend Peter Kingsley's *Ancient Philosophy, Mystery, and Magic*; Robert Bringhurst's "The Philosophy of Poetry
and the Trashing of Doctor Empedokles" (in *Everywhere Being is Dancing*,
93–110); and Siegfried Zielinski's "Attraction and Repulsion: Empedocles"
in *Deep Time of the Media*. You might also want, first of all, to test drive J.
Ellis McTaggart's "The Unreality of Time."

§ A Philology of the Future/Anterior

Assignments: Study Nietzsche's "We Classicists" (translated by Arrowsmith)
and again as "We Philologists" (translated by Kennedy). Then, "Nietzsche
on Classics and Classicists" (parts 1–3) (by Nietzsche, translated by Arrowsmith). And Nietzsche's *Philosophy in the Tragic Age of the Greeks*.

Study Porter's *Nietzsche and the Philology of the Future*. And then, Bill
Readings's "Postmodern Figures of History: Anachronisms and the Imme-
morial," in *Introducing Lyotard* (58–62). Then, reread and study Pollock's
"Future Philology?" And Alan Rosenberg and Steven V. Hicks's "Nietzsche
and Untimeliness," Folks!

Notes: I, of course, am here reconfiguring the notion of a *future philology*, though not refiguring that much in terms of Nietzsche. The phrase
"future anterior" in relation to time (history) is referred to by many. The
phrase, for me, speaks of the past coming to us from the future. And let us
not forget Knox, who writes: "[T]he Greek word *opiso*, which means literally, 'behind' or 'back,' refers not to the past but to the future" (11). Clearly,
as I say, the future anterior is in Nietzsche's dramatic-aphoristic-thinking
practices; and in Heidegger, partially, as *ecstasis* of the future; and Lacan,
and Knox, et al. It can even be found in Aristotle, which is where Heidegger

appropriated many of his ideas. But each thinker is different. A history de/ based on *what will have been* is history that is in *anticipation*. I would keep, however, the notion of "future anterior" radically heterogeneous. Open to what will have taken place.

Your Notes: Write your own notes. T/Here . . . in the torn fabric of time /\/\ /\ /\ searching for a tare. . . . In the mix of . . . this scale . . .

Too early [ ] Too late .

Test Drives: Decide on your own test drives.

Wissenschaft / conscious [ ] unconscious / *Weisheit* .

In Perpetuity

This essay-as-seminar, I can only hope, as I dis/engage my own studies, will continue in multiple *registers* with multiple colleagues in a *Society of the Friends of Philologies and Histories, Writing the Event*.

Seminar Readings

Algra, Keimpe. *Concepts of Space in Greek Thought*.
Auerbach, Erich. "Philology and Weltliteratur."
Bacon, Francis. "The Masculine Birth of Time."
Ballif, Michelle. *Seduction, Sophistry, and the Woman with the Rhetorical Figure*.
Becker, A. L. *Beyond Translation*.
Blanchot, Maurice. *The Writing of the Disaster*.
Blondel, Eric. *Nietzsche: The Body and Culture*.
Bringhurst, Robert. *Everywhere Being Is Dancing*.
Butler, Samuel. The Authoress of the Odyssey, Where and When She Wrote, Who She Was, the Use She Made of the Iliad, and How the Poem Grew under Her Hands.
———. The Humour of Homer, and Other Essays.
Calder III, William Musgrave. "How Did Ulrich Von Wilamowitz-Moellendorff Read a Text?"
———. "The Wilamowitz-Nietzsche Struggle: New Documents and a Reappraisal."
Campbell, Karlyn Kohrs. "Agency: Promiscuous and Protean."
Cerquiglini, Bernard. *In Praise of the Variant*.
Curthoys, Ned. "Edward Said's Unhoused Philological Humanism."
de Man, Paul. "The Return to Philology."
Derrida, Jacques. "Structure, Sign, and Play in the Discourse of the Human Sciences."
Dershowitz, Nachum, and Edward M. Reingold. *Calendrical Calculations*.

Doane, Mary Ann. *The Emergence of Cinematic Time.*
Dries, Manuel, ed. *Nietzsche on Time and History.*
duBois, Page. *Sowing the Body.*
Enos, Richard Leo. "Rhetorical Archaeology."
———. "Notions, Presumptions, and Presuppositions in Hellenic Discourse."
Frank, Roberta. "The Unbearable Lightness of Being a Philologist."
Friedman, Albert. "Ontology Recapitulates Philology."
Giles, Peter, and William Dwight Whitney. "Philology."
Grafton, Anthony. "Joseph Scaliger and Historical Chronology."
———. *Joseph Scaliger: A Study in the History of Classical Scholarship.* Volume 1.
———. *Joseph Scaliger: A Study in the History of Classical Scholarship.* Volume 2.
———. "Prolegomena to Friedrich August Wolf."
Green, Peter. "Mandarins and Iconoclasts."
Gumbrecht, Hans Ulrich. *The Powers of Philology.*
———. *In 1926: Living at the Edge of Time.*
Hadas, Moses. *Ancilla to Classical Reading.*
Hamacher, Werner. "Degregation of the Will."
———. "From '95 Theses on Philology.'"
Hanson, Victor Davis, and John Heath. *Who Killed Homer?*
Hartog, François. "The Double Fate of the Classics."
Hoy, David Couzens. *The Time of Our Lives.*
Irigaray, Luce. *Marine Lover of Friedrich Nietzsche.*
Kingsley, Peter. *Ancient Philosophy, Mystery, and Magic.*
Knox, Bernard. *Backing into the Future.*
Kolfman, Sarah. "Baubô: Theological Perversion and Fetishism."
Kolb, David. *The Critique of Pure Modernity.*
Klossowski, Pierre. *Nietzsche and the Vicious Circle.*
Latour, Bruno. *We Have Never Been Modern.*
Lefebvre, Henri. *Rhythmanalysis.*
Lloyd-Jones, Hugh. *Blood for the Ghosts.*
———. "Nietzsche and the Study of the Ancient World."
Lukacher, Ned. *Primal Scenes: Literature, Philosophy, Psychoanalysis.*
———. *Time-Fetishes.*
McTaggart, J. Ellis. "The Unreality of Time."
Martindale, Charles. "Did He Die, or Was He Pushed?"
Michalski, Mark. "Hermeneutic Phenomenology as Philology."
Miller, Elaine P. "Harnessing Dionysos: Nietzsche on Rhythm, Time, and Restraint."
Most, Glenn. "Heidegger's Greeks."
Nägele, Rainer. *Reading After Freud.*
———. *Theater, Theory, Speculation.*
Nietzsche, Friedrich. *Beyond Good and Evil.*
———. *The Birth of Tragedy and Other Writings.*
———. *Daybreak.*
———. "Description of Ancient Rhetoric."
———. "The Dionysian Worldview."
———. "Homer and Classical Philology."
———. "Homer's Contest."

———. *Human, All Too Human.*
———. "Nietzsche on Classics and Classicists Author(s)."
———. "Nietzsche on Classics and Classicists (Part II)."
———. "Nietzsche on Classics and Classicists (Part III)."
———. "Nietzsche: On the Theory of Quantitative Rhythm."
———. "Nietzsche: Notes for 'We Philologists.'"
———. *On the Genealogy of Morals and Ecce Homo.*
———. "On Rhythm."
———. "On Truth and Lying in an Extra-Moral Sense."
———. *Philosophy and Truth.*
———. *Philosophy in the Tragic Age of the Greeks.*
———. *The Pre-Platonic Philosophers.*
———. "Time-Atom Theory: Nachgelassene Fragmente, Early 1873."
———. *Twilight of the Idols/The Anti-Christ.*
———. *Unmodern Observations.*
———. *Untimely Meditations.*
———. "We Classicists."
———. "We Philologists."
Norton, Robert E. "Wilamowitz at War."
Paden, William D., ed. *The Future of the Middle Ages: Medieval Literature in the 1990s.*
Pfeiffer, Rudolf. *History of Classical Scholarship.*
Phillips, C. Robert. "Classical Scholarship against Its History."
Porter, James I. "Nietzsche's Atoms."
———. "Nietzsche, Homer, and the Classical Tradition."
———. *The Invention of Dionysus.*
———. *Nietzsche and the Philology of the Future.*
Pollock, Sheldon. "Future Philology?"
Poulakos, John. "Nietzsche and Histories of Rhetorics."
———. "Testing and Contesting Classical Rhetorics."
Readings, Bill. *Introducing Lyotard: Art and Politics.*
Reiss, Timothy J. *The Discourse of Modernism.*
Richards, E. G. *Mapping Time: The Calendar and Its History.*
Richardson, John. "Nietzsche on Time and Becoming."
Rosenberg, Alan, and Steven V. Hicks. "Nietzsche and Untimeliness."
Rubin, Andrew N. "Techniques of Trouble: Edward Said and the Dialectics of Cultural Philology."
Said, Edward W. *Humanism and Democratic Criticism.*
Sandys, Sir John Edwin. *A History of Classical Scholarship.*
Settis, Salvatore. *The Future of the Classical.*
Seyhan, Azade. *Representation and Its Discontents.*
Sloterdijk, Peter. *Thinker on Stage.*
Toplin, Robert Brent. "The Filmmaker as Historian."
Toulmin, Stephen. *Cosmopolis.*
Vattimo, Gianni. *The End of Modernity.*
Vico, Giambattista. *The New Science of Giambattista Vico.*
Vitanza, Victor J. "The Hermeneutics of Abandonment."
———. *Negation, Subjectivity, and the History of Rhetoric.*

——, ed. *Writing Histories of Rhetoric.*

Ulmer, Gregory. "The Object of Post-Criticism."

Waite, Geoff. *Nietzsche's Corps/e.*

Wardropper, Bruce W. "An Apology for Philology."

White, Hayden V. "Historiography and Historiophoty."

Whitman, James. "Nietzsche in the Magisterial Tradition of German Classical Philology."

Wilcox, Donald J. *The Measure of Times Past.*

Wilamowitz-Moellendorff, Ulrich von. "Future Philology!"

——. *History of Classical Scholarship.*

——. *My Recollections, 1848–1914.*

Willett, Steven J. "Can Classicists 'Think Like Greeks'?"

Winfree, Jason Kemp. "Before the Subject: Rereading *The Birth of Tragedy.*"

Wittgenstein, Ludwig. *Philosophical Investigations.*

Wolf, Christa. *Cassandra: A Novel and Four Essays.*

Wolf, Friedrich August. *Prolegomena to Homer, 1795.*

Zielinski, Siegfried. *Deep Time of the Media.*

Ziolkowski, Jan, ed. *On Philology.*

Notes

1. Glossings: *Misos*, as "hatred" of reason, is a bit too strong; "distrust" is a more *reasonable* rendering for my allegorical purposes.

2. Years ago, I offered a seminar on "What is it that language [*logos*] wants?" A speaker (writer)? Or a listener (reader) who would be spoken/written? To speak-write as a listener-reader? Thereafter, I made the link to Lyotard's work, most scandalously with *Driftworks* and *Just Gaming.* What *Logos* wants is promiscuity, that is, reading as well as writing (printing) and thinking, promiscuously, as John Milton says in his *Areopagitica.* This promiscuity is not limited to one sex, though historically, for example, the question has been: "What is it that women want?" (given Freud and Lacan's penchant for such questions). *Encore!* Cf. Ballif, on "woman with the rhetorical figure" in *Seduction*; and Campbell, on "Agency."

3. Cf. Avital Ronell's book *The Test Drive.* As for contests-contestations, I have in mind Nietzsche's "Homer's Contest." And I acknowledge John Poulakos's efforts *to write the drama* itself. See his "Testing and Contesting."

4. See Freud, *Interpretation* (460–87); Derrida, "Structure" (279, 329n1). Cf. Latour, *We Have Never.*

5. My allusion here is to Nietzsche's "On Truth and Lying" and to my thoughts concerning *logos* in Samuel Ijsseling's *Rhetoric and Philosophy in Conflict* and, specifically, Isocrates, Freud, and Heidegger, as presented in *Negation* (123–206). Cf. Wolf, *Cassandra* (161–62).

6. Think of Virgil's Dido and Aeneas (*The Aeneid*, bk. 4).

7. Be restlessly assured, mine is no Burkean study in logology or in attitudes toward history, nor Burkean misplaced correction of Nietzsche. And yet, see Becker's *Beyond Translation* (369–403).

8. Source: http://www.perseus.tufts.edu. The passage is from the Chorus of Elders. Given the constraint of length, I cannot give the various translations available,

but the Perseus site gives the *statistical* "readings" (with links to Liddell-Scott et al.) of the individual words in the contexts of the play. The translations into English, say, between Richard Jebb and the translators of Heidegger's translations in German are catastrophically immense.

9. The term "philology" or "classical philology" has been suppressed, and yet, it returns. There is no entry for *philology* in *The Encyclopedia of Philosophy* (Edwards) or *The Encyclopedia of Rhetoric* (Sloane) or *The Encyclopedia of Rhetoric and Composition* (T. Enos), with the exception of a passing reference under "translation" in Enos's volume. Recently, in *The SAGE Handbook of Rhetorical Studies* (Lunsford et al.), a huge tome, there is no reference to philology, though R. Enos has a helpful discussion in "Rhetorical Archeology." Enos, breaking ground earlier, has introduced his "Notions, Presumptions, and Presuppositions" and "argues that rhetorical theory is indispensable in under-standing Hellenic discourse and therefore necessary in philological analysis" (173). Perhaps, it can be thought that "A Philology for the Future Anterior" is an attempt, here, *to date* this work, amorously, in once again re-breaking the ground, but this time, to peer into the abyss of Baubô. Or Dionysos. Or Homer. Or Cassandra.

10. My use of *Ereignis*, rather than Exigency (urgency, Lloyd Bitzer's "rhetorical situation") is crucial. The *event* for Nietzsche brings about the end of determinative thought and, therefore, a reliance on indeterminate judgment (*Gay Science* #125, 343). The event brings forth passive nihilism until an accomplished nihilism, or the revaluation of all values, has taken place. Such, for Nietzsche, is *the writing of the event* (the accident, the limit) of history. (Cf. Maurice Blanchot's *The Writing of the Disaster*.) It is a crucial issue among crucial issues. This event *opens* widely all thinking. Martin Heidegger, in his lectures on Nietzsche, refers to the event as "not an atheistic proclamation: it is a formula for the fundamental experience of an event in Occidental history" (*Nietzsche* 156). The issue here for me is the event, or breach, between Wilamowitz-Moellendorff and Nietzsche. For Heidegger and the Greeks, see Glenn Most. For Heidegger on philology, see Mark Michalski.

11. I have in mind such anthropologists as James Clifford, M. J. Fischer, Clifford Geertz, George E. Marcus, Michael Taussig, Stephen Tyler, and others.

12. But there are equally those scholars who admire and extend the work of Nietzsche (see Nussbaum, *The Fragility of Goodness*; Williams, *Shame and Necessity*; and Henri Lefebvre, *Rhythmanalysis*).

13. See Latour on the modern and time (esp. 67–77). When I say we have never been modern, I claim what Latour says and *some more*.

AFTERWORD: A REMINISCENCE

Sharon Crowley

> The reader of the following pages must therefore bear in mind
> that what is at stake here is not differings in methodology alone
> but varying perceptions of what ought to be discovered for the
> good of the community.
>
> —James J. Murphy, in "Octalog"

In her introduction to this volume, Michelle Ballif, envisioning a sequel to Victor J. Vitanza's 1994 *Writing Histories of Rhetoric*, characterizes the collection as "an attempt to re/write, re/theorize that volume, specifically by querying: Where did all the theory go? That is, what happened to the impassioned fervor generated in the 1980s and 1990s regarding the *theorization* of theories of writing histories of rhetoric?" Having read the essays Michelle gathered in this volume, I think she may have begged her own question, at least in part. Theory did not go away—this collection is rife with it. Some of these pieces plot interesting new theoretical directions for the historiography of rhetoric; another contemplates future histories; and yet another charts a new take on older theoretical approaches.

What is missing is the old fervor. While these pieces are cogently argued, they are not exactly "impassioned." When a serious theoretical disagreement is raised, as in Steven Mailloux's review of his differences with Diane Davis, the tone is collegial. Also missing is debate over the "best" or "proper" way to write the history of rhetoric, and good riddance to that. The standard or "traditional" way was challenged in the 1980s by scholars interested in new theoretical approaches, and the ensuing debate aroused passions because scholarly identities and important professional interests were at stake: a well-defined canon; a "tradition" that defined which texts were rhetorical and which were not; a body of rhetorical theory derived chiefly from Aristotle; and an agreed-upon method of reading that we might call "formal

criticism." Rhetoric scholars in speech departments had slowly won grudg-
ing respect for their field by adopting this program during the 1950s. Those
who were still active in later decades of the twentieth century were loathe to
put it at risk by dabbling in new-fangled theory from the French, or Marx,
or—heaven forbid—feminists. Here, for example, is Forbes Hill in 1983, defending the fort from what he perceived as an attack on it by Philip Wander:

> Professor Wander leads us with his critiques away from the art of
> rhetoric. He tells us almost nothing about the internal structure of the
> work, the traditional *topoi* drawn on, the unique or unusual strategies
> developed, the *pathe* employed, or the kinds of audience it creates or
> seeks to persuade. These matters I take to be the very essence of an
> art [of] rhetoric; the rest is peripheral. (122)

Hill was confident that rhetoric has an "essence" and discernible boundaries; the ideological criticism that Wander called for dealt with non-
essential matters.

At this time English departments pretty much denied that scholarship
in rhetoric existed. At the first "octalog" on historiography, held at a 1988
at a meeting of CCCC in St. Louis, Jerry Murphy remarked: "When I first
sent an article—it happened to be about medieval rhetoric—to *PMLA*, the
only game in town, in 1960 . . . the response, of rejection, of course, came
in two parts: One, rhetoric is not a subject; and if it were, there would be no
history of it" ("Octalog" 33). Hence many English rhetoricians of Murphy's
generation stumbled onto rhetoric, usually because they needed help in
teaching composition. My favorite "finding-rhetoric" story was often told by
E. P. J. Corbett, who remembered searching the library for help with teaching
freshman English, to which he had been assigned with no training whatever
in the teaching of writing. As Corbett told the story, Hugh Blair's *Lectures*
jumped off the shelf and into his hands, open to the chapter on style. When
I returned to graduate school in 1971, after six years of teaching high-school
writing classes without much help from the available textbooks, I asked
my graduate faculty mentors where to look for scholarship on composition
pedagogy. The literature faculty hadn't a clue, but Shirley Carriar—professor
of English education —had the right answer: study rhetoric. So I registered
for courses in the speech department, where I not only learned about Plato
and Aristotle, but read Kennedy and Ong and Howell and other magisterial
historians of the art.

The intellectual disjunction between my literature and rhetoric classes
nearly drove me nuts. In literature classes, we examined *Gulliver's Travels* for
its formal unity, as though Swift wrote for no purpose other than to please

New Critics. I took silent pleasure in the tropes and figures that enliven *The Canterbury Tales* even as my professors assured me that Chaucer's mature art far surpassed whatever minor tactics he had learned from manuals of rhetoric. We studied Milton as though he were an inspired Romantic genius; if my professors knew he learned the art of composition from the rhetorical exercises he composed in school, they never shared that information in class.[1]

In short, English rhetoricians were intellectual orphans on our home campuses. So we made it a point to get to know other rhetoricians when and where we could find them.[2] We sought one another out and huddled together with speech rhetoricians in isolated corners at meetings of CCCC and SCA (now NCA). We phoned one another asking for advice when our nascent programs in rhetoric faced yet another threat from colleagues or administrations. Our arguments about the historiography of rhetoric were staged over dinner in restaurants recommended by a concierge and located in cities none of us called home, or in hallways outside of hotel rooms where raucous parties were in progress. Needless to say, there was nothing like the research apparatus that is currently available to rhetoricians—the known archives were geographically distant, and one had to go to an actual library to read journals.

By the late 1980s, though, the new scholarship—feminist, postmodern, postcolonial, Marxist, gay—was causing sufficient excitement in other fields that a few rhetoricians had begun to practice alternative sorts of history writing. Jim Berlin published two groundbreaking monographs in that decade: *Writing Instruction in Nineteenth-Century American Colleges* (in 1984) and *Rhetoric and Reality* (in 1986). The opening lines of *Writing* can be read as a direct challenge to the research program defended by Forbes Hill: "A rhetoric is a social invention. It arises out of a time and place, a peculiar social context, establishing for a period the conditions that make a peculiar kind of communication possible, and then it is altered or replaced by another scheme" (1). As I recall, Jim's work shook up some folks because he actually took first-year composition seriously enough to attempt writing its history. But it was his historiographical approach—social, located, time-bound, and most of all, political—that was little short of revolutionary. That provocation, in addition to general excitement about high theory, motivated other historians of rhetoric and composition to try on new approaches as well.

As a result, perhaps, the session on historiography drew a fairly large audience at the CCCC meeting in St. Louis in 1988. The now infamous "Octalog," concerning the politics of historiography, was cooked up and hosted by Jerry Murphy, who said in his remarks that "these people [meaning the eight scholars seated with him at a long table: Berlin, Connors, Crowley, Enos,

Jarratt, Johnson, Swearingen, Vitanza] are interested in bringing whatever has already been done by other people into the presence of us, to see whether we're doing new things, old things, bad things, good things" ("Octalog" 11). Interestingly, Berlin was the only one of the assembled historians who had published major historical works by 1988.[3] This tells me that in those days one didn't need to have published a book to be considered a serious scholar in rhetoric or composition—a few essays, well placed or not—sufficed to get invited to a panel reflecting on the politics of historiography.

By the time Vitanza assembled some hundred rhetoricians in Arlington in 1989 to discuss historiography in rhetorical studies, the debate between traditionalist rhetoricians and revisionists of various stripes was in full swing, and it was indeed impassioned. *Writing Histories about Rhetoric* emerged from the deliberations at that conference, but the printed volume conveys only faint echoes of the intellectual heat generated there. I was lucky enough to be in attendance, and my notes are peppered with profanity and exclamation points deeply embedded in the paper. Anger was expressed in women's restrooms between sessions ("Why are we talking about Aristotle and the Sophists all the time? Where are the women? Where is the feminist historiography?") and vociferous arguments broke out in the bar between so-called "traditional" historians and those who advocated newer approaches to the historiography of rhetoric.[4]

With hindsight, though, it's possible to see that attention to theory and the inclusion of formerly excluded groups had barely gotten off the ground in rhetorical studies by 1989. There is no essay devoted to women's rhetorical achievements in *Writing Histories*, and consideration of the rhetorics of formerly excluded groups still had to be argued for (Welch). The collection does attempt to appropriate the occasional neglected white guy—Nietzsche, Agrippa—into the canon (Covino; J. Poulakos).[5] And postmodern thought still had to be defended, if not explained, to rhetorician-readers (T. Poulakos). Janet Atwill, prescient as always, knew what was necessary for real change to occur:

> alternative histories of rhetoric will not be written until alternative subjects begin both to define the functions of those histories and to alter the conditions in which they are produced. In other words, we will only begin to redress the silences created by histories when we are willing to allow our own disciplinary idioms to be challenged. (110–11)

Which brings me, at last, to the present collection. Nearly every writer here draws on some feature of the new approaches being forwarded in *Writing Histories*. Contributors casually cite Anzaldúa, Bakhtin, Derrida,

Foucault, Heidegger, Levinas, Lyotard, assuming their readers are familiar with the work of these figures. That is to say, one issue that brought historians of rhetoric nearly to blows in the late twentieth century has in the meantime been so thoroughly resolved that use of high theory now goes without saying. Other changes are apparent, as well. We read in these pages a careful rationale for writing pan-historiography—history writing on the large scale that was regularly undertaken in the old days, without such justification, by Kennedy and Murphy and Howell (Hawhee and Olson). And the importance of ancient rhetorics seems to have diminished in contemporary historiography—only one essay in this collection rereads Aristotle: Jane Sutton's lovely Deleuzian riff on noses.

And as Byron Hawk remarks, the most recent CCCC octalog on historiography suggested that inclusiveness is now a mandate. In keeping with this trend, here LuMing Mao carefully develops an approach that may allow historians to write about the other without undue appropriation. Jess Enoch traces the history of feminist scholarship in rhetoric, as though recovery of lost voices and gender analysis have always been with us, and urges feminist historians of rhetoric to take advantage of the burgeoning scholarship on public memory. Chuck Morris and K. J. Rawson can speak of generations of queer scholarship, noting the disjunction between the lives of a younger audience and queer history as enacted by an older performer. (Do I need to say that gender and sexuality are not mentioned in *Writing Histories*?)

I dare not speculate about the degree to which the subjectivities of the authors collected here are "alternate" to those of the rhetoricians who argued about the history of rhetoric so long ago in Arlington. But these authors certainly do work under different disciplinary conditions. Because some of the writers whose work appears in the present collection are students of those who wrote essays for the 1994 volume, I take it that they hold doctorates from rhetoric programs, rather than degrees in literature, or history, or political science, or whatever. So they began their careers knowing a good bit more about their discipline than did earlier generations, and in the highly professionalized "New American University," they were taught how to behave professionally from the moment they began graduate study.

So my answer to Michelle's question is this: while the professional stakes are still high for contemporary rhetoricians—often impossibly so in the case of those who run writing programs—the present generation of scholars is better prepared, academically and intellectually, than was the one that preceded it. They have access to more and better archives as well as to older generations of like-minded scholars. In addition, they work in universities and colleges where scholars in other disciplines have become interested in

rhetorical studies because of their own forays into theory and inclusiveness. All of these scholars have discovered that history writing is rhetorical
through and through, as I argued in the conclusion to my own essay in
Writing Histories. Theory of all sorts no longer arouses suspicion within
rhetorical circles except for the exceptional curmudgeonly demur, and in
general, rhetoricians are not particularly anxious about the survival of their
discipline, either locally or globally. As a result they can eschew hierarchies
topped with "the proper way to do history" or "the best that has been thought
or said," and the theories of historiography they create or use need not be
defended with passion. All of which frees them to open exciting new spaces
for historiographical invention, as they have done in these pages.

Notes

1. Had they bothered to read *John Milton at St. Paul's School* by Donald L. Clark,
historian of rhetoric at Columbia, they would have been disabused of this notion.
And James J. Murphy had set the record straight on Chaucer's rhetorical indebted-
ness in 1964 with "A New Look at Chaucer and the Rhetoricians."

2. I am aware that this "we" probably means "I."

3. Connors did not publish a book-length work until nearly ten years after the
first Octalog met (*Composition-Rhetoric* in 1997); Rich Enos published his two volumes on classical rhetoric in 1993 and 1995; Susan Jarratt's *Rereading the Sophists*
appeared in 1991; Nan Johnson's *Nineteenth-Century Rhetoric in North America* and
Jan Swearingen's *Rhetoric and Irony* both came out in 1991; Vitanza's masterwork,
Negation, Subjectivity, and the History of Rhetoric, appeared in 1996; and I published
The Methodical Memory in 1990.

4. Part of the heat was generated by dismay; those of us labeled "traditional" or
"great-man" historians (the ultimate insult) were bewildered by the charge. See the
discussion that took place following the first octalog for examples, and see Brooks 13.

5. By "white guys" I mean "males with access." The notion of "white" doesn't
make much sense prior to the seventeenth century; the label apparently emerged
after that time as a means of distinguishing those with access from those without
it. In other words, "white" as a marker has less to do with a physiological attribute
than with the circulation of power. See T. Allen.

WORKS CITED

CONTRIBUTORS

INDEX

WORKS CITED

Adelman, Jeremy. "The Problem of Persistence in Latin American History." Introduction. *Colonial Legacies: The Problem of Persistence in Latin American History.* Ed. Adelman. New York: Routledge, 1999. 1–14. Print.

Alcoff, Linda. "The Problem of Speaking for Others." *Cultural Critique* 20 (Winter 1991–92): 5–32. Print.

Alexander, Jonathan. "Transgender Rhetoric(s): (Re)Composing Narratives of the Gendered Body." *College Composition and Communication* 57.1 (2005): 45–82. Print.

Alexander, Jonathan, and David L. Wallace. "The Queer Turn in Composition Studies: Reviewing and Assessing an Emerging Scholarship." *College Composition and Communication* 61 (Sept. 2009): 300–320. Print.

Alexander, Jonathan, and Jacqueline Rhodes. "Queer Rhetoric and the Pleasures of the Archive." *Enculturarion: A Journal of Rhetoric, Writing, and Culture* 13 (Jan. 2012). Web. 17 Sept. 2012. <http://enculturation.net/queer-rhetoric-and-the-pleasures-of-the-archive>.

Algra, Keimpe. *Concepts of Space in Greek Thought.* Leiden, Netherlands: E. J. Brill, 1995. Print.

Allen, Theodore W. *The Invention of the White Race: The Origin of Racial Oppression in Anglo-America.* Vol. 2. London: Verso, 1997. Print.

Allen, W. Sidney. *Accent and Rhythm—Prosodic Features of Latin and Greek: A Study in Theory and Reconstruction.* Cambridge: Cambridge UP, 1973. Print.

Ames, Roger T., and David L. Hall. "Glossary of Key Terms." *Dao De Jing.* By Laozi. Trans. Ames and Hall. New York: Ballantine, 2003. 55–71. Print.

———. "Historical Introduction." *Dao De Jing.* By Laozi. Trans. Ames and Hall. New York: Ballantine, 2003. 1–10. Print.

———. "Philosophical Introduction: Correlative Cosmology—An Interpretive Context." *Dao De Jing.* By Laozi. Trans. Ames and Hall. New York: Ballantine, 2003. 11–54. Print.

Anzaldúa, Gloria. "From *Borderlands/La Frontera.*" *The Rhetorical Tradition: Readings from Classical Times to the Present.* Ed. Patricia Bizzell and Bruce Herzberg. 2nd ed. Boston: Bedford/St. Martin's. 1585–604. Print.

"Archivists with an Attitude." *College English* 61 (May 1999): 574–98. Print.

Arendt, Hannah. *The Human Condition.* Chicago: U of Chicago P, 1958. Print.

Aristotle. *Metaphysics.* Trans. Hugh Tredennick. Loeb Classical Library. 2 vols. Cambridge: Harvard UP, 1935–97. Print.

———. *On Rhetoric: A Theory of Civic Discourse.* Trans. George A. Kennedy. New York: Oxford UP, 1991. Print.

———. *On the Soul.* Trans. W. S. Hett. Loeb Classical Library. Cambridge: Harvard UP, 1995. Print.

———. *Physics.* Trans. Philip H. Wicksteed and Francis M. Cornford. Loeb Classical Library. 2 vols. New York: G. P. Putnam and Sons, 1929–34. Print.

———. *Politics.* Trans. H. Rackman. Loeb Classical Library. Cambridge: Harvard UP, 1944. Print.

———. *Problems. The Complete Works of Aristotle.* 2 vols. Ed. Jonathan Barnes. Princeton: Princeton UP, 1984. Print.

———. *Rhetoric.* Trans. John Henry Freese. Loeb Classical Library. Cambridge: Harvard UP, 1994. Print.

Asen, Robert, and Daniel C. Brouwer, eds. *Counterpublics and the State.* Albany: State U of New York P, 2001. Print.

Atwill, Janet M. "Contingencies of Historical Representation." *Writing Histories of Rhetoric.* Ed. Victor J. Vitanza. Carbondale: Southern Illinois UP, 1994. 98–111. Print.

Auerbach, Erich. *Mimesis: The Representation of Reality in Western Literature.* Trans. Willard R. Trask. Princeton: Princeton UP, 1973. Print.

———. "Philology and *Weltliteratur.*" *Centennial Review* 13 (1969): 1–17. Print.

———. *Scenes from the Drama of European Literature.* Minneapolis: U of Minnesota P, 1984. Print.

Baca, Damián. *Mestiz@ Scripts, Digital Migrations, and the Territories of Writing.* New York: Palgrave, 2008. Print.

Baca, Damián, and Victor Villanueva, eds. *Rhetorics of the Americas: 3114 B.C.E. to 2012 C.E.* New York: Palgrave, 2010. Print.

Bacon, Francis. "The Masculine Birth of Time." *The Philosophy of Francis Bacon.* Trans. Benjamin Farrington. Liverpool: Liverpool UP, 1964. 61–72. Print.

Bakhtin, M. M. "The Problem of Speech Genres." *Speech Genres and Other Late Essays.* Trans. Vern W. McGee. Austin: U of Texas P, 1986. 60–102. Print.

Ballif, Michelle. "Re/Dressing Histories; Or, On Re/Covering Figures Who Have Been Laid Bare by Our Gaze." *Rhetoric Society Quarterly* 22.1 (1992): 91–98. Print.

———. *Seduction, Sophistry, and the Woman with the Rhetorical Figure.* Carbondale: Southern Illinois UP, 2001. Print.

———. "Victor J. Vitanza." *Twentieth-Century Rhetorics and Rhetoricians.* Westport: Greenwood, 2000. 336–42. Print.

Bambrough, Renford. "Universals and Family Resemblances." *Proceedings of the Aristotelian Society* 61 (1960–61): 207–22. Print.

Bateson, Gregory, and Mary Catherine Bateson. *Angels Fear: Toward an Epistemology of the Sacred.* Toronto: Bantam, 1988. Print.

Bechdel, Alison. *Fun Home: A Family Tragicomic.* New York: Houghton Mifflin, 2006. Print.

Becker, A. L. *Beyond Translation.* Ann Arbor: U of Michigan P, 2000. Print.

Benjamin, Walter. *Illuminations.* Ed. Hannah Arendt. New York: Schocken, 1969. Print.

———. *Reflections: Essays, Aphorisms, Autobiographical Writings.* Ed. Peter Demetz. New York: Schocken, 1978. Print.

Bergson, Henri. *Creative Evolution.* Trans. Arther Mitchell. Mineola, NY: Dover, 1998. Print.

———. *Matter and Memory.* Trans. N. M. Paul and W. S. Palmer. Brooklyn: Zone, 1990. Print.

Berlant, Lauren, and Michael Warner. "Sex in Public." *Critical Inquiry* 24 (Winter 1998): 547–66. Print.

Berlin, James. *Writing Instruction in Nineteenth-Century American Colleges.* Urbana: NCTE, 1984. Print.

Bessette, Jean. "(Re)making History: The Role of Literacy and Pedagogy in Collective Memory and Identity." Diss. U of Pittsburgh, forthcoming. Print.

Bevernage, Berber. "Time, Presence, and Historical Injustice." *History and Theory* 47 (2008): 149–67.

Biesecker, Barbara A. "Coming to Terms with Recent Attempts to Write Women into the History of Rhetoric." *Philosophy and Rhetoric* 25.2 (1992): 140–61. Print.

———. "Of Historicity, Rhetoric: The Archive as a Scene of Invention." *Rhetoric and Public Affairs* 9.1 (2006): 124–31. Print.

———. "Remembering World War II: The Rhetoric and Politics of National Commemoration at the Turn of the 21st Century." *Quarterly Journal of Speech* 88.4 (2002): 393–409. Print.

Bigwood, J. M. "Aristotle and the Elephant Again." *The American Journal of Philology* 114.4 (Winter 1993): 537–55. Print.

Bizzell, Patricia. "Opportunities for Feminist Research in the History of Rhetoric." *Rhetoric Review* 11.1 (1992): 50–58. Print.

———. "The Praise of Folly, the Woman Rhetor, and Post-Modern Skepticism." *Rhetoric Society Quarterly* 22.1 (1992): 6–17. Print.

———, ed. *Feminist Historiography in Rhetoric.* Spec. issue of *Rhetoric Society Quarterly* 32.1 (Winter 2002). Print.

Black, M. H. "The Printed Bible." *The Cambridge History of the Bible.* Vol. 3. Ed. S. L. Greenslade. Cambridge: Cambridge UP, 1963. 408–75. Print.

Blair, Carole. "Communication as Collective Memory." *Communication as . . . : Perspectives on Theory.* Ed. Dean Gregory J. Shepherd, Jeffrey St. John, and Ted Striphas. Thousand Oaks: Sage, 2006. 51–59. Print.

———. "Contemporary U.S. Memorial Sites as Exemplars of Rhetoric's Materiality." *Rhetorical Bodies.* Ed. Jack Selzer and Sharon Crowley. Madison: U of Wisconsin P, 1999. 16–57. Print.

———. "Reflections on Criticism and Bodies: Parables from Public Places." *Western Journal of Communication* 65.3 (2001): 271–94. Print.

Blanchot, Maurice. *The Writing of the Disaster.* Trans. Ann Smock. Lincoln: U of Nebraska P, 1986. Print.

Blondel, Eric. *Nietzsche: The Body and Culture.* Trans. Seàn Hand. Stanford: Stanford UP, 1991. Print.

Bogle, John C. "Black Monday and Black Swans." *Financial Analysts Journal* 64 (2008): 30–40. Print.

Boorstin, Daniel J. *Cleopatra's Nose: Essays on the Unexpected.* New York: Random, 1994. Print.

Borda, Jennifer. "Feminist Critique and Cinematic Counterhistory in the Documentary *With Babies and Banners.*" *Women's Studies in Communication* 28.5 (2005): 157–82. Print.

Borgo, David. *Sync or Swarm: Improvising Music in a Complex Age.* New York: Continuum, 2007. Print.

Boyd, Nan Alamilla, and Horacio N. Roque Ramírez, eds. *Bodies of Evidence: The Practice of Queer Oral History*. New York: Oxford UP, 2012. Print.

Boym, Svetlana. *The Future of Nostalgia*. New York: Basic, 2001. Print.

Bravmann, Scott. *Queer Fictions of the Past: History, Culture, and Difference*. Cambridge: Cambridge UP, 1999. Print.

Braziel, Jana Evans. "Being and Time, Non-being and Space: Introductory Notes toward an Ontological Study of 'Woman' and *Chora*." *Belief, Bodies, and Being: Feminist Reflections on Embodiment*. Ed. Deborah Orr, Linda Lopez McAllister, Eileen Kahl, and Kathleen Earle. Oxford: Rowman and Littlefield, 2006, 103–26. Print.

Brereton, John C. "Rethinking Our Archive: A Beginning." *College English* 61.5 (May 1999): 574–76. Print.

Brereton, John C., et al. "Archivists with an Attitude." *College English* 61.5 (May 1999): 574–98. Print.

Bringhurst, Robert. *Everywhere Being Is Dancing*. Berkeley: Counterpoint, 2008. Print.

Brody, Miriam. *Manly Writing: Gender, Rhetoric, and the Rise of Composition*. Carbondale: Southern Illinois UP, 1993. Print.

Brooks, Kevin. "Reviewing and Redescribing 'The Politics of Historiography': Octalog I, 1988." *Rhetoric Review* 16.1 (Autumn 1997): 6–21. Print.

Buchanan, Lindal. "Sarah Siddons and Her Place in Rhetorical History." *Rhetorica* 25.4 (2007): 413–34. Print.

Buck, Gertrude. "The Metaphor. 1899." *Rhetorical Theory by Women before 1900*. Ed. Jane Donawerth. Lanham: Rowman and Littlefield, 2002. 274–79. Print.

Buckley, Michael J. *Motion and Motion's God: Thematic Variations in Aristotle, Cicero, Newton, and Hegel*. Princeton: Princeton UP, 1971. Print.

Burke, Kenneth. *A Grammar of Motives*. Berkeley: U of California P, 1969. Print.

———. *Permanence and Change: An Anatomy of Purpose*. 3rd ed. Berkeley: U of California P, 1984. Print.

Burton, Antoinette M. *Archive Stories: Facts, Fictions, and the Writing of History*. Durham: Duke UP, 2005. Print.

Butler, Judith. *Bodies That Matter*. New York: Routledge, 1993. Print.

———. "Performative Acts and Gender Constitution: An Essay in Phenomenology and Feminist Theory." *Writing on the Body: Female Embodiment and Feminist Theory*. Ed. Katie Conboy, Nadia Medina, and Sarah Stanbury. New York: Columbia UP, 1997. 401–17. Print.

Butler, Samuel. *The Authoress of the Odyssey, Where and When She Wrote, Who She Was, the Use She Made of the Iliad, and How the Poem Grew under Her Hands*. 1897. Forgotten, 2008. Print.

———. *The Humour of Homer, and Other Essays*. Ed. R. A. Streatfeild. Freeport: Books for Libraries P, 1967. Print.

Butt, Gavin. *Between You and Me: Queer Disclosures in the New York Art World, 1948–1963*. Durham: Duke UP, 2005. Print.

Bynum, Caroline Walker. *Metamorphosis and Identity*. New York: Zone, 2001. Print.

Byron, Theodora. *Historical Linguistics*. Cambridge: Cambridge UP, 1978. Print.

Calder, William Musgrave, III. "How Did Ulrich Von Wilamowitz-Moellendorff Read a Text?" *Classical Journal* 86.4 (1991): 344–52. Print.

———. "The Wilamowitz-Nietzsche Struggle: New Documents and a Reappraisal." *Nietzsche-Studien* 12 (1983): 214–54. Print.

Campbell, Joann, ed. *Toward a Feminist Rhetoric: The Writing of Gertrude Buck.* Pittsburgh: U of Pittsburgh P, 1996. Print.

Campbell, Karlyn Kohrs. "Agency: Promiscuous and Protean." *Communication and Critical/Cultural Studies.* 22.1 (Mar. 2005): 1–19. Print.

———. "Biesecker Can't Speak for Her Either." *Philosophy and Rhetoric* 26 (1993): 153–59. Print.

———. "Consciousness-Raising: Linking Theory, Criticism, and Practice." *Rhetoric Society Quarterly* 32.1 (2002): 45–64. Print.

Campbell, Thomas J. *The Jesuits, 1534–1921: A History of the Society of Jesus from Its Foundation to the Present Time.* Vol. 1. New York: Encyclopedia P, 1921. Print.

Cannon, Walter B. *Bodily Changes in Pain, Hunger, Fear, and Rage.* New York: Appleton, 1915. Print.

Carpenter, Faedra Chatard. "Robert O'Hara's *Insurrection*: 'Que(e)rying' History." *Text and Performance Quarterly* 23 (Apr. 2003): 186–204. Print.

Carr, Jean Ferguson, Stephen L. Carr, and Lucille M. Schultz. *Archives of Instruction: Nineteenth-Century Rhetorics, Readers, and Composition Books in the United States.* Carbondale: Southern Illinois UP, 2005. Print.

Carroll, David. "Memorial for the *Différend*: In Memory of Jean-François Lyotard." *Parallax* 6.4 (2000): 3–27. Print.

Castiglia, Christopher. "Sex Panics, Sex Publics, Sex Memories." *Boundary* 2.27 (2000): 149–75. Print.

Castiglia, Christopher, and Christopher Reed. "'Ah, Yes, I Remember It Well': Memory and Queer Culture in *Will and Grace*." *Cultural Critique* 56 (Winter 2004): 158–88. Print.

———. *If Memory Serves: Gay Men, AIDS, and the Promise of the Queer Past.* Minneapolis: U of Minnesota P, 2012. Print.

Catano, James V. *Language, History, Style: Leo Spitzer and the Critical Tradition.* Urbana: U of Illinois P, 1988. Print.

Caussin, Nicolas. *Eloquentia sacrae et humanae parallela.* Flexiae, 1619. *Digitale Bibliothek.* Web. 10 Jan. 2011. <http://daten.digitale-sammlungen.de/~db//0002//bsb00026355/images/>.

———. "From *On Sacred and Profane Eloquence*." *Renaissance Debates on Rhetoric.* Trans. and ed. Wayne A. Rebhorn. Ithaca: Cornell UP, 2000. Print.

Cerquiglini, Bernard. *In Praise of the Variant.* Trans. Betsy Wing. Baltimore: Johns Hopkins UP, 1999. Print.

Chadwick, John. *The Decipherment of Linear B.* 2nd ed. Cambridge: Cambridge UP, 1970. Print.

Chauncey, George. *Gay New York: Gender, Urban Culture, and the Making of the Gay Male World, 1890–1940.* New York: Basic, 1994. Print.

———. "'What Gay Studies Taught the Court': The Historians' Amicus Brief in *Lawrence v. Texas*." *GLQ* 10.3 (2004): 509–38. Print.

Chee, Alexander. "After Peter." *Loss within Loss: Artists in the Age of AIDS.* Ed. Edmund White. Madison: U of Wisconsin P, 2001. 20–36. Print.

Chen, Chung-Hwan. "Universal Concrete, a Typical Aristotelian Duplication of Reality." *Phronesis* 9.1 (1964): 48–57. Print.

Chen, Guying. 老子今注今译 (*Laozi Jinzhu Jinyi, Modern Annotation and Translation of the Daodejing*). Beijing: Shangwu, 2003. Print.

Cherniss, Harold. *Aristotle's Criticism of Presocratic Philosophy*. New York: Octagon, 1971. Print.

Cherwitz, Richard. "Rhetoric as 'A Way of Knowing': An Attenuation of the Epistemological Claims of the 'New Rhetoric.'" *Southern Speech Communication Journal* 42 (1977): 207–19. Print.

Chisholm, Dianne. "The City of Collective Memory." *GLQ* 7.2 (2001): 195–243. Print.

Chomsky, Noam. "Language and the Mind." *Readings in the Theory of Grammar*. Ed. Diane D. Bornstein. Cambridge: Winthrop, 1976. 241–51. Print.

Clark, A. Kim. "Indians, the State and Law: Public Works and the Struggle to Control Labor in Liberal Ecuador." *Journal of Historical Sociology* 7.1 (Mar. 1994): 49–72. Print.

Clark, Donald Leman. *John Milton at St. Paul's School*. New York: Columbia UP, 1948. Print.

Clark, William. *Academic Charisma and the Origins of the Research University*. Chicago: U of Chicago P, 2006. Print.

Classen, C. Joachim. "Aristotle's Picture of the Sophists." *The Sophists and Their Legacy*. Ed. G. B. Kerferd. Wiesbaden: Steiner, 1981. 7–24. Print.

Clevenger, Theodore, Jr. "Contemporary Research in Rhetoric." *Today's Speech* 13.4 (1965): 11–14. Print.

Cohen, Cathy J. "Punks, Bulldaggers, and Welfare Queens: The Radical Potential of Queer Politics?" *Black Queer Studies: A Critical Anthology*. Ed. E. Patrick Johnson and Mae G. Henderson. Durham: Duke UP, 2005. 21–51. Print.

Cohen, Richard A. "Levinas: Thinking Least about Death—Contra Heidegger." *International Journal of Philosophy and Religion* 60 (2006): 21–39. Print.

Cohen, Sande. *History out of Joint: Essays on the Use and Abuse of History*. Baltimore: Johns Hopkins, 2006. Print.

———. "The 'Use and Abuse of History' According to Jean-François Lyotard." *Parallax* 6.4 (2000): 99–113. Print.

Combs, Steven C. *The Dao of Rhetoric*. Albany: State U of New York P, 2005. Print.

Confucius. *The Analects*. Trans. D. C. Lau. Hong Kong: Chinese UP, 1992. Print.

Connors, Robert. *Composition-Rhetoric: Background, Theory, Pedagogy*. Pittsburgh: U of Pittsburgh P, 1997. Print.

Cope, Edward Meredith. *The Rhetoric of Aristotle*. Ed. John Edwin Sandys. 3 vols. Cambridge: W. C. Brown Reprint Library P, 1877. 1966. Print.

Cortright, Rupert L. "Our Tomorrow." *Quarterly Journal of Speech* 35 (1949): 149–55. Print.

Covino, William A. "Alchemizing the History of Rhetoric: Introductions, Incantations, Spells." *Writing Histories of Rhetoric*. Ed. Victor J. Vitanza. Carbondale: Southern Illinois UP, 1994. 49–58. Print.

Crowley, Sharon. "Let Me Get This Straight." *Writing Histories of Rhetoric*. Ed. Victor J. Vitanza. Carbondale: Southern Illinois UP, 1994. 1–19. Print.

———. *The Methodical Memory*. Carbondale: Southern Illinois UP, 1990. Print.

———. "Modern Rhetoric and Memory." *Rhetorical Memory and Delivery*. Ed. J. F. Reynolds. Hillsdale: Lawrence Erlbaum, 1993. 31–63. Print.

Curthoys, Ned. "Edward Said's Unhoused Philological Humanism." *Edward Said*. Ed. Curthoys and Debjani Ganguly. Melbourne: Melbourne UP, 2007. 152–75. Print.

Cvetkovich, Ann. *An Archive of Feelings: Trauma, Sexuality, and Lesbian Public Cultures*. Durham: Duke UP, 2003. Print.

Darsey, James. *The Prophetic Tradition and Radical Rhetoric in America*. New York: New York UP, 1997. Print.

Davis, Diane. *Inessential Solidarity: Rhetoric and Foreigner Relations*. Pittsburgh: U of Pittsburgh P, 2010. Print.

———, ed. *The UberReader: Selected Works of Avital Ronell*. Urbana: U of Illinois P, 2008. Print.

De Aldama, Antonio M. *The Formula of the Institute: Notes for a Commentary*. Trans. Ignacio Echániz. St. Louis: Institute of Jesuit Sources, 1990. Print.

de Certeau, Michel. *The Writing of History*. Trans. Tom Conley. New York: Columbia UP, 1988. Print.

Deethardt, John F. "A Future for Speech Communication." *Communication Quarterly* 30 (1982): 274–81. Print.

Del Caro, Adrian. "Nietzsche's Rhetoric on the Grounds of Philology and Hermeneutics." *Philosophy and Rhetoric* 37.2 (2004): 101–22. Print.

Deleuze, Gilles. *Cinema 2*. Minneapolis: U of Minnesota P, 1989. Print.

de Man, Paul. *Blindness and Insight: Essays in the Rhetoric of Contemporary Criticism*. 2nd ed. Minneapolis: U of Minnesota P, 1988. Print.

———. "The Return to Philology." *The Resistance to Theory*. Minneapolis: U of Minnesota P, 1986. 3–20. Print.

Derrida, Jacques. *Aporias*. Trans. Thomas Dutoit. Stanford: Stanford UP, 1993. Print.

———. "Fors." Foreword. Trans. Barbara Johnson. *The Wolf Man's Magic Word*. By Nicolas Abraham and Maria Torok. Trans. Nicholas Rand. Minneapolis: U of Minnesota P, 1986. xi–xlviii. Print.

———. *Memoires for Paul de Man*. Trans. Cecile Lindsay, Jonathan Culler, and Eduardo Cadava. New York: Columbia UP, 1986. Print.

———. "Passages—from Traumatism to Promise." Trans. Peggy Kamuf. *Points . . . : Interviews, 1974–1994*. Ed. Elisabeth Weber. Stanford: Stanford UP, 1995. 372–98. Print.

———. *Specters of Marx*. Trans. Peggy Kamuf. New York: Routledge, 2006. Print.

———. "Structure, Sign, and Play in the Discourse of the Human Sciences." *Writing and Difference*. Chicago: U of Chicago P, 1978. 278–93. Print.

Dershowitz, Nachum, and Edward M. Reingold. *Calendrical Calculations*. 3rd ed. Cambridge: Cambridge UP, 2007. Print.

Dewey, John. *Democracy and Education*. Ed. Jo Ann Boydston. Carbondale: Southern Illinois UP, 1985. Print.

———. *Essays, Reviews, Miscellany, and The Public and Its Problems*. Ed. Jo Ann Boydston. Carbondale: Southern Illinois UP, 1988. Print.

Dinshaw, Carolyn. *Getting Medieval: Sexualities and Communities, Pre- and Postmodern*. Durham: Duke UP, 1999. Print.

Doane, Mary Ann. *The Emergence of Cinematic Time*. Cambridge: Harvard UP, 2002. Print.

Dockhorn, Klaus. "Hans-Georg Gadamer's *Truth and Method*." Trans. Marvin Brown. *Philosophy and Rhetoric* 13.3 (1980): 160–80. Print.

Dodds, E. R. *The Greeks and the Irrational*. Berkeley: U of California P, 1973. Print.

Donawerth, Jane. "Nineteenth-Century United States Conduct Book Rhetoric by Women." *Rhetoric Review* 21.1 (2002): 5–21. Print.

———. *Rhetorical Theory by Women before 1900: An Anthology*. Lanham, MD: Rowman and Littlefield, 2002. Print.

Doty, Mark. "Is There a Future?" *In the Company of My Solitude: American Writing from the AIDS Pandemic*. Ed. Marie Howe and Michael Klein. New York: Persea, 1995: 3–12. Print.

Dow, Bonnie. "Feminism, Difference(s), and Rhetorical Studies." *Communication Studies* 46 (1995): 106–17. Print.

Dries, Manuel, ed. *Nietzsche on Time and History*. Berlin: Walter de Gruyter, 2008. Print.

duBois, Page. *Sowing the Body*. Chicago: U of Chicago P, 1988. Print.

Duggan, Lisa. *The Twilight of Equality? Neoliberalism, Cultural Politics, and the Attack on Democracy*. Boston: Beacon, 2003. Print.

Dunmire, Patricia L. "Preempting the Future: Rhetoric and Ideology of the Future in Political Discourse." *Discourse and Society* 16 (2005): 481–513. Print.

Dunn, Thomas R. "Remembering 'A Great Fag': Visualizing Public Memory and the Construction of Queer Space." *Quarterly Journal of Speech* 97 (2011): 435–60. Print.

Ede, Lisa, Cheryl Glenn, and Andrea Lunsford. "Border Crossings: Intersections of Rhetoric and Feminism." *Rhetorica* 13.4 (1995): 401–41. Print.

Edwards, Mark U. *Printing, Propaganda, and Martin Luther*. Berkeley: U of California P, 1994. Print.

Edwards, Paul, ed. *The Encyclopedia of Philosophy*. 8 vols. New York: Macmillan, 1967. Print.

Eisenstein, Elizabeth L. *The Printing Press as an Agent of Change: Communications and Cultural Transformations in Early-Modern Europe*. Cambridge: Cambridge UP, 1979. Print.

Elkins, James. *Visual Studies: A Skeptical Introduction*. New York: Routledge, 2003. Print.

Enders, Jody. "Delivering Delivery: Theatricity and the Emasculation of Eloquence." *Rhetorica* 15.3 (1997): 253–78. Print.

Eng, David L., Judith Halberstam, and José Esteban Muñoz. "What's Queer about Queer Studies Now?" Introduction. *Social Text* 84–85 (Fall/Winter 2005): 1–17. Print.

Engbers, Susanna Kelly. "With Great Sympathy: Elizabeth Cady Stanton's Innovative Appeals to Emotion." *Rhetoric Society Quarterly* 37.3 (2007): 307–32. Print.

Enoch, Jessica. *Refiguring Rhetorical Education: Women Teaching African American, Native American, and Chicano/a Students, 1865–1911*. Carbondale: Southern Illinois UP, 2008. Print.

———. "A Woman's Place Is in the School: Rhetorics of Gendered Space in Nineteenth-Century America." *College English* 70.3 (2008): 275–95. Print.

Enoch, Jessica, and Dana Anderson. *Burke in the Archives*. Columbia: U of South Carolina P, forthcoming. Print.

Enoch, Jessica, and Jordynn Jack. "Remembering Sappho: New Perspectives on Teaching (and Writing) Women's Rhetorical History." *College English* 73.5 (2011): 518–37. Print.

Enos, Richard Leo. "The Archeology of Women in Rhetoric: Rhetorical Sequencing as a Research Method for Historical Scholarship." *Rhetoric Society Quarterly* 32.1 (2002): 65–79. Print.

———. "The Classical Tradition(s) of Rhetoric: A Demur to the Country Club Set." *College Composition and Communication* 38 (Oct. 1987): 283–90. Print.

———. *Greek Rhetoric before Aristotle*. Rev. and Expanded ed. Anderson, SC: Parlor, 2012. Print.

———. "Notions, Presumptions, and Presuppositions in Hellenic Discourse: Rhetorical Theory as Philological Evidence." *Philosophy and Rhetoric* 14.3 (Summer 1981): 173–84. Print.

———. "Rhetorical Archaeology: Established Resources, Methodological Tools, and Basic Research Methods." *The SAGE Handbook of Rhetorical Studies.* Ed. Andrea A. Lunsford, Kirt H. Wilson, and Rosa A. Eberly. Los Angeles: Sage, 2009. 35–52. Print.

———. *Roman Rhetoric: Revolution and the Greek Influence.* Rev. and Expanded ed. Anderson, SC: Parlor, 2008. Print.

———. "The Secret Composition Practices of the Ancient Spartans: A Study of 'Non-Civic' Classical Rhetoric." *Renewing Rhetoric's Relations to Composition: Essays in Honor of Theresa Jarnagin Enos.* Ed. Shane Borrowman, Stuart C. Brown, and Thomas P. Miller. New York: Routledge, 2009. 236–47. Print.

———. "The Structuring of Rhetorical Theories: The Center of a Central Tradition." *Rhetorical Society Quarterly* 8.1 (1978): 2–7. Print.

———. "Verso: Etymology of 'Rhapsode.'" *Issues in Interpretation* 3 (Winter 1978): n.p. Print.

Enos, Richard Leo, and Roger Thompson et al., eds. *The Rhetoric of St. Augustine of Hippo: De Doctrina Christiana and the Search for a Distinctly Christian Rhetoric.* Waco: Baylor UP, 2008. Print.

Enos, Theresa, ed. *The Encyclopedia of Rhetoric and Composition.* New York: Garland, 1996. Print.

Eves, Rosalyn Collings. "A Recipe for Remembrance: Memory and Identity in African American Women's Cookbooks." *Rhetoric Society Quarterly* 24.3 (2005): 280–97. Print.

Farrell, Allan P. *The Jesuit Code of Liberal Education: Development and Scope of the Ratio Studiorum.* Milwaukee: Bruce, 1938. Print.

Farrell, Thomas. "Sizing Things Up: Colloquial Reflection as Practical Wisdom" *Argumentation* 12.1 (1998): 1–14. Print.

The Fate of the Disciplines. Spec. issue of *Critical Inquiry* 35.4 (2009): 729–1091. Print.

Feinberg, Leslie. *Transgender Warriors: Making History from Joan of Arc to Dennis Rodman.* Boston: Beacon, 1996. Print.

Ferreira-Buckley, Linda. "Rescuing the Archives from Foucault." *College English* 61.5 (May 1999): 577–82. Print.

Fillion, Réal Robert. "Realizing Reason in History: How Cunning Does It Have to Be?" *Owl of Minerva* 23 (1991): 77–92. Print.

Finnegan, Cara A. *Picturing Poverty: Print Culture and FSA Photographs.* Washington, DC: Smithsonian Books, 2003. Print.

Fisher, Walter R. "Rationality and the Logic of Good Reasons." *Philosophy and Rhetoric* 13 (1980): 121–30. Print.

Flynn, Lawrence J. "The *De arte rhetorica* by Cyprian Soarez, S. J.: A Translation with Introduction and Notes." Diss. U of Florida, 1957. Print.

"Forum: The Politics of Archival Research." *Rhetoric and Public Affairs* 9.1 (2006): 113–52. Print.

Foucault, Michel. *The Archaeology of Knowledge and the Discourse on Language.* Trans. A. M. Sheridan. New York: Pantheon, 1972. Print.

———. "Critical Theory/Intellectual History." *Politics, Philosophy, Culture: Interviews and Other Writings, 1977–1984*. Ed. Lawrence D. Kritzman. New York: Routledge, 1988. 17–45. Print.

———. *Discipline and Punish: The Birth of the Prison*. Trans. Alan Sheridan. New York: Vintage, 1977. Print.

———. "The Ethics of the Concern for the Self as a Practice of Freedom." *Ethics Subjectivity and Truth: The Essential Works of Michel Foucault, 1954–1984*. Vol. 1. Ed. Paul Rabinow. New York: New, 1994: 281–302. Print.

———. *Fearless Speech*. Ed. Joseph Pearson. Los Angeles: Semiotext(e), 2001. Print.

———. *The Hermeneutics of the Subject: Lectures at the Collège de France, 1981–1982*. Ed. Frédéric Gros. Trans. Graham Burchell. New York: Palgrave Macmillan, 2005. Print.

———. "History, Discourse, Discontinuity." *Foucault Live: Interviews 1961–1984*. Ed. Sylvere Lotringer. Trans. Lysa Hochroth and John Johnston. New York: Semiotext(e), 1989. 33–50. Print.

———. *History of Sexuality, Volume 1: Introduction*. Trans. Robert Hurley. New York: Vintage, 1990. Print.

———. "Nietzsche, Genealogy, History." *The Foucault Reader*. Ed. Paul Rabinow. New York: Pantheon, 1984. 76–100. Print.

———. "Nietzsche, Genealogy, History." *Language, Counter-Memory, Practice: Selected Essays and Interviews*. Ed. Donald F. Bouchard. Trans. Bouchard and Sherry Simons. Ithaca: Cornell UP, 1977. 139–64. Print.

———. "On the Genealogy of Ethics." *Ethics Subjectivity and Truth: The Essential Works of Michel Foucault, 1954–1984*. Vol. 1. Ed. Paul Rabinow. New York: New, 1994. 253–80. Print.

———. "On the Ways of Writing History." *Aesthetics, Method, and Epistemology: The Essential Works of Michel Foucault, 1954–1984*. Vol. 2. Ed. James D. Faubion. Trans. Robert Hurley. New York: New, 1998. 279–95. Print.

———. "Preface to Transgression." *Language, Counter-Memory, Practice: Selected Essays and Interviews*. Ed. Donald F. Bouchard. Trans. Bouchard and Sherry Simons. Ithaca: Cornell UP, 1977. 29–52. Print.

———. *Religion and Culture*. Ed. Jeremy R. Carrette. Manchester: Manchester UP, 1999. Print.

———. *Remarks on Marx*. New York: Semiotext(e), 1991. Print.

———. "Self-Writing." *Ethics Subjectivity and Truth: The Essential Works of Michel Foucault 1954–1984*. Vol. 1. Ed. Paul Rabinow. New York: New, 1994. 207–22. Print.

———. "Sexual Choice, Sexual Act" *Ethics Subjectivity and Truth: The Essential Works of Michel Foucault 1954–1984*. Vol. 1. Ed. Paul Rabinow. New York: New, 1994. 141–56. Print.

———. *"Society Must Be Defended": Lectures at the College de France 1975–1976*. Ed. Mauro Bertani and Allessandro Fontana. Trans. David Macey. New York: Picador, 1997. Print.

———. "Theatricum Philosophicum." *Language, Counter-Memory, Practice: Selected Essays and Interviews*. Ed. Donald F. Bouchard. Trans. Bouchard and Sherry Simons. Ithaca: Cornell UP, 1977. 165–92. Print.

———. "What Is Enlightenment?" *Ethics Subjectivity and Truth: The Essential Works of Michel Foucault 1954–1984*. Vol. 1. Ed. Paul Rabinow. New York: New, 1994. 303–20. Print.

Fox, Ragan. "Tales of a Fighting Bobcat: An 'Auto-archaeology' of Gay Identity Formation and Maintenance." *Text and Performance Quarterly* 30.2 (2010): 122–42. Print.

Frank, Roberta. "The Unbearable Lightness of Being a Philologist." *Journal of English and Germanic Philology* 96.4 (1997): 486–513. Print.

Fredal, James. *Rhetorical Action in Ancient Athens: Persuasive Artistry from Solon to Demosthenes.* Carbondale: Southern Illinois UP, 2006. Print.

Freeman, Elizabeth. Introduction. *GLQ: A Journal of Lesbian and Gay Studies* 13.2–3 (2007): 159–76. Print.

———. "Packing History, Count(er)ing Generations," *New Literary History* 31 (2000): 727–44. Print.

Freeman, Kathleen. *The Murder of Herodes and Other Trials from the Athenian Law Courts.* New York: Norton, 1963. Print.

Freud, Sigmund. *The Interpretation of Dreams.* Vol. 5 of *The Standard Edition of the Complete Works of Sigmund Freud.* Ed. James Strachey. London: Hogart, 1900. Print.

———. "The Uncanny." *The Uncanny.* Trans. David McLintock. New York: Penguin, 2003. 121–62. Print.

Friedman, Albert. "Ontology Recapitulates Philology." *Pacific Coast Philology* 19.1–2 (1984): 7–11. Print.

Fumaroli, Marc. *L'Âge de l'éloquence: rhétorique et "res literaria" de la Renaissance au seuil de l'époque classique.* Paris: Champion, 1980. Print.

———. "The Fertility and the Shortcomings of Renaissance Rhetoric: The Jesuit Case." *The Jesuits: Cultures, Sciences, and the Arts, 1540–1773.* Ed. John W. O'Malley, Gauvin Alexander Bailey, Steven J. Harris, and T. Frank Kennedy. Toronto: U of Toronto P, 1999. 90–106. Print.

Gaillet, Lynée Lewis, ed. With Winifred Bryan Horner. *The Present State of Scholarship in the History of Rhetoric: A Twenty-First Century Guide.* Columbia: U of Missouri P, 2010.

Gannon, Victoria. "Art Review: Lineage: Matchmaking in the Archive." KQED/Northern California Public Broadcasting. 30 June 2009. Web. 10 Jan. 2011. <http://www.kqed.org/arts/visualarts/article.jsp?essid=24944>.

Garrett, Mary. "Some Elementary Methodological Reflections on the Study of the Chinese Rhetorical Tradition." *International and Intercultural Communication Annual* 22 (1999): 53–63. Print.

Gehrke, Pat J. "The Crisis Fallacy: Egoism, Epistemology, and Ethics in Crisis Communication and Preparation." *Communication Ethics and Crisis: Negotiating Differences in Public and Private Spheres.* Ed. J. M. H. Fritz and S. Alyssa Groom. Madison, NJ: Fairleigh Dickinson UP, 2011. 133–59. Print.

———. *The Ethics and Politics of Speech: Communication and Rhetoric in the Twentieth Century.* Carbondale: Southern Illinois UP, 2009. Print.

Gelb, I. J. "Records, Writing and Decipherment." *Language and Texts: The Nature of Linguistic Evidence.* Ed. Herbert H. Paper. Ann Arbor: Center for the Coordination of Ancient and Modern Studies. University of Michigan, 1975. 61–86. Print.

Genette, Gerard. *Paratexts: Thresholds of Interpretation.* Trans. Jane E. Lewin. Cambridge: Cambridge UP, 1997. Print.

George, Ann, and Jack Selzer. *Kenneth Burke in the 1930s.* Columbia: U of South Carolina P, 2007. Print.

Geuss, Raymond, and Ronald Speirs. Introduction. *The Birth of Tragedy and Other Writings*. By Friedrich Nietzsche. Ed. Raymond Guess and Ronald Speirs. Trans. Speirs. Cambridge: Cambridge UP, 1999. vii–xxxvii. Print.

Giles, Peter, and William Dwight Whitney. "Philology." *Encyclopaedia Britannica*. 11th ed. Vol. 21. 1910. 414–38. Web. 27 June 2010. <http://www.archive.org/details/encyclopaediabri21chisrich>.

Glenn, Cheryl. *Rhetoric Retold: Regendering the Tradition from Antiquity through the Renaissance*. Carbondale: Southern Illinois UP, 1997. Print.

———. "Truth, Lies, and Method: Revisiting Feminist Historiography." *College English* 62.3 (2000): 387–89. Print.

———. *Unspoken: A Rhetoric of Silence*. Carbondale: Southern Illinois UP, 2004. Print.

Glenn, Cheryl, and Jessica Enoch. "Drama in the Archives: Rereading Methods, Rewriting History." *College Composition and Communication* 61.2 (Dec. 2009): 321–42. Print.

———. "Invigorating Historiographic Practices in Rhetoric and Composition Studies." *Working in the Archives*. Ed. Alexis E. Ramsey, Wendy B. Sharer, Barbara L'Eplattenier, and Lisa S. Mastrangelo. Carbondale: Southern Illinois UP, 11–27. Print.

Gold, David. *Rhetoric at the Margins: Revising the History of Writing Instruction in American Colleges, 1873–1947*. Carbondale: Southern Illinois UP, 2008. Print.

Goldstein, R. J. Preface. *Remarks on Marx*. By Michel Foucault. New York: Semiotext(e), 1991: 7–14. Print.

Graff, Richard, and Michael Leff. "Revisionist Historiography and Rhetorical Tradition(s)." *The Viability of the Rhetorical Tradition*. Ed. Graff, Arthur E. Walzer, and Janet M. Atwill. Albany: State U of New York P, 2005. 11–30. Print.

Grafton, Anthony. "Joseph Scaliger and Historical Chronology." *History and Theory* 14.2 (May 1975): 156–85. Print.

———. *Joseph Scaliger: A Study in the History of Classical Scholarship*. Vol. 1: Textual Criticism and Exegesis. Oxford: Oxford UP, 1983. Print.

———. *Joseph Scaliger: A Study in the History of Classical Scholarship*. Vol. 2: Historical Chronology. Oxford: Oxford UP, 1994. Print.

———. "Prolegomena to Friedrich August Wolf." *Journal of the Warburg and Courtauld Institutes* 44 (1981): 101–29. Print.

Graham, A. C. *Disputers of the Tao: Philosophical Argument in Ancient China*. La Salle: Open Court, 1989. Print.

Green, Peter. "Mandarins and Iconoclasts." *Arion* 3rd ser. 6.3 (Winter 1999): 122–49. Print.

Grene, Marjorie. "Is Genus to Species as Matter to Form? Aristotle and Taxonomy." *Synthese* 28.1 (1974): 51–69. Print.

Gross, Daniel. "Caussin's Passion and the New History of Rhetoric." *Rhetorica* 21.2 (2003): 89–112. Print.

Grossberg, Lawrence. *Cultural Studies in the Future Tense*. Durham: Duke UP, 2010. Print.

Gumbrecht, Hans Ulrich. *The Powers of Philology*. Urbana: U of Illinois P, 2003. Print.

———. *In 1926: Living at the Edge of Time*. Cambridge: Harvard UP, 1997. Print.

Gunn, Joshua. *Modern Occult Rhetoric: Mass Media and the Drama of Secrecy in the Twentieth Century*. Tuscaloosa: U of Alabama P, 2005. Print.

Hadas, Moses. *Ancilla to Classical Reading.* Morningside Heights: Columbia UP, 1954. Print.

Hadot, Pierre. *Philosophy as a Way of Life: Spiritual Exercises from Socrates to Foucault.* Trans. Michael Chase. Ed. Arnold I. Davidson. Oxford: Blackwell, 1995. Print.

Halberstam, Judith. *In a Queer Time and Place: Transgender Bodies, Subcultural Lives.* New York: New York UP, 2005. Print.

Hall, David L., and Roger T. Ames. *Anticipating China: Thinking through the Narratives of Chinese and Western Culture.* Albany: State U of New York P, 1995. Print.

Hallas, Roger. "Queer AIDS Media and the Question of the Archive." *GLQ* 16.3 (2010): 431–35. Print.

Halperin, David M. *How to Do the History of Homosexuality.* Chicago: U of Chicago P, 2002. Print.

Halperin, David M., and Valerie Traub, eds. *Gay Shame.* Chicago: U of Chicago P, 2010. Print.

Hamacher, Werner. "Degregation of the Will." *Reconstructing Individualism.* Ed. Thomas C. Heller, Morton Sosna, and David E. Wellbery. Stanford: Stanford UP, 1986. 106–39. Print.

———. "From '95 Theses on Philology.'" *PMLA* 125.4 (2010): 994–1001. Print.

Hanson, Victor Davis, and John Heath. "The Good, the Bad, and the Ugly." *Arion* 3rd ser. 6.3 (Winter 1999): 150–95. Print.

———. *Who Killed Homer?* New York: Encounter, 2001. Print.

Hartog, François. "The Double Fate of the Classics." *Critical Inquiry* 35.4 (2009): 964–81. Print.

Haskins, Ekaterina V. *Logos and Power in Isocrates and Aristotle.* Columbia: U of South Carolina P, 2004. Print.

Havelock, Eric A. *Preface to Plato.* Cambridge: Harvard UP, 1963. Print.

Hawhee, Debra. *Bodily Arts: Rhetoric and Athletics in Ancient Greece.* Austin: U of Texas P, 2004. Print.

———. *Moving Bodies: Kenneth Burke at the Edges of Language.* Columbia: U of South Carolina P, 2009. Print.

Hawk, Byron. *A Counter-History of Composition.* Pittsburgh: U of Pittsburgh P, 2007. Print.

Hegel, G. W. F. *Elements of the Philosophy of Right.* Ed. Allen W. Wood. Cambridge: Cambridge UP, 1991. Print.

Heidegger, Martin. *Nietzsche: Volumes One and Two.* Trans. David Farrell Krell. Harper One, 1991. Print.

———. *The Phenomenology of Religious Life.* Trans. Matthias Fritsch and Jennifer Anna Gosetti-Ferencei. Bloomington: Indiana UP, 2004. Print.

Hendrix, Jerry. "Rhetorical Criticism: Prognoses for the Seventies—A Symposium: An Introductory Prognosis." *Southern Speech Journal* 36 (1970): 101–4. Print.

Herring, Scott. *Another Country: Queer Anti-urbanism.* New York: New York UP, 2010. Print.

Hesiod. *Theogonia.* Print.

———. *Works and Days.* Print.

Hilderbrand, Lucas. "Retroactivism." *GLQ* 12.2 (2006): 303–17. Print.

Hill, Forbes I. "A Turn against Ideology: Reply to Professor Wander." *Central States Speech Journal* 34 (1983): 121–26. Print.

Hoffman, David C. "Concerning *Eikos*: Social Expectation and Verisimilitude in Early Attic Rhetoric." *Rhetorica* 26.1 (2008): 1–29. Print.

Hogg, Charlotte. *From the Garden Club: Rural Women Writing Community.* Lincoln: U of Nebraska P, 2006. Print.

Holtzman, Paul D., ed. "The Year Is 1989: Research Reports." *Today's Speech* 13.4 (1965): 11–14. Print.

Homer. *Iliad.* Print.

———. *Odyssey.* Print.

Howard, Jennifer. "Citation by Citation, New Maps Chart Hot Research and Scholarship's Hidden Terrain." *Chronicle of Higher Education* 11 Sept. 2011. Web. <http://chronicle.com/article/Maps-of-Citations-Uncover-New/128938/>.

Howard, John. "The Talk of the County: Revisiting Accusation, Murder, and Mississippi, 1985." *Queer Studies: An Interdisciplinary Reader.* Ed. Robert J. Corber and Stephen M. Valocchi. Malden: Blackwell, 2003. 142–58. Print.

Hoy, David Couzens. *The Time of Our Lives.* Cambridge: MIT P, 2009. Print.

Hum, Sue, and Arabella Lyon. "Recent Advances in Comparative Rhetoric." *The SAGE Handbook of Rhetorical Studies.* Ed. Andrea A. Lunsford, Kirt H. Wilson, and Rosa A. Eberly. Los Angeles: Sage, 2008. 153–65. Print.

Ibson, John. *Picturing Men: A Century of Male Relationships in Everyday American Photography.* Washington: Smithsonian Institution P, 2002. Print.

Ignatius of Loyola. "The Spiritual Exercises." Trans. George E. Ganss. *Ignatius of Loyola: Spiritual Exercises and Selected Works.* Ed. Ganss. New York: Paulist, 1991. 113–214. Print.

Ijsseling, Samuel. *Rhetoric and Philosophy in Conflict.* Trans. Paul Dunphy. The Hague, Netherlands: Martinus Nijhoff, 1976.

Inayatullah, Sohail. "Deconstructing and Reconstructing the Future: Predictive, Cultural, and Critical Epistemologies." *Futures* 22 (1990): 115–41. Print.

Irigaray, Luce. *Marine Lover of Friedrich Nietzsche.* Trans. Gillian C. Gill. New York: Columbia UP, 1991. Print.

Isocrates. *Panegyricus.* Print.

Jack, Jordynn. "Acts of Institution: Embodying Feminist Rhetorical Methodologies in Space and Time." *Rhetoric Review* 28.3 (2009): 285–303. Print.

———. *Science on the Home Front: American Women Scientists in World War II.* Urbana: U of Illinois P, 2009. Print.

Jarratt, Susan C. "Performing Feminisms, Histories, Rhetorics." *Rhetoric Society Quarterly* 22.1 (1992): 1–5. Print.

———. *Rereading the Sophists: Classical Rhetoric Refigured.* Carbondale: Southern Illinois UP, 1991. Print.

———. "Rhetoric and Feminism: Together Again." *College English* 62.3 (2000): 390–93. Print.

———. "Sappho's Memory." *Rhetoric Society Quarterly* 32.1 (2002): 11–43. Print.

———. "Speaking to the Past: Feminist Historiography in Rhetoric." *Pre/Text* 11.3–4 (1990): 190–209. Print.

Jarratt, Susan C., and Nedra Reynolds. "The Splitting Image: Contemporary Feminisms and the Ethics of êthos." *Ethos: New Essays in Rhetorical and Critical Theory.* Ed. James S. Baumlin and Tita French Baumlin. Dallas: Southern Methodist UP, 1994. 37–64. Print.

Johnson, E. Patrick. "'Quare' Studies, or (Almost) Everything I Know about Queer Studies I Learned from My Grandmother." *Text and Performance Quarterly* 21 (2001): 1–25. Print.

———. *Sweet Tea: Black Gay Men of the South*. Chapel Hill: U of North Carolina P, 2008. Print.

Johnson, Nan. *Gender and Rhetorical Space in American Life, 1866–1910*. Carbondale: Southern Illinois UP, 2002. Print.

———. *Nineteenth-Century Rhetoric in North America*. Carbondale: Southern Illinois UP, 1991. Print.

Johnson, Steven. *Emergence: The Connected Lives of Ants, Brains, Cities, and Software*. New York: Scribner, 2001. Print.

Johnston, Sarah Iles. *Restless Dead: Encounters between the Living and the Dead in Ancient Greece*. Berkeley: U of California P, 1999. Print.

Johnstone, Henry W., Jr. "'Philosophy and *Argumentum ad Hominem*' Revisited." *Validity and Rhetoric in Philosophical Argument: An Outlook in Transition*. University Park, PA: Dialogue P of Man and World, 1978: 53–61. Print.

Juhasz, Alexandra. "Video Remains." *GLQ* 12.2 (2006): 319–28. Print.

Kamuf, Peggy. *Book of Addresses*. Stanford: Stanford UP, 2005. Print.

Kates, Susan. *Activist Rhetorics and American Higher Education, 1885–1937*. Carbondale: Southern Illinois UP, 2001. Print.

Katz, Jerrold J. *The Underlying Reality of Language and Its Philosophical Import*. New York: Harper Torchbooks, 1971. Print.

Kaufmann, Walter, ed. and trans. *The Portable Nietzsche*. Penguin, 1977. Print.

Kellner, Hans. "After the Fall: Reflections on Histories of Rhetoric." *Writing Histories of Rhetoric*. Ed. Victor J. Vitanza. Carbondale: Southern Illinois UP, 1994. 20–37. Print.

———. *Language and Historical Representation: Getting the Story Crooked*. Madison: U of Wisconsin P, 1989. Print.

Kells, Michelle Hall. *Hector P. Garcia: Everyday Rhetoric and Mexican American Civil Rights*. Carbondale: Southern Illinois UP, 2006. Print.

Kells, Michelle Hall, Valerie Balester, and Victor Villanueva, eds. *Latino/a Discourses: On Language, Identity and Literacy Education*. Portsmouth: Boynton/Cook, 2004. Print.

Kennedy, George A. *Classical Rhetoric and Its Christian and Secular Tradition from Ancient to Modern Times*. 2nd ed. Chapel Hill: U of North Carolina P, 1999. Print.

———. *Comparative Rhetoric: An Historical and Cross-Cultural Introduction*. New York: Oxford UP, 1998. Print.

———. *A New History of Classical Rhetoric*. Princeton: Princeton UP, 1994. Print.

———, trans. *On Rhetoric: A Theory of Civic Discourse*. By Aristotle. New York: Oxford UP, 1991. Print.

Kingsley, Peter. *Ancient Philosophy, Mystery, and Magic*. Oxford: Clarendon, 1995. Print.

Kirby, Joan. "'Remembrance of the Future': Derrida on Mourning." *Social Semiotics* 16.3 (Sept. 2006): 461–72. Print.

Kirsch, Gesa E., and Liz Rohan, eds. *Beyond the Archives: Research as a Lived Process*. Carbondale: Southern Illinois UP, 2008. Print.

Kirsch, Gesa E., and Jacqueline J. Royster. "Feminist Rhetorical Practices: In Search of Excellence." *College Composition and Communication* 61.4 (2010): 640–72. Print.

Klossowski, Pierre. *Nietzsche and the Vicious Circle*. Trans. Daniel W. Smith. Chicago: U of Chicago P, 1977. Print.

Knox, Bernard. *Backing into the Future*. New York: Norton, 1994. Print.

Kofman, Sarah. "Baubô: Theological Perversion and Fetishism." *Nietzsche's New Seas*. Ed. Michael Allen Gillespie and Tracy B. Strong. Chicago: U of Chicago P, 1991. 175–202. Print.

Kolb, David. *The Critique of Pure Modernity*. Chicago: U of Chicago P, 1986. Print.

Kraus, Manfred. "Early Greek Probability Arguments and Common Ground Consensus." *Dissensus and the Search for Common Ground*. Ed. H. V. Hansen et al. Windsor: Ontario Society for the Study of Argumentation, 2007. CD-ROM.

Lane, Michael, ed. *Introduction to Structuralism*. New York: Basic, 1970. Print.

Laozi. *Dao De Jing: Making This Life Significant*. Trans. Roger T. Ames and David L. Hall. New York: Ballantine, 2003. Print.

Latour, Bruno. *We Have Never Been Modern*. Trans. Catherine Porter. Cambridge: Harvard UP, 1993. Print.

Lefebvre, Henri. *Rhythmanalysis*. Trans. Stuart Elden and Gerald Moore. New York: Continuum, 2004. Print.

L'Eplattenier, Barbara. "An Argument for Archival Research Methods: Thinking Beyond Methodology." *College English* 72.1 (Sept. 2009): 67–79. Print.

Levinas, Emmanuel. *Totality and Infinity: An Essay on Exteriority*. Trans. Alphonso Lingis. Pittsburgh: Duquesne UP, 1969. Print.

Lipson, Carol S., and Roberta A. Binkley, eds. *Ancient Non-Greek Rhetorics*. West Lafayette: Parlor, 2009. Print.

———, eds. *Rhetoric Before and Beyond the Greeks*. Albany: State U of New York P, 2004. Print.

Liu, Kang. "Is There an Alternative to (Capitalist) Globalization? The Debate about Modernity in China." *The Cultures of Globalization*. Ed. Fredric Jameson and Masao Miyoshi. Durham: Duke UP, 1998. 164–88. Print.

Lloyd, G. E. R. *Adversaries and Authorities: Investigations into Ancient Greek and Chinese Science*. Cambridge, UK: Cambridge UP, 1996. Print.

———. "The Development of Aristotle's Theory of the Classification of Animals." *Phronesis* 6.1 (1961): 59–81. Print.

Lloyd, Geoffrey, and Nathan Sivin. *The Way and the Word: Science and Medicine in Early China and Greece*. New Haven: Yale UP, 2002. Print.

Lloyd-Jones, Hugh. *Blood for the Ghosts*. London: Duckworth, 1982. Print.

———. Introduction. *History of Classical Scholarship*. By Ulrich von Wilamowitz-Moellendorff. Ed. Lloyd-Jones. Trans. Alan Harris. Baltimore: Johns Hopkins UP, 1982. v–xxxii. Print.

———. "Nietzsche and the Study of the Ancient World." *Studies in Nietzsche and the Classical Tradition*. Ed. James C. O'Flaherty, Timothy F. Sellner, and Robert M. Helm. Chapel Hill: U of North Carolina P, 1976. 16–32. Print.

Logan, Shirley. *"We Are Coming": The Persuasive Discourse of Nineteenth-Century Black Women*. Carbondale: Southern Illinois UP, 1999. Print.

Longaker, Mark Garrett. *Rhetoric and the Republic: Politics, Civic Discourse and Education in Early America*. Tuscaloosa: U of Alabama P, 2007. Print.

Loraux, Nicole. *The Invention of Athens: The Funeral Oration in the Classical City*. Trans. Alan Sheridan. New York: Zone, 2006. Print.

Lorch, Paul. "But Who *Was* Harvey Milk?" *Gay and Lesbian Review Worldwide* (May–June 2009): 7. Print.

Love, Heather. *Feeling Backward: Loss and the Politics of Queer History.* Cambridge: Harvard UP, 2007. Print.

Lu, Xing. *Rhetoric in Ancient China, Fifth to Third Century B.C.E.: A Comparison with Classical Greek Rhetoric.* Columbia: U of South Carolina P, 1998. Print.

Lu, Xing, and Herbert W. Simons. "Transitional Rhetoric of Chinese Communist Party Leaders in the Post-Mao Reform Period: Dilemmas and Strategies." *Quarterly Journal of Speech* 92.3 (2006): 262–86. Print.

Lukacher, Ned. *Primal Scenes: Literature, Philosophy, Psychoanalysis.* Ithaca: Cornell UP, 1986. Print.

———. *Time-Fetishes.* Durham: Duke UP, 1998. Print.

Lunsford, Andrea. "On Reclaiming Rhetorica." *Reclaiming Rhetorica: Women in the Rhetorical Tradition.* Ed. Andrea Lunsford. Pittsburgh: U of Pittsburgh P, 1995. 3–8. Print.

———, ed. *Reclaiming Rhetorica: Women in the Rhetorical Tradition.* Pittsburgh: U of Pittsburgh P, 1995. Print.

Lunsford, Andrea A., Kirt H. Wilson, and Rosa A. Eberly, eds. *The SAGE Handbook of Rhetorical Studies.* Los Angeles: Sage, 2009. Print.

Lyon, Arabella. "Confucian Silence and Remonstration: A Basis for Deliberation?" *Rhetoric Before and Beyond the Greeks.* Ed. Carol S. Lipson and Roberta A. Binkley. Albany: State U of New York P, 2004. 131–45. Print.

———. "Rhetorical Authority in Athenian Democracy and the Chinese Legalism of Han Fei." *Philosophy and Rhetoric* 41.1 (2008): 51–71. Print.

———. "Sources of Noncanonical Readings, or Doing History from Prejudice." *Rhetoric Review* 16.2 (1998): 226–41. Print.

———. "Why Do the Rulers Listen to the Wild Theories of Speech-Makers? Or *Wuwei, Shi,* and Methods of Comparative Rhetoric." *Ancient Non-Greek Rhetorics.* Ed. Carol S. Lipson and Roberta A. Binkley. West Lafayette: Parlor, 2009. 176–96. Print.

Lyotard, Jean-François. *The Differend: Phrases in Dispute.* Trans. Georges Van Den Abbeele. Minneapolis: U of Minnesota P, 1989. Print.

———. *Driftworks.* Ed. Roger McKeon. New York: Semiotext(e), 1984. Print.

———. *Just Gaming.* Trans. Jean-Loup Thebaud. Minneapolis: U of Minnesota P, 1985. Print.

———. *The Postmodern Explained: Correspondence, 1982–1983.* Trans. Georges Van Den Abbeele. Minneapolis: U of Minnesota P, 1993. Print.

Maas, Paul. *Greek Metre.* Trans. Hugh Lloyd-Jones. Oxford: Clarendon P, 1972. Print.

Maddux, Kristy. "Winning the Right to Vote in 2004: *Iron Jawed Angels* and the Retrospective Framing of Feminism." *Feminist Media Studies* 9.1 (2009): 73–94. Print.

Mailloux, Steven. *Disciplinary Identities: The Rhetorical Paths of English, Speech, and Composition.* New York: MLA, 2006. Print.

———. "Making Comparisons: First Contact, Ethnocentricism, and Cross-Cultural Communication." *Post-Nationalist American Studies.* Ed. John Carlos Rowe. Berkeley: U of California P, 2000. 110–25. Print.

———. *Reception Histories: Rhetoric, Pragmatism, and American Cultural Politics.* Ithaca: Cornell UP, 1998. Print.

Mao, LuMing. *Reading Chinese Fortune Cookie: The Making of Chinese American Rheto-ric*. Logan: Utah State UP, 2006. Print.

——. "Reflective Encounters: Illustrating Comparative Rhetoric." *Style* 37.4 (2003): 401–25. Print.

——. "Searching for the Way: Between the Whats and Wheres of Chinese Rhetoric." *College English* 72.4 (2010): 329–49. Print.

——. "Studying the Chinese Rhetorical Tradition in the Present: Re-presenting the Native's Point of View." *College English* 69.3 (2007): 216–37. Print.

Marchand, Suzanne L. *Down from Olympus. Archaeology and Philhellenism in Germany, 1750–1970*. Princeton: Princeton UP, 1996. Print.

Marie, Cedar. "The Best Medicine." *Reversing Vandalism Online Gallery*. Web. 20 Aug. 2010. <http://sfpl.org/index.php?pg=2000124801&img=16>.

Marsh, James L., and John D. Caputo, and Merold Westphal, ed. *Modernity and Its Discontents*. New York: Fordham UP, 1992. Print.

Martin, Luther H., Huck Gutman, and Patrick H. Hutton, eds. *Technologies of the Self: A Seminar with Michel Foucault*. Amherst: U of Massachusetts P, 1988. Print.

Martindale, Charles. "Did He Die, or Was He Pushed?" *Arion* 3rd ser. 6.3 (Winter 1999): 103–21. Print.

Maryks, Robert Aleksander. *Saint Cicero and the Jesuits: The Influence of the Liberal Arts on the Adoption of Moral Probabilism*. Burlington, VT: Ashgate, 2008. Print.

Mattingly, Carol. "Telling Evidence: Rethinking What Counts in Rhetoric." *Rhetoric Society Quarterly* 32.1 (2002): 99–108. Print.

——. "Woman's Temple, Women's Fountains: The Erasure of Public Memory." *American Studies* 49.3/4 (2008): 133–56. Print.

McBride, Dwight A. *Why I Hate Abercrombie and Fitch: Essays on Race and Sexuality*. New York: New York UP, 2005. Print.

McKerrow, Raymie E. "Research in Rhetoric: A Glance at Our Recent Past, Present, and Potential Future." *The Review of Communication* 10 (2010): 197–210. Print.

McTaggart, J. Ellis. "The Unreality of Time." *Mind* new ser. 17 (1908): 457–74. Print.

Meyer, Richard. *Outlaw Representation: Censorship and Homosexuality in Twentieth-Century American Art*. New York: Oxford UP, 2002. Print.

Michalski, Mark. "Hermeneutic Phenomenology as Philology." *Heidegger and Rhetoric*. Ed. Daniel M. Gross and Ansgar Kemmann. Albany: State U of New York P, 2006. 65–80. Print.

Miller, Elaine P. "Harnessing Dionysos: Nietzsche on Rhythm, Time, and Restraint." *Journal of Nietzsche Studies* 17 (1999): 1–32. Print.

Miller, Hildy, and Lillian Bridwell Bowles, eds. *Rhetorical Women: Roles and Represen-tations*. Tuscaloosa: U of Alabama P, 2005. Print.

Morris, Charles E. III. "Archival Queer." *Rhetoric and Public Affairs* 9.1 (2006): 145–51. Print.

——. "The Archival Turn in Rhetorical Studies; Or, The Archive's Rhetorical (Re) turn." *Rhetoric and Public Affairs* 9.1 (2006): 113–15. Print.

——, ed. "Forum: The Politics of Archival Research." *Rhetoric and Public Affairs* 9 (Spring 2006): 113–51. Print.

——, ed. "Forum: Remembering AIDS Coalition to Unleash Power (ACT UP), 1987–2012 and Beyond." *Quarterly Journal of Speech* 98 (Feb. 2012): 49–108. Print.

———. "Hard Evidence: The Vexations of Lincoln's Queer Corpus." *Rhetoric, Material-ity, and Politics*. Ed. Barbara Biesecker and John Lucaites. New York: Peter Lang, 2009. 185–214. Print.

———. "My Old Kentucky Homo: Abraham Lincoln, Larry Kramer, and the Politics of Queer Memory." *Queering Public Address: Sexualities in American Histori-cal Discourse*. Ed. Morris. Columbia: U of South Carolina P, 2007. 93–120. Print.

———. "Portrait of a Queer Rhetorical/Historical Critic." Introduction. *Queering Public Address: Sexualities in American Historical Discourse*. Ed. Morris. Columbia: U of South Carolina P, 2007. 1–19. Print.

———, ed. *Remembering the AIDS Quilt*. East Lansing: Michigan State UP, 2011. Print.

Morrison, Toni. "Memory, Creation, and Writing." *Thought* 59.4 (1984): 385–90. Print.

Most, Glenn. "Heidegger's Greeks." *Arion* 3rd ser. 10.1 (2002): 83–98. Print.

Mountford, Roxanne. *The Gendered Pulpit: Preaching in American Protestant Spaces*. Carbondale: Southern Illinois UP, 2003. Print.

———. "Octalog II: The (Continuing) Politics of Historiography." *Rhetoric Review* 16.1 (1997): 22-44. Print.

Muckelbauer, John. "Rhetoric, Asignification, and the Other: A Response to Diane Davis." *Philosophy and Rhetoric* 40.2 (2007): 238–47. Print.

Muñoz, José Esteban. *Cruising Utopia: The Then and There of Queer Futurity*. New York: New York UP, 2009. Print.

———. *Disidentifications: Queers of Color and the Performance of Politics*. Minneapolis: U of Minnesota P, 1999. Print.

Murphy, James J. "A New Look at Chaucer and the Rhetoricians." *Review of English Studies* 15 (1964): 1–20. Print.

———. "Octalog: The Politics of Historiography." *Rhetoric Review* 7.1 (1988): 5–6. Print.

———. *Rhetoric in the Middle Ages: A History of Rhetorical Theory from St. Augustine to the Renaissance*. Berkeley: U of California P, 1974. Print.

Murphy, Roy D. "A Third of a Century of Progress." *The Southern Speech Journal* 30 (1964): 1–7. Print.

Nägele, Rainer. *Echoes of Translation*. Johns Hopkins UP, 1997. Print.

———. *Reading after Freud*. New York: Columbia UP, 1987. Print.

———. *Theater, Theory, Speculation*. Baltimore: Johns Hopkins UP, 1991. Print.

Nestle, Joan. "The Will to Remember: The Lesbian Herstory Archives of New York." *Journal of Homosexuality* 34.3/4 (1998): 225–35. Print.

Newman, Jane O. "The Word Made Print: Luther's 1522 *New Testament* in an Age of Mechanical Reproduction." *Representations* 11 (1985): 95–133. Print.

Newman, Sally. "The Archival Traces of Desire: Vernon Lee's Failed Sexuality and the Interpretation of Letters in Lesbian History." *Journal of the History of Sexuality* 14 (2005): 51–75. Print.

Nichols, Stephen G., ed. *The New Philology*. Spec. issue of *Speculum* 65.1 (1990). Print.

Nietzsche, Friedrich. *Beyond Good and Evil*. Ed. Rolf-Peter Horstmann and Judith Norman. Trans. Norman. Cambridge: Cambridge UP, 2002. Print.

———. *The Birth of Tragedy and Other Writings*. Ed. Raymond Geuss and Ronald Speirs. Trans. Speirs. Cambridge: Cambridge UP, 1999. Print.

———. *Daybreak*. Ed. Maudemarie Clark and Brian Leiter. Trans. R. J. Hollingdale. Cambridge: Cambridge UP, 2009. Print.

———. "Description of Ancient Rhetoric." *Friedrich Nietzsche on Rhetoric and Language*. Ed. and Trans. Sander L. Gilman, Carole Blair, David J. Parent. New York: Oxford UP, 1989. 2–206. Print.

———. "The Dionysian Worldview." Trans. Claudia Crawford. *Journal of Nietzsche Studies* 13 (1997): 81–97. Print.

———. *Ecce Homo*. Trans. Walter Kaufmann. New York: Vintage, 1969. Print.

———. *The Gay Science*. Trans. Walter Kaufmann. New York: Vintage, 1974. Print.

———. "Homer and Classical Philology." Ed. Oscar Levy. Trans. J. M. Kennedy. 2006. Web. 27 June 2010. <http://www.gutenberg.org/files/18188/18188-h/18188-h.htm>.

———. "Homer's Contest." *Portable Nietzsche*. Ed and Trans. Walter Kaufmann. New York: Penguin, 1968. 32–38. Print.

———. "Interpretation in History." *Tropics of Discourse: Essays in Cultural Criticism*. Baltimore: Johns Hopkins UP, 1978. 51–80. Print.

———. *Human, All Too Human*. Trans. R. J. Hollingdale. Cambridge: Cambridge UP, 1996. Print.

———. "Nietzsche on Classics and Classicists Author(s)." Trans. William Arrowsmith. *Arion* 2.1 (Spring 1963): 5–18. Print.

———. "Nietzsche on Classics and Classicists (Part II)." Trans. William Arrowsmith. *Arion* 2.2 (Summer 1963): 5–27. Print.

———. "Nietzsche on Classics and Classicists (Part III)." Trans. William Arrowsmith. *Arion* 2.4 (Winter 1963): 5–31. Print.

———. "Nietzsche: Notes for 'We Philologists.'" Trans. William Arrowsmith. *Arion* new ser. 1.2 (1973/1974): 279–380. Print.

———. "Nietzsche: On the Theory of Quantitative Rhythm." Trans. James W. Halporn. *Arion* 6.2 (Summer 1967): 233–43. Print.

———. "On Redemption. *Thus Spoke Zarathustra*. Trans. R. J. Hollingdale. Penguin, 1961. 159–63. Print.

———. "On Rhythm." *Friedrich Nietzsche on Rhetoric and Language*. Ed. and Trans. Sander L. Gilman, Carole Blair, David J. Parent. Oxford: Oxford UP, 1989. 244–45. Print.

———. *On the Genealogy of Morals* and *Ecce Homo*. Trans. Walter Kaufmann. New York: Vintage, 1969. Print.

———. "On the Uses and Disadvantages of History for Life." *Untimely Mediations*. Trans. R. J. Hollingdale. Cambridge: Cambridge UP, 1988. 57–124. Print.

———. "On Truth and Lying in an Extra-Moral Sense." Trans. David J. Parent. *Friedrich Nietzsche on Rhetoric and Language*. Ed. Sander L. Gilman, Carole Blair, and David J. Parent. Oxford: Oxford UP, 1989. 246–57. Print.

———. *Philosophy and Truth*. Ed. and Trans. Daniel Breazeale. Atlantic Highlands, NJ: Humanities P, 1990. Print.

———. *Philosophy in the Tragic Age of the Greeks*. Trans. Marianne Cowan. Washington, DC: Regnery Gateway, 1987. Print.

———. *The Pre-Platonic Philosophers*. Trans. Greg Whitlock. Urbana: U of Illinois P, 2001. Print.

———. "The Struggle between Science and Wisdom." *Philosophy and Truth*. Ed. and Trans. Daniel Breazeale. Atlantic Highlands, NJ: Humanities P, 1990. 127–46. Print.

———. "Time-Atom Theory: *Nachgelassene Fragmente*, Early 1873." *Pli* 9 (2000): 1–5. Print.

————. *Twilight of the Idols/The Anti-Christ*. Trans. R. J. Holingdale. New York: Penguin, 1968. Print.

————. *Unmodern Observations*. Ed. William Arrowsmith. New Haven: Yale UP, 1990. Print.

————. *Untimely Meditations*. Trans. R. J. Hollingdale. Cambridge: Cambridge UP, 1988. Print.

————. "We Classicists." *Unmodern Observations*. Trans. William Arrowsmith. New Haven: Yale UP, 1990. 305–87. Print.

————. "We Philologists." *The Complete Works of Friedrich Nietzsche*. Ed. Oscar Levy. 3rd ed. Vol. 8 of 18. Trans. J. M. Kennedy. Edinburgh: Scotland. 1911. Web. 27 June 2010. <http://www.gutenberg.org/files/18267/18267-h/18267-h.htm>.

"The 1940s: Jim Kepner." *Southern California LGBT History Website*. 2005. Web. 27 Apr. 2009. <http://www.lgbthistory.org/>.

Nora, Pierre. "Between Memory and History: *Les Lieux de Mémoire*." Trans. Marc Roudebush. *Representations* 26 (1989): 7–24. Print.

North, Helen F. *Sophrosyne: Self-Knowledge and Self-Restraint in Greek Literature*. Ithaca: Cornell UP, 1966. Print.

Norton, Robert E. "Wilamowitz at War." *International Journal of the Classical Tradition* 15.1 (2008): 74–97. Print.

Nussbaum, Martha C. *The Fragility of Goodness*. 2nd ed. Cambridge: Cambridge UP, 2001. Print.

Ochs, Donovan J. *Consolatory Rhetoric*. Columbia: U of South Carolina P, 1993. Print.

"Octalog: The Politics of Historiography." 1988 CCCC Panel. *Rhetoric Review* 7.1 (Fall 1988): 5–49. Print.

"Octalog II: The (Continuing) Politics of Historiography." 1997 CCCC Panel. *Rhetoric Review* 16.1 (Fall 1997): 22–44. Print.

"Octalog III: The Politics of Historiography." 61st Annual Conference on College Composition and Communication. Louisville. 17–20 Mar. 2010. Panel address.

Olson, Lester C. *Benjamin Franklin's Vision of American Community: A Study in Rhetorical Iconology*. Columbia: U of South Carolina P, 2004. Print.

————. *Emblems of American Community in the Revolutionary Era: A Study in Rhetorical Iconology*. Washington: Smithsonian Institution P, 1991. Print.

O'Malley, John W. *The First Jesuits*. Cambridge: Harvard UP, 1993. Print.

O'Malley, Pat. "Risk and Responsibility." *Foucault and Political Reason*. Ed. Andrew Barry, Thomas Osborne, and Nikolas Rose. Chicago: U of Chicago P, 1996. 189–208. Print.

Ong, Walter J. "Literacy and Orality in Our Times." *Profession* 79 (1979): 1–7. Print.

Other People's Pictures. Dir. Lorca Shepperd and Cabot Philbrick. 2004. Film.

O'Toole, James M. "The Symbolic Significance of Archives." *American Archival Studies: Readings in Theory and Practice*. Ed. Randall C. Jimerson. Chicago: Soc. of American Archivists, 2000. 47–72. Print.

Paden, William D., ed. *The Future of the Middle Ages: Medieval Literature in the 1990s*. Gainesville: UP of Florida, 1994. Print.

Palczewski, Catherine H. "The Male Madonna and the Feminine Uncle Sam: Visual Argument, Icons, and Ideographs in 1909 Anti-woman Suffrage Postcards." *Quarterly Journal of Speech* 91.4 (2005): 365–94. Print.

Paré, Ambroise. *On Monsters and Marvels*. Trans. Janis L. Pallister. Chicago: U of Chicago P, 1982. Print.

Parikka, Jussi. *Insect Media: An Archaeology of Animals and Technology*. Minneapolis: U of Minnesota P, 2010. Print.

Parry, Milman. "*L'épithète traditionelle dans Homére*." Paris: Societe d'editions, "Les belles lettres," 1928. Print.

——. *The Making of Homeric Verse: The Collected Papers of Milman Parry*. Ed. Adam Parry. Oxford: Clarendon, 1971. Print.

——. "Studies in the Epic Technique of Oral Verse-Making. II. The Homeric Language as the Language of Oral Poetry." *Harvard Studies in Classical Philology* 43 (1932): 1–50. Print.

Peabody, Berkley. *The Winged Word: A Study in the Technique of Ancient Greek Oral Composition as Seen Principally through Hesiod's* Works and Days. Albany: State U of New York P, 1975. Print.

Perelman, Chaim, and Lucie Olbrechts-Tyteca. *The New Rhetoric: A Treatise on Argumentation*. Trans. John Wilkinson and Purcell Weaver. Notre Dame: U of Notre Dame P, 1969. Print.

Peters, John Durham. *Speaking into the Air: A History of the Idea of Communication*. Chicago: U of Chicago P, 1999. Print.

Pfeiffer, Rudolf. *History of Classical Scholarship: From the Beginnings to the End of the Hellenistic Age*. Oxford: Clarendon, 1971. Print.

Pharr, Clyde. *Homeric Greek*. Norman: U of Oklahoma P, 1970. Print.

Phillips, C. Robert. "Classical Scholarship against Its History." *American Journal of Philology* 110.4 (1989): 636–57. Print.

Phillips, Kendall R. Introduction. *Framing Public Memory*. Ed. Phillips. Tuscaloosa: U of Alabama P, 2004. 1–14. Print.

Pindar. *Olympian Odes*. Print.

Plato. *Ion*. Print.

——. *Phaedo*. Print.

Plutarch. "Alcibiades." *Lives*. Trans. Bernadotte Perrin. Cambridge: Harvard UP, 1916. Print.

Pollack, William. *Real Boys: Rescuing Our Sons from the Myths of Boyhood*. New York: Random, 1998. Print.

Pollock, Sheldon. "Future Philology?" *Critical Inquiry* 35.4 (2009): 931–63. Print.

Porter, James I. "Being on Time." *Nietzsche and the Philology of the Future*. Stanford: Stanford UP, 2000. 127–66. Print.

——. *The Invention of Dionysus*. Stanford: U of Stanford P, 2000. Print.

——. *Nietzsche and the Philology of the Future*. Stanford: Stanford UP, 2000. Print.

——. "Nietzsche, Homer, and the Classical Tradition." *Nietzsche and Antiquity*. Ed. Paul Bishop. New York: Camden House, 2004. 7–26. Print.

——. "Nietzsche's Atoms." *Nietzsche und die antike Philosophie*. Ed. Daniel W. Conway and Rudolf Rehn. Wissenschaftlicher Verlag Trier, 1992. 47–90. Print.

Poulakos, John. "Nietzsche and Histories of Rhetorics." *Writing Histories of Rhetoric*. Ed. Victor J. Vitanza. Carbondale: Southern Illinois UP, 1994. 81–97. Print.

——. *Sophistical Rhetoric in Classical Greece*. Columbia: U of South Carolina P, 1995. Print.

——. "Testing and Contesting Classical Rhetorics." *Rhetoric Society Quarterly* 36 (2006): 171–79. Print.

Poulakos, Takis. "Human Agency in the History of Rhetoric: Gorgias's *Encomium of Helen.*" *Writing Histories of Rhetoric*. Ed. Victor J. Vitanza. Carbondale: Southern Illinois UP, 1994. 59–80. Print.

Powell, Malea. "Dreaming Charles Eastman: Cultural Memory, Autobiography, and Geography in Indigenous Rhetorical Histories." *Beyond the Archives: Research as a Lived Process*. Ed. Gesa E. Kirsch and Liz Rohan. Carbondale: Southern Illinois UP, 2008. 115–27. Print.

Prieto, Mercedes. *Liberalismo y temor: Imaginando los sujetos indígenas en el Ecuador postcolonial, 1895–1950*. Quito: Abya Yala, 2004. Print.

"Project History." *San Francisco Public Library*. Web. 20 Aug. 2010. <http://sfpl.org/index.php?pg=2000111801>.

Pucci, Pietro. *Hesiod and the Language of Poetry*. Baltimore: Johns Hopkins UP, 1977. Print.

Quintilian. *Institutio Oratoria (The Orator's Education)*. Vol. 1. Trans. Donald A. Russell. Cambridge: Harvard UP, 2001. Print.

Rabbow, Paul. *Seelenführung: Methodik der exerzitien in der antike*. Munich: Kössel, 1954. Print.

Ramage, John D. *Rhetoric: A User's Guide*. New York: Pearson, 2006.

Ramírez, Cristina D. "Forging a Mestiza Rhetoric: Mexican Women Journalists' Role in the Construction of a National Identity." *College English* 71.6 (2009): 606–29. Print.

Ramírez, Horacio N. Roque. "A Living Archive of Desire: Terisita la Campesina and the Embodiment of Queer Latino Community Histories." *Archive Stories: Facts, Fictions and the Writing of History*. Ed. Antoinette Burton. Durham: Duke UP, 2005. 111–35. Print.

Ramsey, Alexis E., Wendy B. Sharer, Barbara L'Eplattenier, and Lisa S. Mastrangelo, eds. *Working in the Archives: Practical Research Methods for Rhetoric and Composition*. Carbondale: Southern Illinois UP, 2010. Print.

Ranney, Frances J. "Mining the Collective Unconscious: With Responses from Ruth Ray and Gwen Gorzelsky." *Rhetorica in Motion: Feminist Rhetorical Methods and Methodologies*. Ed. Eileen E. Schell and K. J. Rawson. Pittsburgh: U of Pittsburgh P, 2010. 118–35. Print.

Ratcliffe, Krista. *Anglo-American Feminist Challenges to the Rhetorical Traditions: Virginia Woolf, Mary Daly, and Adrienne Rich*. Carbondale: Southern Illinois UP, 1996. Print.

——. *Rhetorical Listening: Identification, Gender, Whiteness*. Carbondale: Southern Illinois UP, 2005. Print.

"The *Ratio Studiorum* of 1599." Trans. A. R. Ball. *St. Ignatius and the Ratio Studiorum*. Ed. Edward A. Fitzpatrick. New York: McGraw-Hill, 1933. Print.

Rawson, K. J. "Accessing Transgender // Desiring Queer(er?) Archival Logics." *Archivaria* 68 (Fall 2009). 123–40. Print.

——. "Archive This! Queer(ing) Archival Practices." *Practicing Research in Writing Studies: Reflections on Ethically Responsible Research*. Ed. Katy Powell and Pam Takayoshi. New York: Hampton P, 2012. 237–50. Print.

——. "Queering Feminist Rhetorical Canonization." *Rhetorica in Motion: Feminist Rhetorical Methods and Methodologies*. Ed. Eileen E. Schell and K. J. Rawson. Pittsburgh: U of Pittsburgh P, 2010. 39–52. Print.

Ray, Angela G. "The Rhetorical Ritual of Citizenship: Women's Voting as Public Performance, 1868–1875." *Quarterly Journal of Speech* 93.1 (2007): 1–26. Print.

Readings, Bill. *Introducing Lyotard: Art and Politics*. New York: Routledge, 1991. Print.

Reiss, Timothy J. *The Discourse of Modernism*. Ithaca: Cornell UP, 1982. Print.

Ricciardi, Alessia. *The Ends of Mourning: Psychoanalysis, Literature, Film*. Stanford: Stanford UP, 2003. Print.

Richards, E. G. *Mapping Time: The Calendar and Its History*. Oxford: Oxford UP, 2000. Print.

Richards, Laura E., Maud Howe, and Florence Howe Hall. *Julia Ward Howe, 1819–1910, in Two Volumes, with Portraits and Other Illustrations*. Vol. 2. Boston: Houghton Mifflin, 1916. Print.

Richardson, John. "Nietzsche on Time and Becoming." *A Companion to Nietzsche*. Ed. Keith Ansell Pearson. New York: Wiley-Blackwell, 2009. 208–29. Print.

Ritchie, Joy, and Kate Ronald. Introduction. *Available Means: An Anthology of Women's Rhetoric(s)*. Ed. Ritchie and Ronald. Pittsburgh: U of Pittsburgh P, 2001. xv–xxxi. Print.

Roberts, Adrienne Skye. "What We Leave Behind: New Narratives in a Queer Archive." *Open Space: San Francisco Museum of Modern Art*. 8 July 2009. Web. 10 Jan. 2011. <http://blog.sfmoma.org/2009/07/what-we-leave-behind-new-narratives -in-a-queer-archive/>.

Roberts-Miller, Patricia. *Fanatical Schemes: Proslavery Rhetoric and the Tragedy of Consensus*. Tuscaloosa: U of Alabama P, 2009. Print.

Roeder, George. "Filling in the Picture: Visual Culture." *Reviews in American History* 26.1 (1998): 275–93. Print.

Rohy, Valerie. "In the Queer Archive: *Fun Home*." *GLQ* 16.3 (2010): 341–61. Print.

Ronell, Avital. "Is It Happening." *The UberReader: Selected Works of Avital Ronell*. Ed. Diane Davis. Urbana: U of Illinois P, 2008. 324–26. Print.

———. "Preface to *Dictations*." *The UberReader: Selected Works of Avital Ronell*. Ed. Diane Davis. Urbana: U of Illinois P, 2008. 145–55. Print.

———. "Slow Learner." *The UberReader: Selected Works of Avital Ronell*. Ed. Diane Davis. Urbana: U of Illinois P, 2008. 259–92. Print.

———. *The Test Drive*. Chicago: U of Chicago P, 2007. Print.

———. *The UberReader: Selected Works of Avital Ronell*. Ed. Diane Davis. Urbana: U of Illinois P, 2008.

Rosenberg, Alan, and Steven V. Hicks. "Nietzsche and Untimeliness." *Journal of Nietzsche Studies* 25 (2003): 1–34. Print.

Rosenstock, Bruce. "Socrates as Revenant: A Reading of the *Menexenus*." *Classical Association of Canada* 48.4 (Winter 1994): 331–47. Print.

Royle, Nicholas. *The Uncanny*. Manchester: Manchester UP, 2003. Print.

Royster, Jacqueline Jones, ed. *Southern Horrors and Other Writings: The Anti-lynching Campaign of Ida B. Wells, 1892–1900*. Boston: Bedford, 1997. Print.

Rubin, Andrew N. "Techniques of Trouble: Edward Said and the Dialectics of Cultural Philology." *South Atlantic Quarterly* 102.4 (2003): 861–76. Print.

Runia, Eelco. "Burying the Dead, Creating the Past." *History and Theory* 46 (Oct. 2007): 313–25. Print.

Russo, J. A. "Is 'Oral' or 'Aural' Composition the Cause of Homer's Formulaic Style?" *Oral Literature and the Formula*. Ed. Benjamin A. Stolz and Richard S. Shannon.

Ann Arbor: Center for the Coordination of Ancient and Modern Studies. U of Michigan, 1976: 31–71. Print.

Ryan, Kathleen J. "Recasting Recovery and Gender Critique as Inventive Arts: Constructing Edited Collections in Feminist Rhetorical Studies." *Rhetoric Review* 25.1 (2006): 22–40. Print.

Said, Edward W. "The Return to Philology." *Humanism and Democratic Criticism.* Ed. Said. New York: Columbia UP, 2004. 57–84. Print.

Said, Marie, and Edward W. Said, trans. "Philology and Weltliteratur." By Erich Auerbach. *The Centennial Review* 13.1 (1969): 1–17. Print.

Sandys, Sir John Edwin. *A History of Classical Scholarship.* Vols. 1–3. Cambridge: Cambridge UP, 1903. Web. 8 July 2010. <http://www.archive.org/details/historyofclassicoosanduoft>.

Sappho. *Sappho: A New Translation.* Trans. Mary Barnard. Berkeley: U of California P, 1958. Print.

Saussure, Ferdinand de. *Course in General Linguistics.* Peru, IL: Open Court, 1972. Print.

Scaliger, Josephus Justus. *Opus novum de emendatione temporum.* Paris, 1583. Print.

Schiappa, Edward. *The Beginnings of Rhetorical Theory in Classical Greece.* New Haven: Yale UP, 1999. Print.

Schilb, John. "Future Histories of Rhetoric and the Present Age of Anxiety." *Writing Histories of Rhetoric.* Ed. Victor J. Vitanza. Carbondale: Southern Illinois UP, 1994. 128–38. Print.

Schneider, Manfred. "Luther with McLuhan." Trans. Samuel Weber. *Religion and Media.* Ed. Hent de Vries and Samuel Weber. Stanford: Stanford UP, 2001. 198–215. Print.

Schorer, Mark. "An Indignant and Prophetic Novel: George Orwell Looks Thirty-Five Years Ahead into the Age of the Super-State." *New York Times* 12 June 1949, BR1. Print.

Schwartz, Barry. "Postmodernity and Historical Reputation: Abraham Lincoln in Late Twentieth-Century American Memory." *Social Forces* 77 (Sept. 1998): 63–103. Print.

Scott, Joan Wallach. *Gender and the Politics of History.* Rev. ed. New York: Columbia UP, 1999. Print.

Scott, Robert L. "On Viewing Rhetoric as Epistemic." *Central States Speech Journal* 18 (1967): 9–17. Print.

———. "On Viewing Rhetoric as Epistemic: Ten Years Later." *Central States Speech Journal* 27 (1976): 258–66. Print.

Scribner, Robert W. *For the Sake of Simple Folk: Popular Propaganda for the German Reformation.* Cambridge: Cambridge UP, 1981. Print.

Segal, Charles P. "Gorgias and the Psychology of the Logos." *Harvard Studies in Classical Philology* 66 (1962): 99–155. Print.

Sember, Robert. "In the Shadow of the Object: Sexual Memory in the AIDS Epidemic." *Space and Culture* 6 (Aug. 2003): 214–34. Print.

Settis, Salvatore. *The Future of the "Classical."* Trans. Allan Cameron. Cambridge: Polity, 2006. Print.

Seyhan, Azade. *Representation and Its Discontents.* Berkeley: U of California P, 1992. Print.

Sharer, Wendy B. "Disintegrating Bodies of Knowledge: Historical Material and Revisionary Histories of Rhetoric." *Rhetorical Bodies.* Ed. Jack Selzer and Sharon Crowley. Madison: U of Wisconsin P, 1999. 120–39. Print.

———. *Vote and Voice: Women's Organizations and Political Literacy, 1915–1930.* Carbondale: Southern Illinois UP, 2004. Print.

Shaver, Lisa. "Women's Death-Bed Pulpits: From Quiet Congregants to Iconic Ministers." *Rhetoric Review* 27.1 (2007): 1–34. Print.

Shuger, Deborah K. *Sacred Rhetoric: The Christian Grand Style in the English Renaissance.* Princeton: Princeton UP, 1988. Print.

Skinner, Carolyn. "'She Will Have Science': Ethos and Audience in Mary Gove's Lectures to Ladies." *Rhetoric Society Quarterly* 39.3 (2009): 240–59. Print.

Sloane, Thomas O., ed. *The Encyclopedia of Rhetoric.* Oxford: Oxford UP, 2001. Print.

Sloterdijk, Peter. *Thinker on Stage.* Trans. Jamie Owen Daniel. Minneapolis: U of Minnesota P, 1989. Print.

Smith, Barbara Herrnstein. *Contingencies of Value.* Cambridge: Harvard UP, 1988. Print.

Smyth, Herbert Weir. *Greek Grammar.* Gordon M. Messing. Cambridge: Harvard UP, 1972. Print.

Sophocles. *Antigone.* Print.

"So You Want to Be an Archivist: An Overview of the Archival Profession." *Society of American Archivists.* Web. 20 Aug. 2010. <http://www2.archivists.org/profession>.

Spitzer, Leo. *Linguistics and Literary History: Essays in Stylistics.* Princeton: Princeton UP, 1970. Print.

Stoler, Ann Laura. *Along the Archival Grain: Epistemic Anxieties and Colonial Common Sense.* Princeton: Princeton UP, 2009. Print.

Stormer, Nathan. "In Living Memory: Abortion as Cultural Amnesia." *Quarterly Journal of Speech* 88.3 (2002): 265–83. Print.

Stromberg, Ernest, ed. *American Indian Rhetorics of Survivance.* Pittsburgh: U of Pittsburgh P, 2006. Print.

Stryker, Susan. "Transgender History, Homonormativity, and Disciplinarity." *Radical History Review* 100 (2008): 145–57. Print.

Sutton, Jane S. "The Death of Rhetoric and Its Rebirth in Philosophy." *Rhetorica* 4 (1986): 203–26. Print.

———. *The House of My Sojourn.* Tuscaloosa: U of Alabama P, 2010. Print.

———. "Structuring the Narrative for the Canon of Rhetoric." *Writing Histories of Rhetoric.* Ed. Victor J. Vitanza. Carbondale: Southern Illinois UP, 1994. 156–79. Print.

Swearingen, C. Jan. "Plato's Feminine: Appropriation, Impersonation, and Metaphorical Polemic." *Rhetoric Society Quarterly* 22.1 (1992): 109–22. Print.

———. *Rhetoric and Irony.* Oxford: Oxford UP, 1991. Print.

Tacey, William S. "Contemporary Research and Application of Research in Business and Industry Communication." *Today's Speech* 13.4 (1965): 24–26. Print.

Taleb, Nassim Nicholas. *The Black Swan: The Impact of the Highly Improbable.* New York: Random, 2010. Print.

Tasker, Elizabeth, and Frances B. Holt-Underwood. "Feminist Research Methodologies in Historic Rhetoric and Composition: An Overview of Scholarship from the 1970s to the Present." *Rhetoric Review* 27.1 (2008): 54–71. Print.

Taylor, Diana. *The Archive and the Repertoire: Performing Cultural Memory in the Americas.* Durham: Duke UP, 2003. Print.

Taylor, Mark C. *The Moment of Complexity: Emerging Network Culture.* Chicago: U of Chicago P, 2001. Print.

Todorov, Tzvetan. *Genres in Discourse*. Trans. Catherine Porter. Cambridge: Cambridge UP, 1990. Print.

Tonn, Mary Boor. "Militant Motherhood: Labor Mary Harris's 'Mother' Jones." *Quarterly Journal of Speech* 82 (1996): 1–21. Print.

Toplin, Robert Brent. "The Filmmaker as Historian." *American Historical Review* 93.5 (1988): 1210–27. Print.

Toulmin, Stephen. *Cosmopolis*. Chicago: U of Chicago P, 1990. Print.

Traub, Valerie. *The Renaissance of Lesbianism in Early Modern England*. Cambridge: Cambridge UP, 2002. Print.

Ulmer, Gregory. "The Object of Post-criticism." *The Anti-aesthetic*. Ed. Hal Foster. Port Townsend, WA: Bay, 1987, 83–110. Print.

Vattimo, Gianni. *The End of Modernity*. Trans. Jon R. Synder. Baltimore: Johns Hopkins UP, 1988. Print.

Veyne, Paul. "Foucault Revolutionizes History." *Foucault and His Interlocutors*. Ed. Arnold I. Davidson. Trans. Catherine Porter. Chicago: U of Chicago P, 1997. 146–82. Print.

Vico, Giambattista. *The New Science of Giambattista Vico*. Trans. Thomas Bergin and Max Harold Fisch. Ithaca: Cornell UP, 1986. Print.

Virgil. *The Aeneid*. Print.

Vitanza, Victor J. "An After/word: Preparing to Meet the Faces That 'We' Will Have Met." *Writing Histories of Rhetoric*. Ed. Vitanza. Carbondale: Southern Illinois UP, 1994. 217–51. Print.

———. "The Hermeneutics of Abandonment." *Parallax* 4.4 (1998): 123–39. Print.

———. *Negation, Subjectivity, and the History of Rhetoric*. Albany: State U of New York P, 1997. Print.

———. Preface. *Writing Histories of Rhetoric*. Ed. Vitanza. Carbondale: Southern Illinois UP, 1994. vii–xii. Print.

———. "Taking A-Count of a (Future-Anterior) History of Rhetoric as 'Libidinalized Marxism' (A PM Pastiche)." *Writing Histories of Rhetoric*. Ed. Vitanza. Carbondale: Southern Illinois UP, 1994. 180–216. Print.

———. "Three Countertheses: Or, A Critical In(ter)vention into Composition Theories and Pedagogies." *Contending with Words*. Ed. Patricia Harkin and John Schilb. New York: MLA, 1991. 139–72. Print.

———, ed. *Writing Histories of Rhetoric*. Carbondale: Southern Illinois UP, 1994. Print.

Vivian, Bradford. *Public Forgetting: The Rhetoric and Politics of Beginning Again*. University Park: Pennsylvania State UP, 2010. Print.

Vogel, Shane. "Closing Time: Langston Hughes and the Queer Poetics of Harlem Nightlife." *Criticism* 48 (2006): 397–426. Print.

Waite, Geoff. *Nietzsche's Corps/e*. Durham: Duke UP, 1996. Print.

Walker, Jeffrey. *Rhetoric and Poetics in Antiquity*. New York: Oxford UP, 2000. Print.

Walzer, Arthur E, and David Beard. "Historiography and the Study of Rhetoric." *The SAGE Handbook of Rhetorical Studies*. Ed. Andrea A. Lunsford, Kirt H. Wilson, and Rosa A. Eberly. Los Angeles,: SAGE, 2009. 13–33. Print.

Wang, Bo. "'Breaking the Age of Flower Vases': Lu Yin's Feminist Rhetoric." *Rhetoric Review* 28.3 (2009): 246–64. Print.

———. "Engaging *Nuquanzhuyi*: The Making of a Chinese Feminist Rhetoric." *College English* 72.4 (2010): 385–405. Print.

Wardropper, Bruce W. "An Apology for Philology." *MLN* 102.2 (Mar. 1987): 176–90.

Warner, Michael. "Publics and Counterpublics." *Public Culture* 14.1 (Winter 2002): 49–90. Print.

———. *The Trouble with Normal: Sex, Politics, and the Ethics of Queer Life.* Cambridge: Harvard UP, 1999. Print.

Watkins, Calvert, ed. *The American Heritage Dictionary of Indo-European Roots.* 2nd ed. Boston: Houghton Mifflin, 2000. Print.

Watson, Lyall. *Jacobson's Organ and the Remarkable Nature of Smell.* New York: Norton, 2000. Print.

Weinberg, Harry L. "The Contemporary Emergency in Speech Pedagogy Research." *Today's Speech* 13.4 (1965): 27–29. Print.

Welch, Kathleen Ethel. "Interpreting the 'Silent Aryan' Model of Histories of Classical Rhetoric: Martin Bernal, Terry Eagleton, and the Politics of Rhetoric and Composition Studies." *Writing Histories of Rhetoric.* Ed. Victor J. Vitanza. Carbondale: Southern Illinois UP, 1994. 38–48. Print.

Wertheimer, Molly Meijer, ed. *Listening to Their Voices: The Rhetorical Activities of Historical Women.* Columbia: U of South Carolina P, 1997. Print.

Wessels, Aaron. "Media Release: GLBT Historical Society and First Artist-in-Residence Debut New Exhibit during Pride Week." *GLBT Historical Society.* Web. 22 May 2009. <http://www.glbthistory.org/news/releases/20090522_Lineage.html>.

West, Cornel. *The American Evasion of Philosophy: A Genealogy of Pragmatism.* Madison: U of Wisconsin P, 1989. Print.

———. *The Cornel West Reader.* New York: Basic Civitas, 1999. Print.

White, Hayden V. "The Burden of History." *Tropics of Discourse: Essays in Cultural Criticism.* Baltimore: Johns Hopkins, 1978. 27–50. Print.

———. "Historiography and Historiophoty." *American Historical Review* 93 (1988): 1193–99. Print.

———. "Interpretation in History." *Tropics of Discourse: Essays in Cultural Criticism.* Baltimore: Johns Hopkins UP, 1978. 51–80. Print.

Whitman, James. "Nietzsche in the Magisterial Tradition of German Classical Philology." *Journal of the History of Ideas* 47.3 (1986): 453–68. Print.

Wilamowitz-Moellendorff, Ulrich von. "Future Philology!" Trans. Gertrude Postl. *New Nietzsche Studies* 4.1–2 (2000): 1–32. Print.

———. *History of Classical Scholarship.* Ed. Hugh Lloyd-Jones. Trans. Alan Harris. Baltimore: Johns Hopkins UP, 1982. Print.

———. *My Recollections, 1848–1914.* Trans. G. G. Richards. London: Chatto and Windus, 1930. Print.

Wilcox, Donald J. *The Measure of Times Past.* Chicago: U of Chicago P, 1987. Print.

Willett, Steven J. "Can Classicists 'Think Like Greeks'?" *Arion* 3rd ser. 6.3 (Winter 1999): 84–102. Print.

Williams, Bernard. *Shame and Necessity.* 2nd ed. Berkeley: U of California P, 2008. Print.

Wilson, Kirt. *The Reconstruction Desegregation Debate: The Politics of Equality and the Rhetoric of Place, 1870–1875.* East Lansing: Michigan State UP, 2002. Print.

Winfree, Jason Kemp. "Before the Subject: Rereading *The Birth of Tragedy.*" *Journal of Nietzsche Studies* 25 (2003): 58–77.

Wittgenstein, Ludwig. *Philosophical Investigations.* 3rd ed. Trans. G. E. M. Anscombe. New York: Macmillan, 1973. Print.

Wolf, Christa. *Cassandra: A Novel and Four Essays*. New York: Noonday, 1984. Print.

Wolf, Friedrich August. *Prolegomena to Homer, 1795*. Trans. Anthony Grafton, Glenn W. Most, and James E. G. Zetzel. Princeton: Princeton UP, 1985. Print.

Work, William. "Employment Opportunities in Speech: Fact and Prophecy." *Central States Speech Journal* 18 (1967): 18–35. Print.

Wu, Hui. "Historical Studies of Rhetorical Women Here and There: Methodological Challenges to Dominant Interpretive Frameworks." *Rhetoric Society Quarterly* 32.1 (2002): 81–97. Print.

——. "The Paradigm of Margaret Cavendish: Reading Women's Alternative Rhetorics in a Global Context." *Calling Cards: Theory and Practice in the Study of Race, Gender, and Culture*. Ed. Jacqueline Jones Royster and Ann Marie Mann Simpkins. Albany: State U of New York P, 2005. 171–86. Print.

You, Xiaoye. "The *Way*, Multimodality of Ritual Symbols, and Social Change: Reading Confucius's *Analects* as a Rhetoric." *Rhetoric Society Quarterly* 36.4 (2006): 425–48. Print.

Yu, Anthony C. "Reading the *Daodejing*: Ethics and Politics of the Rhetoric." *Chinese Literature: Essays, Articles, Reviews* 25 (2003): 165–87. Print.

Zaeske, Susan. "Signatures of Citizenship: The Rhetoric of Women's Antislavery Petitions." *Quarterly Journal of Speech* 88.2 (2002): 147–68. Print.

Zelizer, Barbie. "Reading the Past against the Grain: The Shape of Memory Studies." *Critical Studies in Mass Communication* (June 1995): 214–39. Print.

Zerubavel, Eviatar. *Time Maps: Collective Memory and the Social Shape of the Past*. Chicago: U of Chicago P, 2003. Print.

Zhang, Longxi. *Mighty Opposites: From Dichotomies to Differences in the Comparative Study of China*. Stanford: Stanford UP, 1998. Print.

Zielinski, Siegfried. *Deep Time of the Media*. Trans. Gloria Custance. Cambridge: MIT P, 2006. Print.

Zimmerman, Eugenia N. "Managing Chaos: *Dea Fortuna* in Classical Antiquity and in the Medieval World." *The Canadian Journal for Rhetorical Studies/La Revue Canadienne d'Études Rhétoriques* 5 (1995): 1–15. Print.

Ziolkowski, Jan, ed. *On Philology*. University Park: Pennsylvania State UP, 1990. Print.

CONTRIBUTORS

Michelle Ballif is an associate professor of English at the University of Georgia. Her research focuses on the intersections between classical rhetoric and poststructuralist theory and its implications for historiography. She is the author of *Seduction, Sophistry, and the Woman with the Rhetorical Figure*, coauthor of *Women's Ways of Making It in Rhetoric and Composition*, and coeditor of *Twentieth Century Rhetoric and Rhetoricians* and *Classical Rhetorics and Rhetoricians*.

Sharon Crowley is a professor emerita from Arizona State University, now happily retired. In the distant past she wrote books called *Toward a Civil Discourse, Composition in the University*, and *The Methodical Memory*. In addition, she published a few essays in rhetoric and composition journals. In 2008, she was named a Fellow of the Rhetoric Society of America.

Jessica Enoch is an associate professor of English at the University of Maryland, where she teaches courses in rhetoric, feminist rhetoric, and pedagogy. She published *Refiguring Rhetorical Education: Women Teaching African American, Native American, and Chicana/o Students, 1865–1911* in 2008. "Claiming Space: Feminist Rhetorical Investigations of Educational Geographies" is the title of her current book project. Her coedited collection with Dana Anderson, *Burke in the Archives: Using the Past to Transform the Future of Burkean Studies*, is forthcoming from University of South Carolina Press.

Richard Leo Enos is a professor and the holder of the Lillian B. Radford Chair of Rhetoric and Composition in the Department of English at Texas Christian University. His research emphasis is in the history of rhetoric with a specialization in classical rhetoric. Much of his work deals with understanding the relationship between thought and expression in antiquity. He is the recipient of many awards, including the Rhetoric Society of America's George E. Yoos Distinguished Service Award (2006) and the Chancellor's

Award for Distinguished Achievement as a Creative Teacher and Scholar (2008). He also was named Piper Professor for the State of Texas (2009), was inducted as a Fellow in the Rhetoric Society of America (2006), and serves on the Managing Committee of the American School of Classical Studies at Athens.

G. L. Ercolini is an assistant professor in the Program in Speech Communication and Rhetoric and the Department of English at University of South Carolina. Her research primarily concerns the history of rhetoric, the relationship between rhetoric and philosophy, Enlightenment rhetoric, and contemporary rhetorical theory. She has published on Kenneth Burke's reading of Soren Kierkegaard; Hannah Arendt's and Theodor Adorno's portraits of Walter Benjamin; Immanuel Kant's rhetorically inflected anthropological ethics; and with Pat J. Gehrke, on humanism and the films of Stanley Kubrick. Her current book project reexamines the legacy of Immanuel Kant on the question of his treatment of rhetoric.

Pat J. Gehrke is an associate professor in the Program in Speech Communication and Rhetoric and the Department of English at the University of South Carolina. He is the editor of the *Review of Communication* and author of *The Ethics and Politics of Speech*, as well as numerous essays published in journals such as *Philosophy and Rhetoric, Critical Studies in Media Communication*, and *Philosophy Today*.

Debra Hawhee is a professor of English at Penn State University, where she teaches the history of rhetoric (ancient and modern) and oral and written communication. She is the author of *Bodily Arts: Rhetoric and Athletics in Ancient Greece* and *Moving Bodies: Kenneth Burke at the Edges of Language* and is coauthor, with Sharon Crowley, of *Ancient Rhetorics for Contemporary Students*.

Byron Hawk is an associate professor of English at the University of South Carolina. His research interests are histories and theories of composition, rhetorical theory and technology, and rhetorics of popular music. He is the author of *A Counter-History of Composition: Toward Methodologies of Complexity*, which won *JAC*'s W. Ross Winterowd Award and received honorable mention for MLA's Mina Shaughnessy Prize.

Steven Mailloux is currently the President's Professor of Rhetoric at Loyola Marymount University. Previously, he taught rhetoric, critical theory, and

US cultural studies at the University of California, Irvine. His books include *Interpretive Conventions: The Reader in the Study of American Fiction*; *Rhetorical Power*; *Reception Histories: Rhetoric, Pragmatism, and American Cultural Politics*; and *Disciplinary Identities: Rhetorical Paths of English, Speech, and Composition*.

LuMing Mao is chair and professor in the Department of English at Miami University. His teaching and research interests center on rhetorical studies in a historical, global context, intersecting writing, Asian and Asian American studies, cross-cultural communication, and critical discourse analysis. His previous publications include *Reading Chinese Fortune Cookie: The Making of Chinese American Rhetoric* and *Representations—Doing Asian American Rhetoric* (coedited with Morris Young), which received honorable mention for the 2009 Mina P. Shaughnessy Prize from MLA. He is currently working on a book project, *Searching for a Tertium Quid: Studying Chinese Rhetoric in the Present*.

Charles E. Morris III is a professor of communication and rhetorical studies and LGBT studies at Syracuse University. He is the editor of *Remembering the AIDS Quilt* and *Queering Public Address*, cofounding editor of *QED: A Journal in GLBTQ Worldmaking*, and a two-time recipient of the National Communication Association's Golden Monograph Award.

Christa J. Olson is an assistant professor of composition and rhetoric in the Department of English at the University of Wisconsin—Madison. Her work on Latin American rhetorical history and visual culture has appeared in *Rhetoric Society Quarterly*, *College Composition and Communication*, and the *Quarterly Journal of Speech*.

K. J. Rawson is an assistant professor in the Department of English at the College of the Holy Cross. At the intersections of queer, feminist, and rhetorical studies, his scholarship focuses on the rhetorical dimensions of queer and transgender archiving in both traditional and digital collections. With Eileen E. Schell, he coedited *Rhetorica in Motion: Feminist Rhetorical Methods and Methodologies* (2010), and his scholarship has also appeared in *Archivaria* and several edited collections.

Jane S. Sutton is a professor of communication arts and sciences at the Pennsylvania State University, York, where she teaches undergraduates and is faculty advisor for Lambda Pi Eta, Pi Rho chapter. She has published articles and book reviews in journals such as *Rhetorica, Rhetoric Society Quarterly, Advances in the History of Rhetoric, Philosophy and Rhetoric,* and *Quarterly Journal of Speech*. In addition to contributing chapters in books such as *Writing Histories of Rhetoric*, edited by Victor J. Vitanza, and *Rethinking the History of Rhetoric*, edited by Takis Poulakos, she wrote *The House of My Sojourn: Rhetoric, Women, and the Question of Authority* (2010), which won the Bonnie Ritter Book Award in Feminist/Women's Studies in Communication, National Communication Association, in 2011. She is past president of the American Society of the History of Rhetoric.

Victor J. Vitanza is a professor of English and rhetorics at Clemson University and is the founding director of the rhetorics, communication, and information design PhD program in the College of Architecture, Arts, and Humanities. He is a professor of rhetoric and philosophy as well as the Jean-François Lyotard Chair at the European Graduate School, in Saas-Fee, Switzerland.

INDEX

accidental, 5, 82, 130–38, 161, 172

agency: animal, 97; discursive, 51; female rhetorical, 63, 141n; homosexual, 79, 80, 84, 86; political, 54, 94, 102; rhetorical, 27, 61

Alcoff, Linda, 45, 47, 56, 57n1

Alexander, Jonathan, 71, 74, 82

allegory, 108, 188n1

alterity (*see also* other; otherness), 47, 149

anachronism, 143n2, 144n, 174, 175, 179, 183, 184

ancient rhetorics, 1, 11, 13, 103, 194; Greek, 10, 22, 23, 137, 143n2, 152, 182; non-Greek, 41, 43, 54

animal, 90, 92–98, 100, 101, 103, 133

Anzaldua, Gloria, 135, 136, 193

appropriation, of otherness, 4, 26–31, 38, 39, 42–45, 95, 102, 177, 194

archive, 4, 5, 66, 74–89, 91, 96–105, 106, 111, 192

Aristotle, 36, 103, 128–38, 184, 190, 191, 193, 194

art, 82, 86, 88, 94, 99, 101, 111, 161, 180

artifacts, 3, 4, 5, 9, 13–15, 95, 100, 101

Aspasia, 61, 143–144, 152

audience, 12, 32, 36, 63, 85, 86, 113, 117

Augustine, 32, 33, 38, 39

Ballif, Michelle, 24, 190, 194; "Re/Dressing," 73n8, 74; *Seduction*, 183, 188n2; "Victor," 3

being, 139, 141, 155, 179; and accidents, 161; being-in-the-world, 31, 140; in time, 181–84

Berlin, James A., 125, 150, 192, 193

Biesecker, Barbara, 1, 73, 79

Binkley, Roberta A., 11, 41

Blair, Carole, 62, 64, 65

body (*see also* embodiment), 100, 126n11, 129, 144; body language, 117; as gendered, 64, 69, 71, 72; performance, 37, 64, 68, 87, 92, 102; political body, 38, 131; physiology, 180, 182; and science fiction, 166, 167

Borgo, David, 114–22, 125, 126n9, 127n14

Buchanan, Lindal, 61

Buck, Gertrude, 130, 131, 132

Burke, Kenneth, 98, 107, 184, 188n7; and identification, 42, 43, 95

Butler, Judith, 70, 143

Campbell, Karlyn Kohrs, 1, 73n1, 188n2

Caussin, Nicolas, 31, 32, 37, 40n6

chronology, 111, 174, 176, 177, 182, 183, 184

Cicero, 36, 37

class, 21, 61, 69, 71, 72, 75, 86, 87, 88

Cohen, Sande, 107, 112–13, 114, 121, 126n7

comedy, 107, 108, 147, 168, 171

complexity theory, 5, 110, 114–27

Confucius, 41, 49, 56; Confucian rhetoric, 43, 44, 57

Crowley, Sharon, 2, 65, 126n6, 192, 195n3

counterpublics, 27, 62, 86, 96

Davis, Diane, 26–29, 31, 40n2, 40n5, 127n15, 153, 190

theorhetoric, 32, 33, 34, 35, 36, 37, 38, 40

third man, 3–4, 6, 152

time (*see also* future; past; present; space; temporality), 4, 5, 56, 148, 167, 174, 176, 177, 192; affective relations across, 86; being in, 181–85; and music, 115; out of joint, 112, 141, 183; rhetorics of, 69, 71; time-slicing, 92, 96, 97, 101

topoi, 5, 90, 93, 95, 96, 97, 100, 182, 191

tragedy, 61, 171, 175, 183

transgender, 71, 75, 80, 84, 87

transgression, 5, 155, 166, 174

trauma, 183

trope, 25, 32, 33, 43, 53, 61, 137, 144n, 146, 192

uncanny, 140, 141, 145, 148, 149; Freud's "The Uncanny," 147, 153, 150

unconscious, 17, 182, 185

untimely (unmodern), 172, 174, 175

virtue, 36, 51, 69

Vitanza, Victor J., 5, 174; and language games, 151–52; *Negation*, 6, 139, 142n, 150n3, 195n3; and Octalog I, 193; and the sophists, 152; and the "third man" 3; and *Writing* 2, 104n4, 106, 107, 125, 165, 190, 193

Vivian, Bradford, 62, 66

Walker, Jeffrey, 22, 90, 94

White, Hayden, 110–12, 113–14, 125, 126n6, 184

Wilamowitz-Moellendorff, Ulrich von, 175, 176, 177, 178, 179, 180, 189n10

wisdom, 36, 49, 140, 154, 176, 180

woman (*see also* historiographical methods, feminist), 1, 188n2; women in the history of rhetoric, 3, 10, 11, 21, 58–73, 135, 136, 141n

Zelizer, Barbie, 62, 63, 66